AF564703

University Library System

M. Ram

RANDOM PUBLICATIONS
NEW DELHI (INDIA)

ISBN 978-93-5111-562-5

Published in 2015 in India by

RANDOM PUBLICATIONS

4376-A/4B, Gali Murari Lal, Ansari Road
New Delhi-110 002
Phone : +9111-43580356, 011-23289044, 011-43142548
e-mail: sales@randompublications.com,
info@randompublications.com, randomexports@gmail.com

Type Setting by : Friends Media, Delhi-110089
Printed at Thomson Press(India) Limited

Preface

The University Library subscribes to more than 300 distinct online information services that provide scholarly content generally unavailable through free Web search utilities. We have an outstanding collection of textbooks, scholarly journals, multimedia content, current industry periodicals, and much more. The Library's collection of resources is continually updated and expanded to provide the most up-to-date and relevant information.

Academic libraries today vary in regard to the extent to which they accommodate those who are not affiliated with their parent universities. Some offer reading and borrowing privileges to members of the public on payment of an annual fee; such fees can vary greatly. The privileges so obtained usually do not extend to such services as computer usage, other than to search the catalog, or Internet access. Alumni and students of cooperating local universities may be given discounts or other consideration when arranging for borrowing privileges. On the other hand access to the libraries of some universities is absolutely restricted to students, faculty, and staff. Even in this case, they may make it possible for others to borrow materials through inter-library loan programs.

In library information system, information technology has had a clear and persuasive impact in almost every area of the library. The most significant development in information technology over the last few years or so is digital technology. Digital technology is revolutionizing the traditional concepts of preservation and access in library and archive communities. The applications of digital system and computing system in the libraries have been a subject of interest to present day professional librarians.

Present book has been complete to cater to the requirements of the teachers, researchers and students.

I would like to thank my team for standing beside me throughout my career and writing this book. My special thanks go to "Random Publications" who have published the book.

– M. Ram

Contents

1

Library Automation in University Libraries

The real boost in library automation came from the establishment of the INFLIBNET Centre. Before Inflibnet scattered efforts were being made in academic libraries specially in the institutions of special characters like IITs, IIMs, etc. INFLIBNET proved a real catalyst. Inflibnet started with scratch. At that time there were no financial assistance available to the University Libraries for automation. For the first time it was established that automation was the need of hour. The finances were allocated for the first time. The standards were established about the data capturing. The format was finalised and the Karvan started. As one estimate at present about 120 university libraries have been using computers in their activities. Some of the University libraries are even establishing digital libraries not only of already available digital resources but are digitising their own litreature. About 50 university libraries have their web pages.

TECHNOLOGICAL PROBLEMS IN LIBRARY AUTOMATION

Technological problems include both the hardware, *i.e.*, the computer as an instrument for information processing, and the software, *i.e.*, the methodology which is applied. The major problems faced today in terms of the hardware are due to the variety of computers being used in different types of research and business institutions. The computers, manufactured by various firms are not compatible. Developing countries sometimes receive sophisticated technology like computers as gifts from more developed countries; these often become obsolete from the manufacturer's point of view.

Such machines are not only unsuitable for most complex work but any technical problems which come up cannot be repaired. Information retrieval work requires machines more sophisticated than those manufactured indigenously, and few imported machines are capable of handling information retrieval applications. The random access facility and disks large enough for storage of bibliographic information are not readily available.

In most institutions, organisational goals receive priority over the library's requirements, meaning that the librarian must use the computer available rather than what is actually required according to specifications. Library activities in all institutions are done through sharing disk space as well as computer time. Therefore, when the storage capacity is not large enough to accommodate various types of data, bibliographic data are given the lowest priority. On-line facilities are rare in India. In fact, only TIFR's library has access to an on-line terminal for bibliographic data, the DEC-1077 computer of the National Centre for Software Development and Computing Techniques.

The communication infrastructure of India is still not suitable for extensive on-line information facilities; the telephone system is not reliable enough to support an effective network facility. Software problems arise because programmes must be developed in terms of the machine on which they are to operate. Therefore, the incompatibility of equipment tends to make the software incompatible as well, especially when programmes are written in machine or assembly language. While using languages which are not machine-bound, such as FORTRAN, COBOL, ALGOL, etc., may seem like a solution, in actual practice such languages cannot be interchanged without suitable modifications.

A software package developed for the IBM 360 model 30 would require many changes not only in the programme but also in the programming language if it were to run on any other computer. Development of a programme suitable for the available machine is therefore preferable to acceptance of a package programme. This makes the development and use of package programmes difficult and leads to a lack of standardisation in programming language as well as in output. Machine-readable data bases are byproducts of international information network systems and are available on magnetic tapes.

These are useful in building information resources and for retrospective search and current awareness services. Again, however, the tape service is expensive and suitably sophisticated computers are scarce. The data bases have a standard format which requires extensive changes to fit existing hardware and other system requirements. Also, relevant bibliographic information has to be selected from the data base and stored. Often this storage space is scarce and expensive.

ECONOMIC PROBLEMS

The major obstacle for any innovations in developing countries is the lack of resources. The initial cost of establishing a computer system is beyond the reach of most organisations and institutions. Library and information processing is done either with spare computer capacity made available by the institution itself, or with computer time hired from another institution.

The cost of hiring computer time and storage space is very high and often cannot be justified at the management level by cost-benefit analysis. At IIT, for example, CPU time per hour costs ₹ 1000 for educational purposes and ₹.2000 for business and industrial use.

Moreover, the computer provides only paper printout, and the paper often costs more than the processing. Few developing countries can afford the machine-readable data bases, either. The tapes are very expensive and because foreign exchange is involved in subscribing to them, it is even more difficult for most organisations in India and other developing countries to afford them. The annual subscription rate of one data base is now $8000. Library tasks often overlap and their peculiar nature seldom makes the advantages of computerisation seem very convincing in the light of cost-benefit analysis.

In India, libraries and information centres are attached to government organisations or research institutions, so library services cannot be calculated on a profit/loss basis. Long-term benefits have to be kept in mind while justifying such services. The libraries that have computerised some of their services or operations often have not taken such steps as a result of serious thought. Computerisation has a glamour of its own in the minds of many librarians. Overly enthusiastic librarians often run uneconomical programmes, producing lengthy listings, for instance, in the name of computerised service.

Often the manual method is used concurrently with the computerised system because of a lack of faith on the part of staff and users. The duplication of work and the cost involved in these cases is obviously unjustifiable; the librarian should know which aspects of service should be mechanised. An example of an economically viable computerised library activity is the centralised acquisition of periodicals in operation at INSDOC. This facility serves thirty laboratories, which not only frees the facilities from the tedious task of periodical acquisitions but also eliminates the cost of duplicate purchasing.

ATTITUDINAL PROBLEMS

Computers appear very awesome to developing countries. They are powerful machines which can perform many functions and therefore offer a solution to the many types of manual inefficiency which often plague the developing countries. Among librarians there are two different attitudes towards computerised facilities. One group is taken in by the glamour of modern technology and believes that computers can perform miracles. Members of this group often give insufficient thought to the real value of the computer to the organisation/institution and make uneconomical, haphazard use of the facility.

The other group, still the majority in developing countries, lacks knowledge of the potential and consequences of library automation. There is constant tension between this traditional librarian group and the 'new-wave' librarians. Professionals of the majority group do not realise that computers cannot replace human intelligence. Due to the accuracy essential for data input in library services, the librarian/information scientist is indispensable. The National Library of Calcutta conducted an experiment to computerise the Indian National Bibliography in 1968.

The scheme failed, however, because labour unions opposed it fearing retrenchment of library staff. Among developing countries, the attitudes of India's librarians are typical. They are not confident about automated services. Library staffs should therefore be trained in programming and thus be made aware of the work involved in automation. They will then realise that automation will not take away their jobs. They will also realise that computers are machines which have their limitations as well as their advantages. The communication gap between the librarian and the computer specialist is another major hindrance in establishing any effective automated system in a library.

There is often disagreement among the librarian, the programmer and the systems analyst. Librarians should be trained in computer programming and computer specialists should be versed in the special needs of library automation. Only then can a common language evolve among the three and a project be started.

Administrative personnel assume a very important role in decisionmaking. Their enthusiasm, support and conviction can help realise any new plan, just as their apathy and lack of understanding of the need for accurate and speedy information can jeopardise any effort. Although many things have taken a favourable turn in India, the majority of those at the management level unfortunately are not conversant with the development of information science and are unaware of the important role of information in all areas of national development.

This very often results in insufficient planning, which in turn curbs the enthusiasm of imaginative information scientists and librarians. Due to this lack of appreciation, priorities are poorly ordered and funds are not well allocated. Administrators also have a tendency to underestimate or overestimate the capacity of automation. Any information system or service is planned for the best possible benefit to its users. Unless the users are mentally prepared to accept a new system, however, it cannot be effective. Indian users are still unfamiliar and overawed by computers, so computer awareness and interest has to be fostered to enable proper utilizaton of a system.

They should neither overestimate computer capabilities nor be afriad of interacting with the computer systems. Another obstacle is that, because batch processing systems are still in use in India, there are bulky printouts in monotonous type faces and formats which prove to be a headache not only for the librarian, but also for the user.

There is no dearth of manpower in systems analysis and computer programming in India. We are already exporting software packages to countries that find them less expensive than developing their own. Library automation is still neglected, however; it is an area which has not attracted young people with appropriate expertise. Training should be given to both the librarian and the computer specialist about each other's functions and possibilities. Both INSDOC and DRTC conduct courses on automated systems in libraries. Under the forthcoming NISSAT plan, steps are being taken to build the requisite technical manpower.

Moreover, the Indian government's Department of Electronics is developing training programmes for the National Informatics Centre. There are two main objectives in training for library automation: to orient the programmers and system analysts to writing programmes suitable for automating library facilities, and to persuade librarians to accept the utility of automation and teach them to prepare accurate inputs to make the system worthwhile.

AUTOMATED CATALOGI

Descriptive cataloging is an intellectual activity requiring considerable decision-making and one that is time-consuming. As a result, many libraries experience cataloging backlogs which impede the flow of materials into circulating and reference collections thereby preventing library catalogs from representing those collections fully and accurately. Recognizing that the cost of descriptive cataloging can approach or even exceed the value of certain materials, many libraries do not catalog paperbound books, low-cost government publications, or other relatively inexpensive items.

In some research libraries, materials of presumably limited interest may be placed in off-site storage facilities with only an abbreviated catalog record created. In most libraries, conventional descriptive cataloging is not even considered for individual titles in large microform sets, even though such materials may significantly augment a library's resources in particular subject areas, and the failure to catalog them impairs their utility.

To simplify decision-making, to save time, and to reduce costs associated with descriptive cataloging, libraries have historically relied on cataloging copy, i.e., descriptive cataloging information prepared by other libraries, especially the Library of Congress.

The automation of descriptive cataloging depends on the availability of such cataloging copy in computer-processible form. In the late 1960s, the Library of Congress developed the MARC format for the communication of bibliographic data on magnetic tape and began distributing machine- readable cataloging copy through its MARC Distribution Service.

Since the late 1960s, MARC formats have been developed for various types of library materials, and the scope of the MARC programme-once limited to English-language monographs-has broadened steadily and significantly.

The LC MARC database-the accumulation of Library of Congress cataloging data in machine-readable form-now contains more than 2.5 million records, most of them cataloged since the inception of the MARC programme. Although MARC tapes can be purchased from the Library of Congress for input to local computer systems, most libraries obtain access to MARC data through products and services developed by publishers, computer system developers, time-sharing services, and other intermediaries.

Among the earliest of these MARC-derivative products were computer-generated micro publications such as MARCFICHE, produced by MARC Applied Research, and Books in English produced by the British Library.

Created by computer-output microfilm (COM) technology, both products provided more timely and varied access to LC cataloging data than could be obtained through the conventionally printed National Union Catalog, which was itself discontinued in Favour of a COM implementation in the early 1980s.As an equally timely and flexible alter- native, several search services, including DIALOG and WILSONLINE, offer online access to the LCMARC database. A growing number of vendors supply the MARC database on CD-ROM disks or digital optical videodiscs accompanied by software which supports the retrieval of specific cataloging records and the printing of card sets. Examples include the BIBLIOFILE system from the Library Corporation in Washington, D.C., the LASERSEARCH system from General Research Corporation, and the MINI MARC I1 system from Library Systems and Services Incorporated.

Although these products and services are important, most libraries obtain access to machine-readable cataloging records through one of the bibliographic utilities-organizations which maintain large databases of cataloging records and offer online access and other services to subscribing libraries.

Examples include the Online Union Catalog implemented by the Online Computer Library Center (OCLC), the Research Libraries Information Network (RLIN) operated by the Research Libraries Group, the cataloging support service operated by the Western Library Network (WLN), the Cataloging Support System (CATSS) offered by Utlas International, the LIONS system operated by the New York Public Library, the AGILE I1 service offered by Auto- Graphics Incorporated, and Brodart's Interactive Access System (IAS).

While they differ in database size and composition, the number and nature of their subscribers, and the specific capabilities they support, these bibliographic utilities each maintain a database of MARC records obtained from the Library of Congress and other sources, supplemented by original MARC-format cataloging contributed by subscribing libraries.

Working at local terminals, participating libraries can retrieve cataloging copy, modify it to meet local requirements, and order printed card sets, machine-readable cataloging records on magnetic tape, and other bibliographic products.

Local workstations are also used to input original cataloging records for use by other subscribers. Supporting thousands of online terminals accessing millions of machine-readable records, the bibliographic utilities are among the world's largest and most intensively utilized computer-based information services.

COMPUTER-PRODUCED CATALOGS

The automation of descriptive cataloging addresses only one part of the cataloging activity. In addition to using computers to facilitate access to cataloging copy, libraries are interested in computer-based solutions to the much discussed problems of card catalogs. The most frequently cited of such problems include substantial space consumption; the purchase of expensive cabinets and supporting furniture; Labour-intensive and time-consuming catalog maintenance routines which are intensified by changes in cataloging rules affecting the choice and form of entries; and limited convenience and retrieval capabilities.

These problems can be minimized or eliminated by the replacement of card catalogs with computer-based book-form or online catalogs. Broadly defined, a book-form catalog contains successive bibliographic records listed in a page format on paper or microforms.

Among the earliest applications of library automation, computer preparation of book-form catalogs can lower production time and costs while eliminating the Labour-intensive file maintenance routines associated with card catalogs. As an alternative to computer printed or typeset catalogs, computer-output microfilm catalogs have been widely implemented by libraries and library systems since the early 1970s.

A number of service bureaus, book jobbers, bibliographic utilities, and other vendors have developed software to produce COM catalogs from library-supplied data, thereby eliminating the need for in-house COM recorders and customized programming catalogs. Broadly defined, an online catalog is an organized, machine-readable accumulation of bibliographic records which are maintained on disks or other direct-access computer storage media for retrieval by library users and staff members working at inter- active terminals or appropriately configured microcomputer workstations.

In addition to saving space and automating file maintenance, online catalogs permit remote access by authorized persons equipped with compatible terminals, and they can support information retrieval operations-such as keyword searching of titles and series names- which are not conveniently possible with card or book-form catalogs. Online catalogs may be custom-developed for specific library installations or purchased as prewritten software packages or turnkey systems.

Examples of custom-developed online catalogs include the Library of Congress Computerized Catalog, the MELVYL system at the University of California, the LIAS system at Pennsylvania State University, the Library Computer System (LCS) at Ohio State University, and the Dartmouth College Online Catalog. Prewritten software packages suitable for online catalog implementations include BRS/SEARCH from BRS Information Technologies, a powerful information retrieval programme that is available in mainframe, minicomputer, and microcomputer versions; INMAGIC, a versatile data management programme for dominated by integrated library systems which combine database management and catalog access capabilities with circulation control, acquisitions, serials control, and other operations. Such systems may be implemented as complete turnkey configurations of hard-ware and software or as prewritten software packages designed to operate on a library owned mainframe, minicomputer, or microcomputer.

Vendors include CLSI, Geac, Notis, Dynix, OCLC, Virginia Tech, Data Research Associates, Carlyle, Comstow Information Systems, Universal Library Systems, Sobeco, Sigma Data/Centel, George- town Medical Library, Washington University, IBM, Inlex, Sirsi, Utlas, Innovative Interfaces, Eyring Research Institute, Easy Data, Data Trek, and Unisys. Among the newest and most widely publicized approaches to online catalog implementation, a growing number of vendors offer public access catalog systems which employ CD-ROM storage technology.

Examples include the IMPACT system from Auto-Graphics, Laserguide from General Research, The Intelligent Catalog from the Library Corporation, and the LEPAC system from Brodart. In such implementations, the library provides a machine- readable version of its catalog, typically consisting of MARC format records on magnetic tapes obtained from bibliographic utilities or other sources, to a CD-ROM system vendor who indexes and otherwise pre- pares it for conversion to one or more CD-ROM disks.

The disks themselves are created by a mastering process in special manufacturing facilities, and the library receives a specified number of disk copies plus menu-driven software designed for public catalog access at microcomputer-based workstations. Updated by periodic replacement in the manner of book-form catalogs, such CD-ROM catalogs are increasingly mentioned as an alternative to computer output microfilm for union catalogs and similar implementations.

AUTOMATED REFERENCE SERVICE

Since the late 1960s, many publishers of printed bibliographies, indexing and abstracting journals, and other reference works have offered machine-readable versions of their products for use in computer assisted reference applications. Initially intended for government, corporate, and academic libraries supporting research in scientific and technical disciplines, such machine-readable reference sources have become widely available in business, the social sciences, and the humanities. In addition to databases which correspond to printed publications, a growing number of reference sources have been developed specifically for use in computer-based systems and have no printed counterparts. While the earliest machine-readable databases were bibliographic in character, non-bibliographic numeric and directory-type databases are increasingly commonplace. During the late 1960s and early 1970s, a number of libraries purchased machine-readable bibliographic and non-bibliographic databases for processing on in-house computers using custom-developed information retrieval software. Most libraries, however, lacked access to the hardware and software resources required to implement such systems.

Through the early 1970s,the needs of such libraries were addressed by fee-based search services operated by the producers of machine-readable databases or other organizations such as large research libraries. Such services, which operated in the offline, batch processing mode, were replaced in the mid-1970s by services offering online database searching on a time sharing basis to libraries equipped with conventional terminals. Now widely utilized by libraries of all types and sizes, online search services can be divided into two broad groups:

- Multidisciplinary services-including DIALOG, BRS, ORBIT, WILSONLINE, DATA- STAR, and ESA-IRS-that provide database coverage of a varied range of subjects for a broad clientele; and
- Specialized services-such as the NLM SEARCH SERVICE, STN INTERNATIONAL, LEXIS, and WESTLAW-that provide online access to one or more databases relevant to a single subject discipline, profession, or activity, such as medicine, law, or engineering.

Various types of specialized search services provide online access to databases containing a specific type of information such as news. Examples include the NEXIS, VUITEXT, DATA TIMES, and NEWSNET search services.

While they differ in the number and type of databases offered and in the specific retrieval capabilities supported, multidisciplinary and specialized search services share a common operating methodology: they purchase or otherwise obtain bibliographic and non-bibliographic data- bases in machine-readable form from their producers, convert the data- bases to a form required for storage on their computers, and allow libraries or other subscribers to perform various retrieval operations on such data using prewritten database management software.

The software features a non-procedural query language which permits a user at an online terminal to initiate literature searches or other information retrieval operations by entering specified commands. While their query languages are relatively easy to learn, online search services are more often providing menu-driven interfaces for novice users. Some services also offer private file capabilities which allow libraries to establish their own databases. As a recently implemented supplement or alternative to online search services, an increasing number of bibliographic and non-bibliographic databases are available on CD-ROM disks. Accompanied by information retrieval software, such CD-ROM reference products permit database searching at local microcomputer workstations (over 100 titles were available at the time of this writing). Offered on a subscription basis, they can prove less expensive than online searching for databases that are accessed frequently, although infrequent updating, slow response time for complex searches, and other performance limitations may make them unsuitable for some applications. As a hybrid implementation with potentially attractive cost/performance characteristics, several vendors combine CD-ROM searching of back file data with online access to the most current information.

AREAS WHERE COMPUTERS ARE BEING USED

The following are the areas where computer are being used at present:

- Online public access catalogue
- Circulation
- Acquisition
- Serial control
- Intranet
- Internet
- CD-ROM services
- Online Public Access Catalogue (OPACs)

The problem being faced by the users in locating the document was the first to be targeted in the library automation. As a result the work first started in this direction. There was one more reason for this and that was the availability of CDS/ ISIS software which had the facility of catalogue only. It was in contrast of the special libraries where the work first started on providing information services like CD-ROM search.

Even today this area of automation has more activity than any other area. It has now graduated to Web-OPAC (web based online public access catalogues) where university libraries have made their databases available on their web sites. This has eliminated the need of installation of search software on the user's terminal. One potential which remains unutilised is the use of search data for research purpose as the search history can provide very useful tools for the librarians to formulate their collection development plans.

CIRCULATION

Circulation is one of the main activities of a university library or any library per say. In university libraries, however, the number of books issued and retuned are more than in special libraries. Therefore, the next area which was taken up was the circulation. In some of the libraries the number of books issued/ returned may be more than one thousand per day. We at IIT Roorkee (formerly University of Roorkee) has experience of issuing 1500 books in six working hours. Sometimes there used to be a queue of more than 100 students, since, the free hours for all students used to be the same, before automated circulation started.Use of barcodes had made the life very simple due to added accuracy and speed. Besides speeding up the issue/return, printing reports, sending reminders also become very easy. Circulation data also provides a very important insight into the book use pattern. Librarians should try to use this data for research and development purpose.

ACQUISITION

Use of computers in acquisition remains a low priority area. Not many libraries are using computers in acquisition. On reason may be the continuously reducing budget for purchase of books. But this area needs to be strengthened. Computerisation at the stage can help not only in order processing but also can be a very effective tool in budget control. You can allocate funds to different departments based on a set formula, can send department heads about non-availability of funds, can control over ordering and also utilise the data entered at this stage for technical processing and OPAC.

SERIAL CONTROL

Idiosyncracies involved in serial control affects the use of computers in serial control and hence, the area is not very well represented at automation scenario. One more reason is the unsuitability of serial control modules available in most of the library Management Softwares. The procedures developed by these softwares are so cumbersome that sometimes it looks easier to use normal method rather than automation. However, this area provides very good stage for use of computers as it can help tracking the missing issues very efficiently and provide the current awareness services and even the SDI services besides budget control.

INTRANET

Making the information available on intranet is also growing popularity as it eliminates the need of installing the software on the users' terminals. Users can access the catalogue through intranet or they can find the status of the books issued to them through web access. CD-ROM resources and other digital resources can be accessed on intranet. The beauty is that one need not be conversant with the software as the web links are available through the web page. Growing installation of campus wide networks is also playing a positive role in this direction.

INTERNET

Use of Internet for academic purposes is also increasing day by day. More and more libraries are putting their resources on Internet. Internet is the medium both to access and disseminate information. Internet has emerged as a very big virtual library which has information on practically every subject and in every media may it be text, audio or video. Libraries should use this facility to the best of their capability. They should provide links to similar type of libraries through web pages. One very good use can be designing of e-gates where user can have access to the electronic resources through a common user interface.

DIGITAL LIBRARIES

Digital library has recently become the buzzword for librarians. In the last year most of the seminars and the conferences had 'digital libraries' as their theme. Digital libraries can be of two types, *i.e.*, digital libraries of the digital text available in the market such as e-journals, CD-ROM databases, e-books, software, etc., or it can be developed from the printed text available in the library. If a library takes a decision to develop a digital library of its collection specially theses, dissertations and old journals, it can solve the problem of space and preservation both. But the decision about creating such decision is taken to be very carefully as it will prove a very costly venture both in terms of money and manpower.

PROSPECTS

Having talked about the problems and areas of applications let us talk about future prospects. I can definitely say that the things are changing for the good. Now University authorities are realising that there is no way to escape library automation. They are finding various ways to finance their library automation projects. Librarians are also realising that they can not remain indifferent to the change, otherwise they will be labelled outdated. One area of concern is the library science graduates being produced by our library schools It is surprising that UGC is giving responsibility of refresher courses of library science to the library science school and not to the libraries who are established themselves as advanced libraries and uses the technology far ahead than the library science schools. Existing staff is getting rid of the fear of computerisation. They are coming forward to learn and make themselves suitable to face the challenges of the new millennium. Standardisation is increasing and the better softwares are available.

NEED FOR LIBRARY AUTOMATION

Even though this question seems to be very fundamental it is essential to emphasise this aspect, as the library automation is yet to take off in majority of the Indian libraries. Secondly, while justifying need for library automation more than cost-effectiveness the benefits derived by the library users become the major consideration. To appreciate the advantages it becomes necessary to highlight the different levels of library automation.

Following are considered as important factors for Library Automation:

- Information explosion.
- Increase in the collection of libraries.

- Inability of users to explore the unlimited litreature and information of their interest.
- Advances in the computer and communication technology.
- Wastage of user/ staff time in locating the information.
- Provide wide access to resources within the libraries and elsewhere.
- Better access.
- Quality in service.
- Cooperative efforts (Resource Sharing).

Out of all libraries an academic library has a difficult task of defining its mission and operating objectives. The automation programme will have to mange a wide range of litreature associated with numerous departments and educational programmes of the academic institution. Furthermore, in an academic library the collections will be diverse unlike a special research library where the collection is relatively homogeneous.

The user group will also range widely, including faculty, staff, students, scholars, administrators and the general public. The position of an academic library funded largely by the government further complicates the process of identifying and prioritising objectives. As difficult as the task might at first appear, it is nevertheless essential to the process of establishing automated systems of any type. In addition the overall health of ones library operation will benefit from a modicum of intellectual rigour in this area.

PLANNING OF LIBRARY AUTOMATION

Planning for library automation has been defined as planning for 'integrated systems' that computerise an array of traditional library functions using a common database. While this is still generally true, rapid technological change is forcing a re-examination of what it means to 'automate the library.' As physical, spatial and temporal barriers to acquiring information are crumbling, libraries must plan for a broader and more comprehensive approach to providing automated services.

DEVELOPING A LIBRARY 'PROFILE'

One of the most important planning tools involves collecting basic statistical information on the library and its operations. You will find that the same basic data will be needed again and again–whether for vendors from whom you are requesting cost estimates, or for other libraries with whom you may be seeking to cooperate in implementing automation.

The following are examples of commonly needed data:

- Number of titles and volumes in the collection, current and projected.
- Number of borrowers, current and projected.
- Number of materials circulated, current and projected.
- Number of new materials acquired, current and projected.
- Interlibrary loans, lent to and borrowed from other libraries.

- Description of any cooperative arrangements involving the library.
- Library address and hours of operation.

In addition, it is important to take stock of any existing automation in the library by compiling the following data:

- Percentage of collection that has catalogue records in machine-readable form.
- Description of collection without machine-readable records, by category, (, monographs, audiovisuals).
- Description of currently-automated library functions (if any).
- Estimates of the location and number of workstations (to show where you intend to have equipment in any future system).
- Specifications for any existing equipment to be re-used with any future system (if any).

At the same time that this data is being assembled, it is important to assess user needs and set service priorities. This can be accomplished by undertaking a focused, strategic planning process designed to involve the library's 'stakeholders.'

DEVELOPING A STRATEGIC PLAN

A library planning to automate should undertake a process by which representative staff and users can identify service needs and objectives. The purpose of such an effort is to allow participants to articulate their interests and concerns, share perspectives and learn about possibilities in a collaborative setting.

Group interaction is an important contributing factor in the success of the goal, which is to develop and sustain library automation in the years ahead.

Here are the basic steps involved in this process:

- Plan on a two-day, intensive planning effort.
- Ask participants to identify strengths, weaknesses, opportunities and threats in the library's environment (known as 'SWOT' factors in strategic planning) that are characteristic of or that confront the library.
- Group these factors into critical issue areas that are likely to have an impact on the libraries' future in developing and sustaining automation.
- *Ask participants to identify ideas and perceptions in relation to the question*: "How do you see the library providing user-friendly, cost-effective automated services in five years?
- Through a method of your own devising, ask participants to prioritise all of the ideas that come out of the above two 'brainstorming' exercises.
- Ask participants to shape these priorities into the draft of a strategic 'vision' for automation development consisting of a statement of purpose, goals and objectives for the library.

SETTING SERVICE PRIORITIES

Your strategic vision must now provide the framework or context for the next step in the automation process, which is to determine which library functions should be automated and in what order of priority. For example, processes that are repetitive, occupy large amounts of staff time, require retrieving information from large, unwieldy files, or are high-profile functions of the library (such as the public catalogue) are prime candidates for automation. Determining the functions that you wish to automate and their priorities relative to each other is important for all sorts of reasons.

If needs and priorities are clear, functions can be automated in phases, allowing for more effective use of frequently scarce funding. Moreover, it is a way to develop credibility with funding agencies and be able to take advantage of 'sudden' funding opportunities. Finally, evaluations of systems and options will be easier and more productive if you are able to match your highest functional priorities against the corresponding modules available in the marketplace.

A WORD ABOUT COSTS

Speaking of funding, planners need to be aware that there are certain cost elements involved in the installation and operation of any automated system.

These may be summarised as follows:

- Planning and consulting costs include direct, out-of-pocket costs, (*e.g.*, hiring a consultant) and indirect costs, (*e.g.*, training staff) associated with getting started.
- Purchase of the system includes the cost of acquiring the initial system hardware and software, as well as the cost of preparing a site for the computer system.
- Telecommunication costs are those fees paid to telephone companies for connecting remote terminals or workstations to a central computer system.
- Conversion costs are those associated with the creation of machine-readable bibliographic and, for circulation systems, patron, records.
- On-Going Operating costs include:
  - Maintenance fees
  - Utility costs
  - Bar code labels
  - Miscellaneous supply costs
  - Telecommunications costs
  - Salaries and benefits (if extra staff are hired).
- Additions to the existing system may be required to maintain performance specifications, to accommodate new users, or to allow for additional automated functions.

SYSTEM SPECIFICATIONS

At some point, you will need to re-formulate your functional priorities into 'functional specifications,' which may be defined as what you want an automated system to do for you, including things that your current manual system cannot do. '

Technical specifications' must also be established. These include standards that must be adhered to, system performance, operation, and maintenance, as well as infrastructure requirements, such as stable sources of electricity and telecommunications, and sufficient bandwidth.

Developing clear and accurate functional and technical specifications that are specific to your library is one of the most important, if not THE most important, activity that you will engage in as you plan for your automated system.

These specifications will carry you through the entire procurement process, and will ensure that the system which most closely matches them will be the most useful and the most responsive to your needs.

DEVELOPING A FORMAL SPECIFICATIONS DOCUMENT

It is very difficult to compare systems sensibly and pragmatically solely by randomly looking at systems, talking to sales representatives, reading litreature or comparing broad cost quotations. For this reason, libraries use a formal document–often known as a 'Request for Proposal,' or RFP–that organises and standardises the information provided to and requested from the various system vendors. Utilising an RFP to solicit written responses from vendors makes it possible for you to systematically compare functionality, cost, maintenance, support, and all the other issues that are involved in system procurements. The process can save you money and will result in a wiser decision.

An RFP document should include these essential elements, among others:

- Background information on the library.
- A description of how the proposals should be arranged and submitted.
- Instructions on receiving vendor business and financial information.
- Criteria the library will use to evaluate vendor proposals.
- Questions regarding vendor training and documentation.
- Your functional and technical specifications.

Also, vendors should be asked to describe:

- How they will create bibliographic, item and borrower databases.
- Their system maintenance programmes and services.
- Their site preparation requirements.
- Their delivery and installation methodologies.
- Their system performance guarantees.
- Their pricing and cost strategies, in detail.

EVALUATING VENDOR PROPOSALS

Upon the receipt of vendor proposals, it will be time to begin the process of system evaluation and selection.

This process involves a number of key steps:

- If possible, form a project team of persons to assist with the evaluations and the selection who have some knowledge of automation or who work in the area(s) being automated. People involved in the strategic planning process would be a good choice.
- Try to weed out proposals that are 'fatally flawed,' *e.g.*, where the vendor fails to reply to any of the functional specifications or the system is missing a module for a high-priority function.
- Begin in-depth reading of the 'surviving' proposals, carefully noting both deviations from the requirements as defined by the RFP and any aspect that is handled unusually well. Make a list of any parts of the response that are not clear and require further clarification.
- Schedule system demonstrations. They are an important component of the evaluation process. Allow the vendors to show off the vendor's system in the most attractive light; however, be prepared with a list of what you want to see along with questions you would like answered. Use the same list with each vendor. This permits more effective cross-comparisons.
- Consider using computerised spreadsheet software in order to compare and evaluate vendor cost proposals. Costs may not be what they seem at first glance.
- Contact some of each vendor's current clients–sites of the same library type, and of similar size, where the hardware and software modules that have been proposed to you are currently in use.
- Assign point values to the criteria listed in the RFP and assign scores to the different proposals. The system with the highest score becomes the number one finalist, the system with the second highest score number two and so on.

  To maintain a negotiating edge, it is better to cut to two vendors rather than one. If that is impossible, maintain the illusion anyway. Remember: The selection process is not over until the contract is signed. Until that point, never let any vendors know that they have been eliminated, including those with fatal flaws.

DEVELOPMENT OF LIBRARY : PROBLEMS AND SOLUTIONS

Libraries have been part of the world, including South Asia, for centuries. Who can forget the University of Taxila and Nalanda Libraries which flourished in India during the fifth and seventh century AD respectively? Nalanda University Library was the biggest in Asia during the seventh century and at its peak of reputation and international glory in the ninth century AD. These libraries had thousands of books and even hand-written manuscripts and other types of materials for the benefit of their users, including scholars from many Asian countries. It has not been established whether or not the Asian libraries during the ancient times had periodicals in their collections.

According to various dictionaries, a periodical is "a publication with a distinctive title which appears at stated or regular intervals ...". The birth of the first periodical took place on January 5, 1665, at Paris, France. On this historic day, the first scientific journal, entitled Journal des Scavans, was published. It was the creation of Denys de Sallo, who was a counsellor of the French Court of Parliament. The first issue of this journal had only twenty pages and included ten short articles, a few letters and notes. It is a well known fact that the field of library and information science is relatively new in the modern world.

The first library school in the world, known as the Columbia School of Library Economy, was opened by the late Melvil Dewey in the United States in 1887 at New York. He was also the first editor of the Library Journal, which started publication in 1876 by R.R. Bowker from New York, and is still being published on a regular basis. The growth of journals in all fields of study was slow during the late nineteenth and early twentieth centuries but it picked up rapidly in the second half of the present century, including in the field of library and information science.

"Regardless of the publication medium, serials [periodicals] remain the key tool for scholarship and the primary source of current information and topical news in all fields of endeavor.". According to the 37th edition of Ulrich's International Periodicals• Directory, about 157,173 serials were published in the world during 1998, including 1,600 journals in the field of library and information science and computer applications.

These figures include 110 journals published from Asia. According to my research, Asian countries publish over 200 journals in our field in English as well as in vernacular languages. Therefore, the information contained in Ulrich's International Periodicals Directory is not complete.Unfortunately, only 22 Asian titles have been abstracted in Library and Information Science Abstracts (LISA), published in the UK, and Library Literature, published in New York, has only four titles published from Asia, and two Asian titles published in the UK and USA.Japan took the lead in Asia by publishing in 1907 the first library journal, entitled Toshokan Zasshi, which is still being published on a regular basis. In 1912, India followed by publishing the first Indian library journal in English, entitled Library Miscellany.

It was the brainchild of William Borden, an American librarian who was working in Baroda at the time. Unfortunately, Library Miscellany ceased publication in 1920.

In 1916 Iyyanki Venkata Ramanayya started a publication in Telugu, entitled Granthalaya Sarvastvamu, which is still published on a regular basis.

China, known for inventing paper and having a long tradition of scholarship going back to 26 BC, was behind in publishing library literature. The most populous country in the modern world, China published its first journal in librarianship in 1972 in the Chinese language.

The title of this journal is Tushu Gongzuo Tongsum (Book Services Newsletter). At present, 92 journals are published in China, including 62 journals in library science and 30 in information science, the majority in Chinese. In the view of Cheng, "there are 12 excellent journals of library science in China. They are the most representative core journals in library science research in China." During the first half of the present century, about ten library journals were published in Asia. But during the second half, from 1950 to 1999, about 200 new journals started publication, including titles like Herald of Library Science, Pakistan Library Bulletin, and Eastern Librarian. Many good journals such as Modern Librarian and Indian Librarian ceased publication for various reasons, which will be discussed later in the paper. At present, Japan publishes 63 journals but only seven of them are in English

SOUTH ASIA

South Asia has a long history of excellent libraries dating back to the fourth century BC. This area includes Bangladesh, Bhutan, India, the Maldives, Nepal, Pakistan, and Sri Lanka.

INDIA

The Republic of India is the largest country and occupies the major part of the South Asian region. India has the advantage over other Asian countries in publishing library journals in the English language because it has the largest English-speaking population in the world. It publishes 57 journals in the field of library and information science, a majority of them in English. According to my research, India is the leader in publishing journals in the field but only a handful of them are known and available outside India.

There are a few other good journals published in India, including the Bulletin of ILA (Indian Library Association). It was launched in 1933 when the ILA was formed, but it has changed its title many times. Professor P.N. Kaula started his own journal, entitled Herald of Library Science, in Varanasi in 1962 and it also has been published on a regular basis for the last 37 years. Prof. Kaula edits a few other journals, including International Information, Communication and Education; it is a multi-disciplinary journal, published semiannually, and was launched in 1982. Granthalaya Vijnona, also published semiannually, in Hindi, started publication in 1970. In 1998, Prof. Kaula launched another journal, Ranganathan Research Bulletin: Supplement to the Herald of

Library Science. It is the only journal in Asia, rather I should say in the world, that is devoted exclusively to a particular school of thought in the field of library and information science. It seems that it will be an "effective medium to propagate Ranganathan's ideology and his school of thought.". Other notable Indian journals in the field are: IASLIC Bulletin (1956-), International Library Movement (1979-), and Journal of Library and Information Science (1976-). In my view, one of the best Indian journals is Library Science with Slant to Documentation and Information Science. It was started by Ranganathan in 1964, and is a publication of the Sarada Ranganathan Endowment for Library Science in Bangalore. In addition, there are a few journals published in regional languages, including Bengali, Gujarati, Hindi, Kannada, Malayalam, Marathi, Tamil, and Telugu.

Bangladesh is situated in the northeast corner of the South Asian sub-continent. Before becoming an independent country in 1972, it was part of Pakistan from 1947 to 1972, and part of India until 1947, when the country was divided by the British at the time of independence. Bangladesh publishes only two journals in the field of library and information science. The Eastern Librarian is a publication of the Library Association of Bangladesh and has been published on a regular basis since 1966, though issues do not always appear on time. The last issue of this publication was a combined volume 20-22, published in the spring of 1998. A new journal was launched earlier this year in 1999: Bangladesh Journal of Library and Information Science. In addition, a few newsletters in Bangla are also published in Bangladesh, including Informatics.

Bhutan is a small country in the Himalayan region between India and Tibet. The development of libraries and librarianship is still very limited. According to my information, no library journals are published from this country.

The Maldives is the smallest country in the region, south of India. It publishes no library and information science journals.

Nepal is another small country, which divides India from China on the foothills of the Himalayas. There are no major publications reported in the field of librarianship, with the exception of an annual publication of the National Council for Science and Technology, which deals with libraries in the country.

Pakistan was created in 1947, when the British divided India in two regions at the time of independence. It is situated in the northwest of India. Pakistan has "1,500 libraries and 3,000 professional librarians... [and] six library schools.". There were no major library journals in Pakistan until the Pakistan Library Association was founded in 1964.

The Pakistan Library Bulletin, a quarterly journal, started publication in Karachi in 1968. At present, there are eleven journals and newsletters published in Pakistan, of which ten are in English and one in Urdu. It is possible that there may be a few journals published in regional languages such as Punjabi and Sindhi, but I am not aware of them.

Sri Lanka is an island to the southeast of the southernmost point of India in Tamil Nadu. It has a good working network of libraries and a few library schools. At present, four library journals are published in Sri Lanka. They are Sri Lanka Library Review, published semiannually in English, and Journal of University Librarians Association of Sri Lanka, an annual publication in English, and two other quarterlies, which are trilingual (Sinhalese, Tamil, and English).

A limited number of journals (ranging from one to four) are published in various other Asian countries in both English and regional languages. They include two each in English and Indonesian from Indonesia; one in English and three in Malay/English from Malaysia; four (in English) from the Philippines; three from Singapore; two from Korea; one in English and four from Taiwan (including one in English); two from Thailand; and four from Vietnam.

PROBLEMS AND SOLUTIONS

It is certainly good to know that Asia produces over 200 journals in the field of library and information science which includes over 70 journals from South Asia. I have been editor of Library Times International since 1984, and associate editor of International Leads since 1996. I have been interested in research, writing, and publishing since my high school days. At present, I read many library journals regularly to enhance my knowledge, and to see the quality of the library journals from an editor's viewpoint. I have examined a majority of South Asian and many other library journals for this paper. From an editor's view, I must say that there are many problems with Asian journals including South Asian journals which need immediate attention.

A majority of library journals in Asia, including South Asian countries, are published quarterly, a few semiannually, a few yearly, and some even published irregularly. It is very disappointing that many journals do not appear on time. Sometimes a few issues, or even a few volumes, are combined. The editors are to be blamed for this unprofessionalism. They should know the importance of research and timely information needed by scholars, researchers, faculty members, librarians, students, and other users. A journal is a "primary means of scholarly communication... [it] offers authors and readers some advantages over the monograph:... [including] intensive study of very specific questions or aspects of large problems, and the timely publication of intended communication.". Therefore, all library journals must be published on time for the benefit of interested users and readers.

The invention of printing in 1440 provided a new tool for sharing and communicating thoughts with others in a form which led to the birth of periodicals. Unfortunately, the paper used by a majority of publishers for printing library journals is of very poor quality. It becomes yellow within a few years. Maybe, it is not acid-free, thus shortening the life of paper. Therefore, it is very important to use an acid-free quality paper to preserve the writings of all scholars in every language of Asia including English, and to make microfilm copies of all important library journals.

Many articles in South Asian English-language journals are of very poor quality. First, writers do not make sense and write poor sentences. Many times there is no link between paragraphs. It seems that the editors are desperate to get articles and publish them in their journals without looking at their quality. They need to be edited properly, and good proofreading should be done before the final copy of any journal is approved for printing. Perhaps poor quality of the paper, poor writing and poor editing are the main reasons that these journals are not subscribed to by many libraries, and as a result they have small circulation. Even Ulrich's International Periodicals Directory does not give circulation figures of many journals published from South Asia and other Asian countries. Many editors have started their own journals in South Asia without proper planning, finances, and marketing.

This has resulted in the premature death of many journals. A majority of the editors are part-time, without any proper help, which makes it very difficult to run a quality and profitable business. Even many library associations have part-time editors for their journals. It helps to have full-time staff for those journals and newsletters that appear monthly or more frequently. It is important to include only the best articles on important topics to attract more readers and subscribers. It is always good to have a few referees to read manuscripts and act on their advice. I would like to know how many manuscripts are rejected by editors.

Another problem with a few South Asian journals is that their foreign subscription rates are very high, with the exception of a few journals and newsletters from Sri Lanka, making it very difficult for Western countries to subscribe to them. It seems that editors and/or publishers want to become rich overnight without delivering the product on time and in many cases without the necessary quality in their publications. If the price is right and you have a quality journal, you will certainly attract more subscribers, and you will make more money, if that is your motive. Otherwise, subscription figures will not improve.

Excellent marketing of library journals is the key to success. I have been very active in the field of librarianship for over twenty-five years. During these years, I have not seen any letters or sample copies of journals from any editor or publisher from South Asia. I have not seen any advertisements for Asian journals in publications of South Asia and North America. It is very important to have a good plan to market a library journal. It should be done on a regular basis by advertising in various library journals, direct marketing by sending sample issues to prospective subscribers, distributing free copies to librarians at various regional and national conferences, calling people on the phone, hiring firms to do marketing for you, and even giving discounts to various subscription agencies to market and sell your publication Another problem with a few publishers is that lost and damaged copies of their journals are never replaced free. Often even authors do not receive free copies of journals and/or offprints of their articles.

Times have changed due to the introduction of technology. Many journals are available in full text on various databases on the Web and on CD-ROM. It helps readers to do research much faster. But I have yet to see a South Asian journal on any North American database on the web and/or on CD-ROM. A majority of good South Asian and other Asian journals in the field of library and information science should be made available electronically as soon as possible for the benefit of researchers and other users. It will help in publicity also.

I have been an advocate of excellent service and quality journals. As editor of Library Times International since 1984, I believe we have succeeded because of our commitment to excellence, good marketing, and assistance from a team of 55 reporters. Our reporters from many countries, including a few from South Asia, send in their reports on a regular basis for every issue, our editors and staff work very hard to gather stories, and we publish each issue on time. We have subscribers in over sixty countries. We have heard only good comments from libraries and librarians. Everything is possible in the world with hard work, determination, and goals, and we know that the sky is the limit.

Not all western journals and newsletters are of top quality, but many of them have succeeded because of their excellent services, and publishing every issue on time with a few exceptions. There are 56 ALA-accredited library schools in Canada and the United States. I conducted a survey of the holdings of Asian library journals in their libraries. Only 32 schools responded by fax, mail, e-mail, and voice mail. Ten schools do not get any library journals from Asia. The University of Hawaii receives 54 journals, followed by the University of Illinois at Urbana-Champaign, and University of Pittsburgh. Other schools subscribe to only a few journals. According to deans/librarians of these schools, budget is the main problem for not ordering any journals from Asia.

A second reason is that there is no interest in the faculty or students to read these journals. Another reason mentioned was the Asian languages with which their students are not familiar. A few librarians and library educators have even mentioned poor quality of journals, and others mentioned self-promotion by one editor of an Indian library journal.

It is unfortunate that a majority of these schools do not offer any courses in Asian librarianship, comparative librarianship, or international librarianship to their students. The American Library Association with its 57,000 members is the largest and the oldest library association (founded in 1876) in the world. It has been advocating "Local Touch and Global Reach." How can it achieve this goal when a majority of the accredited schools in North America do not offer any courses in librarianship in Asia, where over two billion people live, and do not subscribe to Asian journals? Martin Richardson, Journals Director of Oxford University Press, is of the opinion that "both authors and readers of learned journals are increasingly expecting their publishers to exploit the many advantages of online distribution. Important research can be disseminated faster, and relevant material can be found more precisely. But this will not happen if each publisher erects ring fences around their own portfolio of information."

He added, "Clearly, there is a need for a 'one-stop shop' where all the major journals from whatever publishers can be searched and accessed without time-consuming visits to a succession of different web sites [or journals] ... [Therefore, we should] maximize the exposure of our authors' research to the global community of academics, researchers, and practicing professionals.". The publishers of Asian, including South Asian, library journals must work together and include their journals on major Web site databases. It will give them more publicity, and their material will be used by many interested scholars, researchers, students, and others for their needs. If no action is taken by publishers and editors, they will be left behind in this race on the Information Superhighway of the twenty-first century.

A few more observations from an editor's point of view. As noted earlier, many journals do not appear on time. The same is true of abstracts and indexes. For example, Indian Library Science Abstracts, Guide to Indian Periodicals, and Index India are also published late. All journals, abstracts and indexes should be published on time for the benefit of researchers. All journals should also include an index for each volume and letters to the editor. Publishers may consider including a few advertisements from other publishers, booksellers, vendors, and subscription agencies; this may give their publications more visibility, increase subscriptions, and improve cash flow. Perhaps it is time for commercial publishers to take the responsibility and start publishing a few quality monthly library journals and newsletters in South Asia and other Asian countries.

Excellent product and service should be the main concern of all editors and publishers. It will not hurt the editors and publishers to take a few courses in journalism and editing to enhance their knowledge. Even an internship with a leading journal and/or a newspaper would help present and future editors. There are many good books in the market on publishing including a new publication, entitled Journal Publishing, which can teach all of us a few important and basic principles of editing and publishing, which in the long run will benefit everyone.

2

Design of Universe Digital Library System

INTRODUCTION

A Digital Library is a live organization that comes to existence through a series of development steps that bring together all necessary constituents. Figure presents this process pictorially and indicates three distinct notions of "systems" that are developed along the way: Digital Library, Digital Library System, and Digital Library Management System. These also correspond to three different levels of conceptualization of the universe of Digital Libraries.

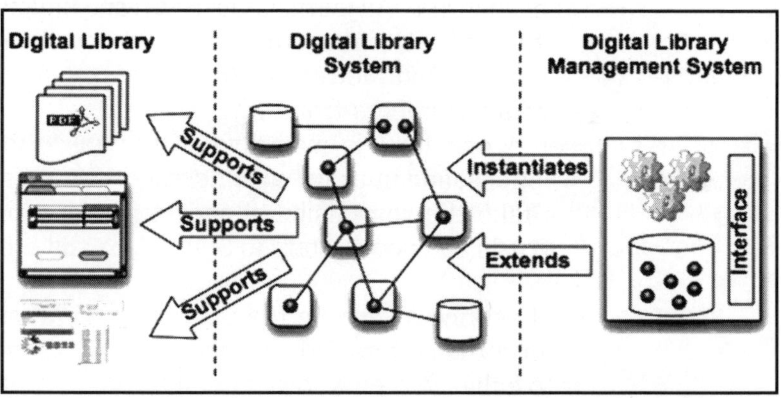

Fig. DL, DLS, and DLMS: A Three-Tier Framework.

Unfortunately, these three system notions are often confused and used interchangeably in the literature.

Nevertheless, as shown in Figure, they play a central and distinct role in the Digital Library development process.

To clarify their differences and their individual characteristics, they are explicitly defined here as follows:

- *Digital Library (DL): A (potentially virtual) organization that comprehensively collects, manages, and preserves for the long term rich digital content and offers to its user communities specialized functionality on that content, of measurable quality, and according to prescribed policies.*

- *Digital Library System (DLS): A software system that is based on a (potentially distributed) architecture and provides all functionality that is required by a particular Digital Library. Users interact with a Digital Library through the corresponding Digital Library System.*
- *Digital Library Management System (DLMS): A generic software system that provides the appropriate software infrastructure to both:*
  - Produce and administer a Digital Library System that incorporates all functionality that is considered foundational for Digital Libraries and
  - Integrate additional software offering more refined, specialized, or advanced functionality.

A Digital Library Management System is what one may call "system software". As in several other domains (e.g., operating systems, databases, user interfaces), such kernel software may be used as a foundation to produce Digital Library Systems. Depending on the philosophy it follows, a DLMS belongs to one of the following three categories:

- *Extensible Digital Library System:* A complete Digital Library System that is fully operational with respect to basic/foundational functionality required. It is based on an open software architecture, so that further software components can be incorporated on top of the ones already there with ease. DelosDLMS is a prototypical example of a system that is based on this philosophy.
- *Digital Library System Warehouse:* A collection of software components that cover all basic/foundational functionality required and a set of tools that can be used to combine these components in arbitrary ways (in Lego-like fashion) to create Digital Library Systems offering diverse sets of functionality. New software components can easily be incorporated into the Warehouse for subsequent combination with those already there. BRICKS and DILIGENT are two prototypical examples of systems that are based on this philosophy.
- *Digital Library System Generator:* A highly parameterized software system that encapsulates templates for a broad range of functionality, which includes all basic/foundational as well as any advanced functionality that has been deemed appropriate. Through an initialization session, the appropriate parameters are set and tuned; at the end of that session, software is automatically generated that constitutes essentially a Digital Library System ready to be installed and deployed.

Note that, while the concept of Digital Library is intended to capture an abstract system that consists of both physical and virtual components, the remaining two capture concrete software systems. For every Digital Library, there is a unique Digital Library System in operation (possibly consisting of many interconnected smaller DLSs in the most general case), whereas all Digital Library Systems are based on a handful of Digital Library Management Systems.

It is also important to note that until now, most Digital Libraries have been created by developing DLSs from scratch without any basis on a DLMS. The notion of DLMS has been recently introduced by the DL community in order to overcome the many drawbacks arising from the current DL development process. When the digital library field reaches maturity, one should expect that only a small number of industrial-strength Digital Library Management Systems will be available on the market.

DESIGN OF DIGITAL LIBRARY MEDIND WEB SITE

The medIND project is having its own domain name at the Internet (http://medind.nic.in). It has pneumonic value and stands for Medical Journals on Internet [from India]. Home page gives details of the project listing of the participating journals.

This listing is hyperlinked to each participating journal home page at the medIND web site. The site provides two approaches to access the journal articles.

BROWSING

Journals are hyperlinked and arranged in alphabetical order. Such hyperlinked list leads to pages giving details of selected journals such as editors, instructions to authors, contact address, parent body etc.

Further, this leads to listing of issues of the journal by years/volume wise. The content page provides hyperlinks to the individual article.

SEARCHING

The searching is being provided through the bibliographic database IndMED. Each record of the IndMED has been linked to the individual article in the MedIND site. The searching of the articles can be achieved through from http://indmed.nic.in as well as from http://mednic.nic.in web sites.

The references will display icons indicating the availability of the full text. In developing digital collection, issues of intellectual property rights have been dealt to strengthen the cooperation between editors and content service provider to facilitate access to digital content through Internet to end users in the area of biomedicine on non-commercial basis.

The design of digital collection should be usable, flexible and simple enough to accommodate future changes and also enables other applications to utilize data for development of future applications.

The naming convention of digital collection is acted as bridge between metadata base and full text of content. This project fulfills the demand of providing full text of documents to health professionals free of cost throughout the world.

It serves as a model for the development of similar collections in others SandT areas, medIND is a step in the process of making it as an open archive source where Indian journals covered in Medline database as well in IndMED database will be stored and will be provided access free of cost to health professionals throughout the world.

This will give enough visibility and exposure to Indian biomedical journals and demand for Indian literature would be met through the medIND project. In future, more visibility to articles included in medIND journals would be provided by adopting and exposing metadata in OAI-PMH and RSS protocols.

THE TASK FORCE ON ARCHIVING OF DIGITAL INFORMATION

An important contribution to the debate over long-term archiving of digital information came from the Task Force on Archiving of Digital Information, organized jointly by the Commission on Preservation and Access and the Research Libraries Group (RLG). The Task Force, in effect, was asked to report on ways that society should work with respect to the cultural record it is now creating in digital form – not only through conversion from print to digital but, perhaps more important – through a record that is "born digital."

Consider that, by the year 2000, an estimated 75per cent of all U.S. Federal transactions will be handled electronically. When President Clinton leaves office, it is estimated that his administration will hand over eight million electronic files to the National Archives; and these administration files are but a minuscule portion of the electronic record generated by the corporate world. Most of this information is born digital and there is no printed record to fall back on.

The Task Force's 1996 report argues that "the problem of preserving digital information for the future is not only – or even primarily – a problem of fine tuning a narrow set of technical variables." Rather, "it is a problem of organizing ourselves over time and as a society to maneuver effectively in the digital landscape.

It is a problem of building – almost from scratch – the various systematic supports, or deep infrastructure, that will enable us to tame our anxieties and move our cultural records naturally and confidently into the future". The Task Force's report is available in full at the web site of the Research Libraries Group (http://www.rlg.org).

The Task Force was co-chaired by Donald J. Waters, now the Director of our Digital Library Federation. Among the report's conclusions and recommendations are:

- The Task Force recognizes that most of the challenges associated with digital preservation are organizational, not technical.

- The first line of defence against loss of valuable digital information rests with the creators, providers, and owners of digital information.
- Certified digital archives must have the right and duty to exercise an aggressive rescue function as a fail-safe mechanism for preserving digital information that is in jeopardy of destruction, neglect, or abandonment by its current custodian.

The final report focuses on three essential questions: What does digital preservation entail? How do we organize ourselves to do it? What steps should we take to move forward?

Time will not permit covering these questions in detail, but one major conclusion of the report cannot be emphasized enough: Our greatest challenges in the digital age are organizational rather than technical. Because we currently lack the infrastructure of practices, standards, and organizations needed to support preservation of digital information, the following elements of infrastructure must be considered:

- Legal bases for deposit and rescue. Nationally and internationally, legislation and agreements are needed to encourage legal deposit of electronic resources in archival repositories, to enable rescue of abandoned resources, and to facilitate access and use of archival files.
- Standards for description. Current library cataloging standards are not sufficient to describe access and contextual information about digital resources. Several efforts to address this issue are underway internationally. For example, existing registers of microform masters are examined for expansion to include digital items. In this context, see also the final report of the *RLG Working Group on Preservation Issues of Metadata* (http://www.rlg.org/preserv/presmeta.html).

There is more, and the need for sharing information about best practices across the wide spectrum of communities is overwhelming. Preservation of digital materials has emerged as a new, critically important field of interdisciplinary and international activity, and much work needs to be done.

INTRODUCTION TO THE FILM "INTO THE FUTURE"

[Addressing our digital memory crisis begins with dialogue. CLIR prepared a discussion paper on digital preservation. Copies of the discussion paper are available, but first, if I may, I would like to show the documentary movie "Into the Future," on the preservation of knowledge in the electronic age. The movie was commissioned by the Commission on Preservation and Access and the American Council of Learned Societies.

Funding was provided by the Alfred P. Sloan Foundation, the National Endowment for the Humanities, and the Xerox Corporation. It was shown on U.S. national television last January and created much discussion. The mainstream press picked up on the issue and several thoughtful articles appeared on the subject of digital preservation. The discussion paper raises the question "Why should we be concerned?" "Into the Future" provides several answers.

SHOWING OF THE 1/2 HOUR VERSION OF "INTO THE FUTURE."

After the showing: The movie sounds an alarm and raises questions; it does not provide answers. We hope that the answers will eventually be provided by groups such as represented at this conference, the Digital Library Federation (DLF) and its members, and other groups and individuals. The Digital Library Federation (DLF) (For this part, I'm relying extensively on information provided by Donald J. Waters, Director of the Digital Library Federation.

The Council on Library and Information Resources is administrative home to the Digital Library Federation, which includes 19 members – university research libraries, the Library of Congress, the National Archives, and the New York Public Library. The primary mission of the DLF is to establish the necessary conditions for creating, maintaining, expanding, and preserving a distributed collection of digital materials accessible to scholars and a wider public.Participants in the Federation are committed to a shared investment in developing the infrastructure needed for libraries of digital works.

The infrastructure is intended to enable digital libraries to bring together, or "federate," the works they manage for their readers. The DLF has set the following programme priorities:

- DLF will focus on libraries of materials born digital. It is critical that the library community moves from conversion – except in specialized and well-justified cases – to organization, access, and preservation of materials born digital. A high priority is developing the archival mechanisms that preserve the integrity and usability of these digital works over a long term. The Federation is increasingly turning the attention of libraries to the numerous – and difficult – issues associated with works born in, rather than converted to, digital form.
- DLF will help integrate digital materials into the fabric of acadmic life. A critical focus for such integration is to define the circumstances under which conversion to digital form is justified. Conversion projects that facilitate the extension of higher education and promise to improve the quality and lower the cost of research and education deserve special attention.
- DLF will help stimulate the development of a core digital library infrastructure. The highest priorities for attention at the present time are the network and systems requirements and means of authentication and authorization, the means of discovery and retrieval, and archiving.
- DLF will help define and develop the organizational support needed

for effectively managing digital libraries. Organizational issues requiring early attention include identifying institutional values and strategies for managing intellectual property in digital form, and creating the conditions for the development of the professional skills needed for digital library management.

CLIR AND DLF PLANS FOR DIGITAL ARCHIVING

As one of its primary agenda items, CLIR and the DLF aim to ensure the persistence of digital information, both born digital or created by conversion. Much has been written about the need to document digital information in order for it to serve the role of "record" in an archival sense, as well as about the need to "migrate" digital information to new media in order to prevent loss from media decay and obsolescence.However, relatively little effort has gone towards answering the more fundamental question of how to ensure that digital documents will remain readable and understandable in the future. At this time, one might usefully distinguish the following strategies:

- Copying (no changes to the information)
- Migration (adpation to new hardware and software)
- Emulation (new platforms mimicking previous platforms)
- Archeology (doing nothing and trying to salvage neglected information when needed)

CLIR and the DLF commissioned Jeff Rothenberg, author of "Ensuring the Longevity of Digital Documents" (*Scientific American*, January 1995) to investigate approaches currently being considered to ensure the future accessibility and readability (i.e., longevity) of digital material. His preliminary findings challenge the concept of "migration." Since migration involves translation of each different type and format (text, images, sound video, animation, etc.), the process is highly labour-intensive.

If a document is accepted for long-term storage based on an assumed migration strategy, Rothenberg argues, it is impossible to give even gross estimates of what will have to be done to it in the future, when this will have to be done, how much it will cost, or how long it will be before the document is corrupted by inappropriate translation.In his further research, Rothenberg will concentrate on emulation as a solution to the problem of digital preservation, one that is predictable and testable and eliminates repeated translation of documents "which must inevitably lead to their corruption and loss."Others argue that "migration" is, at least for the shorter term, the only viable solution. Stay tuned.

OTHER ACTIVITIES OF THE DLF THAT RELATE TO ARCHIVING ARE

- Digital collections of licensed works. Libraries are pouring substantial resources into developing licenses for access to electronic journals, while still maintaining subscriptions to print copies of the same materials.

Not all contracts provide for long-term access to the licensed materials, but terms in some licenses require the publisher to provide the library with a tape or CD-ROM containing a copy of the licensed work. The Copyright Division of the Library of Congress is developing the means to accept archival quality versions of copyrighted works deposited there, but project work is needed to ensure that the tapes and CD-ROMS deposited with libraries and archives as archival copies can and will serve the fail-safe purpose for which they are intended.

- Institutionalizing digital information. Much scholarly information in digital form is currently being managed as a cottage industry by individual faculty on behalf of a particular discipline. The directors of the DLF institutions are considering how DLF can provide leadership in bringing products emerging from this cottage industry into a more stable, institutional environment.
- Cornell has developed a proposal that DLF will support, to explore the requirements and means for preserving materials converted to digital form in a subset of genres.
- Extension of reach: *Making of America* Phase III. Conversion, as the Library of Congress has demonstrated, is a significant means of extending the reach of library collections in the service of general education. One of the founding goals of the DLF is to find ways to aggregate the existing digitized collections. This effort will focus primarily at the level of descriptive metadata as a means of integration and provide a testbed for exploring intersystem searching methods.

There is another important dimension to the project: In several institutions (e.g., Yale and Cornell), large quantities of digitized Americana are inaccessible because the digital platforms on which the collections were built have become obsolete. *Making of America* Phase III thus affords the opportunity to develop and demonstrate migration techniques as a means of preservation of digital information.

Perhaps we should add a fifth strategy to the four already mentioned – prayers. James Gleick reported in *The New York Times* ("The Digital Attic: An Archive of Everything," 12 April 1998) that "the Daiho Temple of Rinzai Zen Buddhism held a `memorial service for lost information' in Kyoto and online." Gleick adds that "of course, the details are lovingly preserved, in English and Japanese, at its web site.

A look at the web site reveals that there is much common ground between this conference and the Rinzai Zen Buddhists (http://www.thezen.or.jp/jomoh/kuyo.html): "After the effort of transforming all this knowledge into electronic information has been completed, is it enough then to say that we are finished? And from there, can we truly make effective use of that which we have created? Sometimes, the answer is 'no.' To provide an example, there are many 'living' documents and softwares that are thoughtlessly discarded or erased without even a second thought. It is this thoughtlessness that has drawn the concern and attention of Head Priest Shokyu Ishiko.

Head Priest Ishiko hopes that through holding an 'Information Service' and by teaching the words of Buddha, that this 'information void' will cease to exist." We will all have to help him.

CONCEPTS OF THE DIGITAL LIBRARIES UNIVERSE

Despite the great richness and diversity one finds among existing digital libraries, there are still a rather small number of concepts that are considered fundamental and essentially characterize all relevant systems and, in fact, the entire field.

These concepts are identifiable in every digital library and should be the starting point for any researcher who wants to study and understand the field, for any system designer and developer who is about to embark in an effort to build a Digital Library, and for any content owner who wants to offer it externally. In this section, we identify these concepts and briefly discuss their roles.

Given that there are three kinds of "systems" in the digital library world, in principle each one may have, in addition to the common fundamental concepts, a number of other related concepts associated with it.

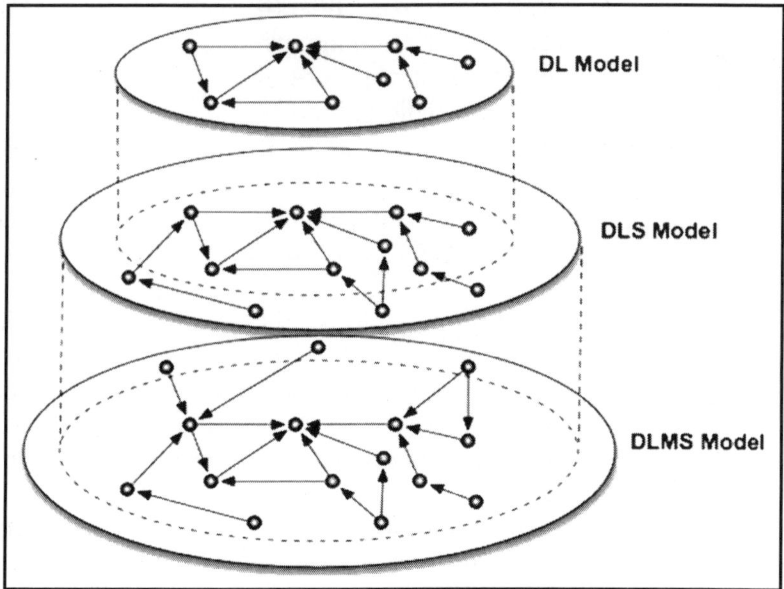

Fig. Hierarchy of Conceptualizations.

Nevertheless, from the definitions of these systems in the previous section, one may easily derive that there is a natural inclusion relationship on the concepts that refer to these systems: the set of concepts used to define the Digital Library is completely included in that used for Digital Library System, which is in turn completely included in that characterising the Digital Library Management System. This inclusion relationship is depicted in Figure.

As a consequence of the above, we introduce below each of these concepts in reference to the highest level of a system (in the three-tier framework) for which it makes sense.

All concepts, however, could also be described in reference to lower-level systems, focusing on the characteristics that are of primary concern there. More details can be found elsewhere.

The main concepts that are foundational in the Digital Library world are six. Five of them have been alluded to in the definition of Digital Libraries and are introduced in reference to them: *Content*, *User*, *Functionality*, *Quality*, and *Policy*; one of them has been alluded to in the definition of a Digital Library Systems and is introduced in reference to them: *Architecture*.

All six concepts are shown together, influencing the Digital Library framework, in Figure and are defined immediately after that.

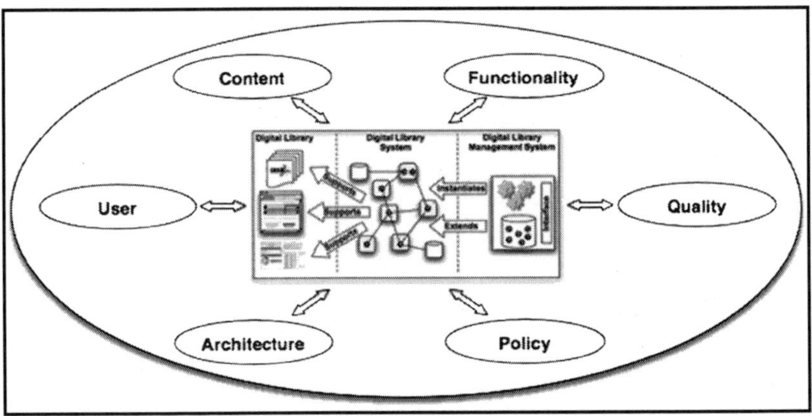

CONTENT

The Content concept represents the data and information that Digital Libraries handle and make available to their users. It is composed of a set of information objects organised in collections. Content is an umbrella concept that is used to aggregate all forms of information that a Digital Library may require to offer its services.

For example, metadata play an important role in the information domain because they describe the contents of other information objects and express their structure.

USER

The User concept represents the actors (whether human or not) entitled to interact with Digital Libraries. The aim of Digital Libraries is to connect such actors with information and to support them in consuming already available information and produce new information.

As in the case of the previous concept, User is an umbrella concept that covers all notions related to the representation and management of actor entities within a Digital Library, i.e., the digital entities representing the actors, the rights that they have within the system, the profiles of the actors with characteristics that personalize the system's behaviour or represent these actors in collaborations, and others.

FUNCTIONALITY

The Functionality concept represents the services that Digital Libraries offer to their users. In the most general case, the functionality expected from Digital Libraries is extremely rich. One may not expect, however, that all Digital Libraries must support the complete spectrum. Some core functionality represents the bare minimum that is required by all Digital Libraries, e.g., new information object registration, search, and browse.

Beyond that, depending on the particular needs of its community of users and/or the information it is aimed to manage, each Digital Library may offer diverse additional functionality to serve those needs.

QUALITY

The Quality concept represents the parameters that can be used to characterize and evaluate the content and behaviour of Digital Libraries. It potentially includes several diverse parameters associated with each class of content or functionality, possibly even with each distinct information object or service. Some of these parameters are objective in nature and can be automatically measured, whereas others are subjective in nature and can only be measured through human experiments.

POLICY

The Policy concept represents a set of rules that govern the interaction between users and Digital Libraries. Several mechanisms should be available to enable such interaction and the Digital Library should activate those mechanisms in the form prescribed by its policies. The policy concept includes all aspects of system security, digital rights management, system load control, and other similar issues.

ARCHITECTURE

The Architecture concept (which refers to a Digital Library System) represents a mapping of the functionality and content offered by a DL onto hardware and software components6. Having this as a main concept is important due to the following considerations:

- Digital Libraries are often assumed to be among the most complex and advanced forms of information systems ;
- Interoperability of Digital Libraries is one of the greatest challenges of the research community. Having a clear architectural understanding of Digital Library Systems offers ammunition in addressing both the above issues effectively.

In addition to the above primary Digital Library concepts, there is one more that is a derivative of them and is also very useful. That is the concept of Resource, which aggregates the concepts of Content, User, Functionality, and Policy, i.e., all concepts that refer to internal entities of a Digital Library and can be sensed by the external world. There are several aspects of all these concepts that are very similar or identical.

Approached as instances of the more general concept of Resource, the Digital Library should treat them in the same fashion. Having described the main concepts characterising the foundation of the digital library universe, we proceed in introducing four main roles of actors that interact with digital libraries at different levels and for different purposes.

ACTORS OF THE DIGITAL LIBRARY UNIVERSE

We envisage four different and complementary roles of actors interacting with digital libraries: *DL End-Users*, *DL Designers*, *DL System Administrators*, and *DL Application Developers*.

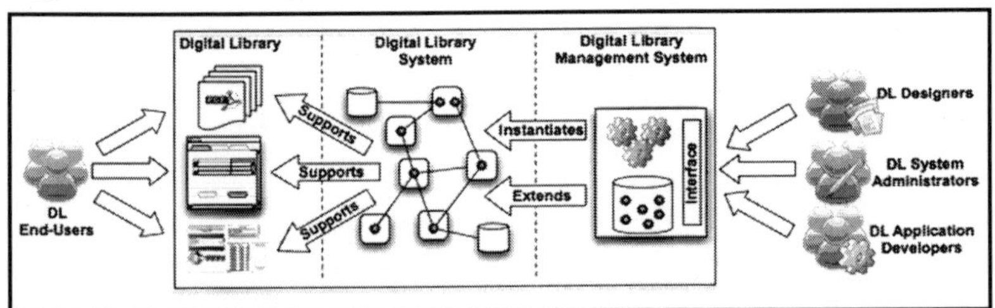

Fig. The Main Roles of Actors versus the Three-tier Framework

As depicted in Figure, each role is primarily associated with one of the three "systems" in the three-tier framework and, therefore, has the view that corresponds to that system. These roles are defined below.

DL END-USERS

These exploit the DL functionality for providing, consuming, and managing the DL Content as well as some of its other constituents. They perceive the DL as a stateful entity that serves their functional needs. The behaviour and output of the DL depend on its state at the time a particular part of its functionality is activated. The state of the DL corresponds to the state of its resources, i.e., it consists of the collections of information objects managed by the DL, its set of authorized users, its functionality, and its set of policies. This state changes during the Digital Library lifetime according to the functionality activated by the users and their inputs. DL end-users may be further partitioned into *Content Creator*, *Content Consumer*, and *Librarian*.

DL DESIGNERS

These exploit their knowledge of the application semantic domain to define, customise, and maintain the Digital Library so that it is aligned with the information and functional needs of its end-users.

To perform this task, they interact with the DLMS providing functional and content configuration parameters. The former capture aspects of the DL functionality perceived by the end-users, e.g., the result set format, the query language, the user profile formats, and the document model.

The latter capture third-party resources that are exploited by the specific DL, e.g., repositories of content, ontologies, classification schemas, authority files, and gazetteers. The values of these parameters, which can be modified during the DL lifetime, configure the specific DL perceived by the end-users because they determine the particular Digital Library System instance serving the Digital Library.

DL SYSTEM ADMINISTRATORS

These select the software components necessary to create the Digital Library System needed to serve the required DL and decide where and how to deploy them. They interact with the DLMS by providing architectural configuration parameters, such as the selected software components, the hosting nodes, and the components allocation.

Their task is to identify the architectural configuration that better fits the DLS in target ensuring the appropriate level of quality. The value of the architectural configuration parameters can be changed over the DL lifetime. Any change of these parameters may result in the provision of different DL functionality and/or different quality.

DL APPLICATION DEVELOPERS

These develop the software components of DLMSs and DLSs, realizing the necessary functionality.

These four roles cover the whole spectrum of actors interacting with digital libraries. Their models of the digital library universe are linked together in a hierarchical fashion as depicted in Figure. This is a direct consequence of the above definitions since DL end-users act on the Digital Library, whereas the remaining three roles operate on the DLMS and consequently on the DLS and DL as well. This relationship ensures that roles designed to directly co-operate share a common vocabulary/knowledge. For instance, the DL end-user expresses its requirements in terms of the DL model and, subsequently, the DL designer understands these requirements and defines the DL accordingly.

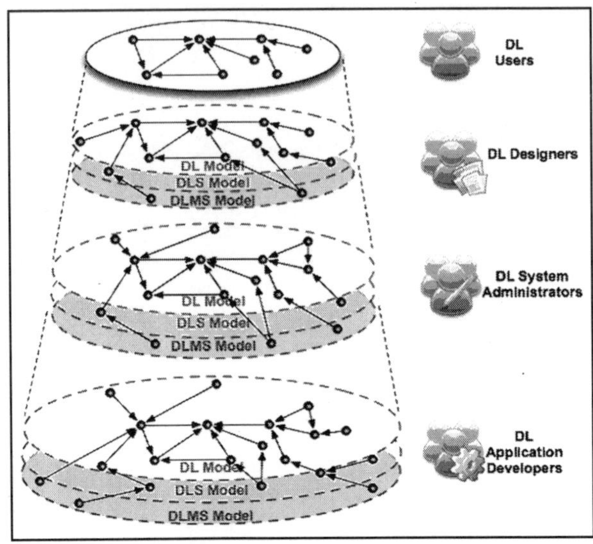

Fig. Hierarchy of Users' Views

REFERENCE FRAMEWORKS

The Digital Library Universe is quite complex and comprises multiple elements. The representation of the details of these elements requires the introduction of several frameworks at different levels of abstraction:

Reference Model

It is a set of inter-related concepts that collectively circumscribe and capture the essence of a distinct part of human knowledge, be it a whole scientific field or an individual idea or anything in between. It is a framework that helps in understanding of the basic elements of its concept(s) of concern.

As stated in, "A Reference Model consists of a minimal set of unifying concepts, axioms and relationships within a particular problem domain, and is independent of specific standards, technologies, implementations, or other concrete details".It can be established at various levels of abstraction, from very high-level and flexible to very concrete and precise. Although independent of them, it often leads to standards that have to be followed by all systems dealing with the particular parts of knowledge corresponding to it.

Digital libraries need to obtain a corresponding reference model in order to consolidate the diversity of existing approaches into a cohesive and consistent whole and provide a common basis for further advancement.

Reference Architecture

it is an architectural design pattern indicating an abstract solution in implementing the concepts and relationships identified in the Reference Model. Essentially, the reference architecture acts as a blueprint for the implementation of a DLS. There may be more than one reference architecture that addresses how to design digital libraries systems.

Each of them proposes an optimal architectural pattern for a particular class of DLSs serving the needs of DLs characterised by similar goals, motivations and requirements. For example, we might have a reference architecture for DLSs supporting federated DLs, i.e. DLs built by federating local resources of multiple organizations, and another one for personal DLs, or for specialised applications.

Concrete Architecture

It introduces additional elements making the reference architecture more concrete, e.g. replaces the mechanisms envisaged in the Reference Architecture with concrete standards and specifications. For example, it may specify that the run-time environment deployed on the hosting nodes is CORBA or the Web Services Application Framework, and that the Search functional component is implemented by four specific communicating Web Services.

The three frameworks above are shown in Figure in relationship to the general digital library environment. At the top is the most abstract Reference Model, which guides the more specific Reference Architecture and Concrete Architecture further down. In turn, these should constrain the development of any actual Implementation of a system.

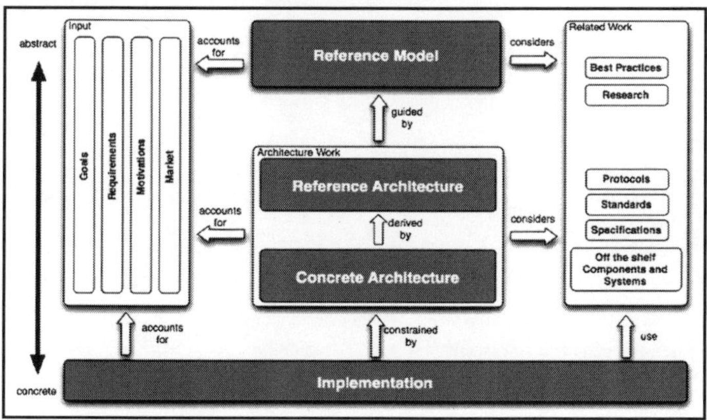

Fig. The Digital Library Universe

The three reference frameworks are the outcome of an abstraction process that has taken into account all the natural Inputs, shown to the left, e.g., the systems already existing on the market, and has taken into consideration all existing Related Work, shown to the right, e.g., best practices and relevant research.When these frameworks are adopted and followed by the community, the resulting systems will be largely compatible with each other; the interoperability thus afforded will open up significant new horizons for the field.

The goal of *'The Digital Library Manifesto'* has been to set the foundations and identify the entities of discourse within the universe of digital libraries. It has introduced the relationships among three kinds of relevant "systems" in this area: Digital Library, Digital Library System, and Digital Library Management System.

It has presented the main concepts characterising the above, i.e., content, user, functionality, quality, policy, and architecture, and has identified the main roles that actors may play within a digital library, i.e., end-user, designer, administrator, and application developer. Finally, it has described the reference frameworks that are needed to clarify the digital library universe at different detailed levels of abstraction, i.e., the Reference Model and the Reference and Concrete Architectures.

'The Digital Library Manifesto' is accompanied currently by two other documents, which correspond precisely to the aforementioned reference frameworks. These documents come as a first attempt to fulfil the needs of the field in these areas.

Clearly, diversity of needs among different digital libraries will continue to introduce new concepts that will require incorporation into the Reference Model and the Reference and Concrete Architectures. Hence, these documents should be considered as first versions of otherwise dynamic documents that will keep evolving, having the Manifesto as a firm foundation.

The *'Digital Library Manifesto'* has been based on the experience and knowledge gained by many previous efforts that have gone on for the past fifteen years around Europe and the rest of the world. We hope it will serve as a basis for new advances in research and system development in the future.

DIGITAL LIBRARY DESIGN INTO THE REALM OF ENTERPRISE ARCHITECTURE

Previous digital library research and initiatives have conceptualised and proposed several frameworks for the design, development, evaluation and interaction of digital library systems. Levy and Marshall discussed a work-oriented perspective of digital library research that is based on the work people do, and how digital libraries assist in the completion of work related tasks. Their framework highlights three crucial characteristics of digital libraries: document, technology and work. Moen and McClure identified a framework of five interacting dimensions in digital library of Government Information Locator Service (GILS): policy, users, technology, contents, and standards. The evaluation framework also includes three perspectives, representing the "views" of the stakeholders in the GILS: users, agencies, and the government. Marchionini and Fox identified four dimensions of digital library development: community, technology, service and content. Researchers presented a framework, consisting seven levels, for examining digital libraries: social, institutional, individual, interface, engineering, processing and content. Another holistic framework is presented by Fuhr consisting four major dimensions, namely data/collection, system/ technology, users and usage. Sandusky developed a list of six attributes in framing digital library usability research: audience, institution, access, content, services, and design and development. Soergel offered a digital library research framework consisting of three guiding principles and eleven specific themes for research and development.

Researcher introduced 5S and formalisms for Streams, Structures, Spaces, Scenarios, and Societies - as a framework for providing theoretical and practical unification of digital libraries. All these frameworks emphasise the importance of a holistic approach rather than examine digital libraries as a single view, which would be limited in their utility. However, the absence of common frameworks in the digital library development practices undermines the ability to develop and design digital library systems efficiently, to create large-scale collaborative activities, and to communicate the value of the systems to other communities.

Researcher wrote that the broad and deep requirements of digital libraries demand new frameworks and theories in order to understand better the complex interactions among their components. Supporting this claim, the summary report of the Joint NSF-European Union (EU) Working Groups on Future Directions of Digital 1 Libraries Research recommended that "new frameworks and theories be developed in order to understand the complex interactions between the various components in a globally distributed digital library". Formal frameworks are crucial to specify and understand clearly and unambiguously the characteristics, structure, and behaviour of complex information systems such as digital libraries.

The Digital Library Federation (DLF) in 2005 sponsored the formation of the Service Framework Group (SFG) to consider a more systematic, community-based approach to align the functions of digital libraries in fulfilling the needs of information environments. DLF envisaged that digital library functionalities be generated from the library business processes, considering the architectures as information systems with specific business requirements.

It is in this context, and in recognition of visions already underway to align digital library development with the emerging perspective of the Enterprise Architecture, the authors conducted a study that seeks to understand and model the digital library services adopting a framework that give preference to scopes, goal requirements and processes - those concepts already common in Enterprise

Architecture processes Abdullah and Zainab regard a digital library as an enterprise that requires architecting.

An Enterprise Architecture for the digital library is a framework or blueprint which shows how the digital library organisation carries out an intended task and how the digital library will or can improve the processes.

It shows how a digital library represents a special workspace for the user community, not only for search and access but also for the process or workflow management, information creation, sharing and exchange, and distributed workgroup communication. In order to identify what is required of a digital library in a specific context, a sound methodology is needed to establish an understanding of the digital library entire structure.

A multi-faceted information services such as digital libraries may be examined along different dimensions and from different perspectives or views of the stakeholders. There is a need to identify potential users, their involvement and roles in the digital library, their attitude towards the technology, their perception of its potential use and how it fits within the digital library goals in general.

ENTERPRISE ARCHITECTURE

In general, Enterprise Architecture is a framework that describes how an organisation develops, manages and uses information technology to optimally support its business functions. Sometimes, the term refers to the group of people responsible for modeling and then documenting the information architecture; other times the term denotes the process of doing this work.

More commonly, Enterprise Architecture refers to the models, documents and reusable items that reflect the actual architecture. In the EA Community Enterprise Architecture is a framework or blueprint for how the organisation achieves the current and future business objectives.It examines business processes, information technology, software and hardware, local and wide area networks, people, operations and projects with an organisation's overall strategy. Each of these strategies has a separate architectural discipline and Enterprise Architecture is the "glue" that integrates each of these disciplines into a cohesive framework.

From these definitions, it is understood that Enterprise Architecture consists of the various structures and processes of an organisation. Following this understanding, it is known that an Enterprise Architecture model is a representation of those structures and processes. A good Enterprise Architecture model will depict the organisation both as it is today and as it is envisioned in the future, and will map the various views representing the architecture to one another.

These views include both business-oriented perspectives as well as technical perspectives. The blueprint or framework of the enterprise would reveal detailed statements and processes that characterised architectural drawings. The detail drawings would be in any form, such as rich pictures, structured charts, data flow diagrams, Unified Modelling Language (UML) activity diagrams, database tables and entity-relationship model.

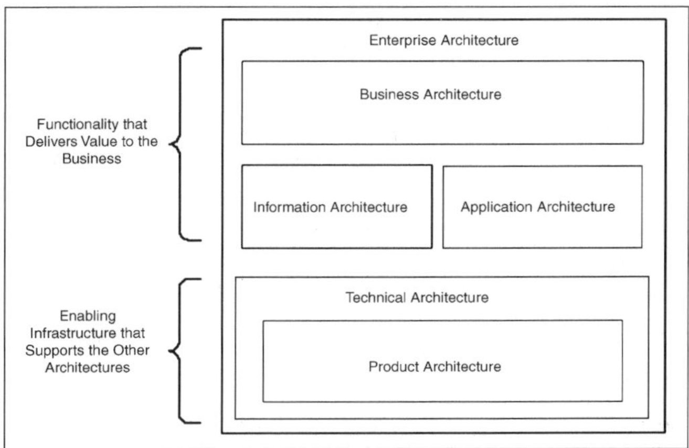

Fig. Enterprise Architecture Relationship.

FORMULATION OF AN INTEGRATED FRAMEWORK FOR THE COLLABORATIVE DIGITAL LIBRARY

Collaborative digital libraries are constructed, collected and organised by a community of users and their functionalities support the information needs and uses of that community. Researchers viewed a digital library as a collaborative working and meeting space of people sharing common interests. Through a case study method, Zachman Framework is used as a basis to investigate the existing stakeholder's conditions and environment that would ensure the reception of a collaborative digital library for urban secondary schools use in Malaysia.

In this digital library environment, students collaboratively build the digital library resources, which indirectly allow members of the community to be aware and be actively involved in local content development. The collaborative digital library would benefit both the students who would be the creator and publisher of digital project works and the teachers who would be given the experience of managing digital resources.

The multi-method approach used in the case study, to ensure the consideration of all the aspects (dimensions) of a digital library system and the relationship of these dimensions in the framework used, has been reported elsewhere. Findings were used to populate the Zachman Framework with contextual, conceptual, logical and module diagrams at every intersection between the columns (why, what, who, how, where, when) and the rows (scope, business model, system model).The framework abstracts the characteristics and features of the digital library based on the following six dimensions:

- Motivation factor, requiring the planner and owner to solicit answers to the "why" question, why there is need for the digital library? Why does the current business process need special handling such as those provided by the digital library?
- Data factor abstracts the "what" aspects of the digital library. What data that is currently handled by the stakeholders? What format would the data take in the digital library environment? What are the characteristics of the data used, processed, stored and presented or disseminated in terms of quality, accuracy, usability, description and organisation?
- People factor looks at the "who" questions or the roles of people in the digital project environment. Who will be instructing? Who will be handling the data? Who will be reporting the collated or processed data? Are the players in the digital library environment "ready" to participate and contribute to the digital library initiative? Are they able to do so?
- Function or Process factor defines the "how" of the activities in the digital environment. How will users search for data, how will they store the data? How will students write, present and submit their project report? How will the teachers ensure that the students know what is required? How do they grade the reports? How will they keep the reports submitted for the specified time required by the Malaysian Ministry of Education? How can the school library or resource centre accommodate these reports?
- Place or Networks looks at the "where" factor. Where will the digital library be located? Where will it be accessed by the stakeholders?
- Time looks at the "when" aspects of the digital library. When will submission of reports take place? This is useful for designing schedules, the processing and control architecture and timing systems.

The next section illustrates the use of Zachman Framework in design of the digital library, focusing on all six dimensions of the framework from three perspectives. Each of these dimensions is investigated from the perspective of the planner, owner and designer of the digital library. These perspectives help ensure that everything relevant to the digital library enterprise is covered. The columns, comprising the six dimensions, are arranged so that the most important column or the focus of attention is presented first. At the end, the outcome would be in the form of listings and diagrams depicting the scope, business and system model of the digital library. Rows 4, 5 and 6 are beyond the scope of this chapter.

Motivation: Why the Digital Library is Needed

Why (Motivation) column of Zachman Framework extracts the motivation of the people that support the realisation of the digital library. This reveals the reasons for creating the digital library, as well as the establishment of goals, objectives and business plan of the digital library. The authors felt motivation aspect (stakeholders' motivation) of the framework should be first populated and given the most importance. The case study revealed that the educational community is ready to collaboratively build the digital library as reflected by the following findings:

- Students are "Internet ready", as indicated by:
  - High home computer ownership as such they are ready to utilise the digital library;
  - High Internet penetration either at home, school, cyber cafes or friend's houses;
  - A high number of students either have 3-4 years or more than 5 years experience in computer usage;
  - Students regularly go online, between either every alternate days or everyday.
- Students are "digital ready" as indicated by their awareness, experience in using and preferring digital sources. The survey indicates that all students know how to word process; they know how to prepare slide presentations or draw using the computer, edit images, create multimedia and scan images, create web pages, database or undertake simple programming. This results show that they are aware and competent in handling digital resources, which is necessary when using digital library.
- Students are also moderately "Web ready" as they know how to use the web. Although most had no formal training, they learn how to use the Web by self-teaching, from books and people. The students also learn how to find sources on their own, from their parents and siblings or from their classmates and friends.
- Students are ready to collaboratively develop digital resources as they indicated sharing the resources they create or found with their friends either by e-mailing the URLs of web sites, informing others through chat room or social networks or creating links to web sites.
- Some students are "ready web publishers", as many of them either maintain a group web page, have their own personal web page or have been creating page pages for others. The results also show that the students have experience in creating digital resource over the Internet using webpage creator tools or HTML to develop their sites.
- Students do use the Internet for school related assignments or as a major source for their school project. Students sampled highly use the Internet resources to get information for the following subjects, History, Science and Geography. The results indicate that students believe that the Internet helps them with their school work.

- All students feel that there is a need for digital library of local information and feel that this would definitely benefit them. The results indicated very significant correlation between positive perception of the digital library with high Internet use, length of Internet experience, accessibility of Internet from home high self ratings of Internet skills.
- Teachers in the case study see the value of digital resources and online publishing for their students. They expressed the willingness to play the role as a facilitator in the digital library environment. They were keen on the digital library because students could contribute original works to be shared with other students, especially where some local contents are not available in textbooks. They believed students would be more careful in preparing their project report if they make it available to wider audience in the digital library environment.
- Teachers felt that a digital library would solve problem of storage and retrieval of reports submitted Since, project reports kept in resource room could only be retrieved by class name and level, and difficult to be retrieved by subject or topics of report or by specific student's name.
- The school's infrastructural facilities are ready to support a digital library as students can gain access to computers at self-accessed learning centres, especially for students and teachers who do not have computers or Internet access at their homes.

The findings indicated that the readiness factors serve as motivating indicators, goals and objectives that support the plan for developing the digital library.

Figure presents the motivating factors that support the plan of the collaborative digital library. The findings of the case study were plugged into the first three rows of the motivational aspect of Zachman Framework.

In Row 1, the Planner's goals and objectives are defined in the form of vision statement that provides the strategic direction for the digital library.The digital library will support secondary students' information needs in conducting research projects through project-based learning (PBL).

In PBL, students interpret, analyse, synthesise, generate, and evaluate information about a topic, collaborate with others, and produce a report.To support students in these types of activities, a full complement of tools is needed to meet the unique needs of learners, and Internet technologies such as digital libraries have the affordances to support students in these activities.

Based on this premise, as well as building from various illustrations of digital library initiatives' vision statement, the planner establishes the vision of the collaborative digital library to populate Row 1 of the Motivation column. The planner's vision of the digital library is as follows:

- "The collaborative digital library should enable secondary students conducting history1 school projects to access the information they need any time and any where, in a friendly, efficient and effective way, by overcoming the barriers o distance and language. The digital library should enable students to collaboratively contribute resources as the digital library is seen as a growing repository on Malaysian local history for education".With the vision in mind, the planner establishes the following goals for developing and implementing the collaborative digital library:
- The development of local historical resources;
- Provision of resources for lifelong learning;
- Provision of round-the clock access; and
- Development of community of users.

In this capacity, it establishes "a digital library service environment" - that is, a networked, online information space in which students can discover, locate, acquire access to and, increasingly, use information.

School's Technical Readiness • ICT Infrastructure is in Place • New Infrastructure is Planned • Awareness of ICT Support System • Implementation of ICT Mediated Learning	Students' ICT Readiness • High Computer Ownership • Ease of Internet Access • Home Access to Internet • Frequent Users • Technologically Skilled	Students' Digital Readiness • Could Use Digital Resources • Strong Preference for Digital Resources • Adequate Searching Skills • Familiar with Search Agents
Teacher's Ready to Collaborate • Value of Integrating with Subject Learning • See the Value of Digital Resources • See the Value of Online Publishing	Motivating Factors Strategic Readiness • Master Plan for ICT Integration • Budget Borne by Government and Parent-Teacher Association	Acceptance of Digital Library • Perceive Digital Library as Useful • Willingness to Contribute Contents

Fig. Motivating Factors that Support the Plan for Realization of the Digital Library.

The objective of the digital library is therefore to provide a learning environment and resources network for history education which is:

- Designed to meet the information needs of learners, in both individual and collaborative settings (enable the creation, organisation and maintaining of local history resources);
- Constructed to enable use of a broad array of materials for local history learning, primarily in digital format submitted by the educational community themselves (they themselves become resource providers); and
- Managed actively to promote reliable access anytime-anywhere to quality collections and services (provided over the Internet), available both within and outside the network.

Row 2 of the figure of the Motivation column identifies the owners' business plan that is the approach to use the collaborative digital library. The digital library is modelled to focus on serving students information needs in conducting research projects. As such, in the implementation of this digital library project, the use of the online resources would be an integral part of history projects-based learning activities.

The digital library may move the student community towards an emerging digital resources and the submission of reports in the electronic form is therefore feasible. The implementation of the business plan is consistent with the Ministry of Education's implementation and evaluation of History project, which will make the accomplishment of the goals and objectives feasible.

The teachers on the other hand will be given the opportunity to validate the quality of submissions to maintain the quality of the digital library, grade the report online and add links to resources found on the Internet.

Row 3 spells out the the designer's perspectives which expressed the motivation of the digital library in the form of behavioural objectives.

The objectives of the collaborative DL from the designer's perspectives are to:

- Enable students to search and browse the digital library resources through various access points regarding the topics they are exploring
- Allow the students to sequence and organise their project reports in various styles, construct references and append digital objects or pictures to their report.
- Provide the students with the experience of publishing their project report, allow teachers grade and their friends to view the repot. The motivation for this is to satisfy their innate need to share their work, so that their peers can give comments for improvements before the report is finally submitted.
- Allow teachers to check the suitability of submissions, maintain quality of contents of the digital library and grade the submissions.
- Allow teachers and students to provide metadata for resources submitted to the digital library. A metadata schema will be applied for this purpose.
- Enable students and user groups to register as members to login and submit and describe resources
- Allow users to submit feedback or submit useful links to other resources in the Internet.
- Guide and assist users in using the digital library functions and services.
- Allow authorised users to add, modify or delete submitted resources to the digital library.

These behavioural objectives of the digital library would assist the designer in developing the required digital library. The motivation and objective statements subsequently assist in the development of the user requirement and detailed definitions of the digital library services required in the Function column of the Framework.

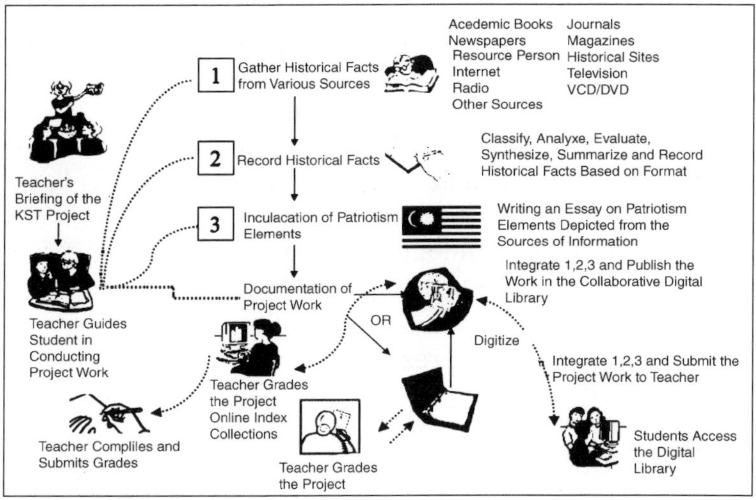

Fig. The Business Plan to Use the Collaborative Digital Library.

Data: What Resources Constitute the Digital Library

What (Data) column of the Zachman Framework describes the digital library resources students used to fulfill their research needs. The data component, at the macro level identifies the information resources included or covered in the collaborative digital library, and at the micro level, concerned the collections, quality, accuracy, usability, description and organisation of the resources in the digital library.

Findings from the case study revealed that the students and teachers emphasised the needs for contents to be "clear, accurate, adequate, organised, valid, reliable, informative and resourceful" To cater for students' information needs, in Row 1, the planner describes the three main categories of resources, without policy-controlled access.

The types of resources are:

- Resources that are born digital;
- Digitised resources or digital proxies for physical items; and
- Links to other resources relevant to the domain focus of the digital libbrary.

The digital library collections incorporates not only digital resources in different media types such as text, images, web documents, audio and video, but also in different formats with different levels of content quality and metadata.

History has been chosen as the domain of the digital library test-bed based on the survey findings that indicated the students surveyed mainly use Internet resources to get information for their History project. Case findings revealed that the project reports are typically made available in the form of collections, which refers to groups of resources organised around three themes or topic namely prominent personalities, historical events and historical buildings.

Figure presents the semantic description of the domain focus, contents, content criteria and scope of the collaborative digital library, which populates the Data component of the Zachman Framework. The stakeholders' needs for contents to be "clear, accurate, adequate, organised, valid, reliable, informative and resourceful" are therefore used as a set of general guidelines or selection criteria of resources accepted for submission.

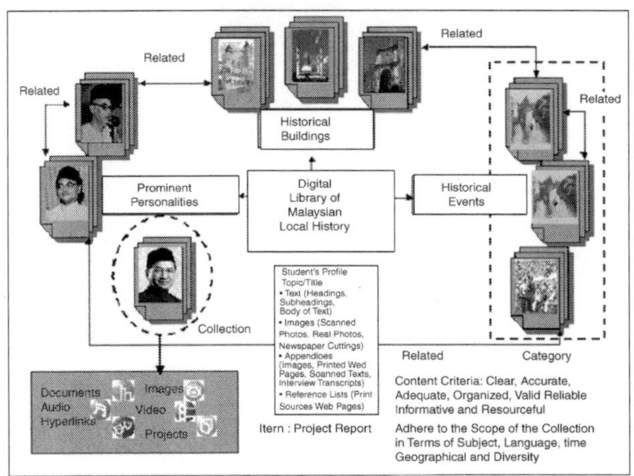

Fig. Domain Focus, Contents, Content Criteria and Scope of the Collaborative Digital Library (Owner's View of Data).

From the designer's perspective, the data of the digital library is expressed as table definition for the digital library data (comprising digital objects data and metadata, user information, annotation and static information pages) and metadata profile for the digital object resource description (comprising administrative, technical and descriptive metadata). Administrative metadata is created by the author, technical metadata is automatically generated and descriptive metadata is assigned by the content access provider (human indexer). The descriptive metadata schema used for the object data description is the Dublin Core (DC) Metadata.The digital library has altogether 16 metadata elements and incorporates DC's 14 out of 15 elements, namely title, creator, subject, description, publisher, contributor, date, type, format, identifier, language, relation, coverage and rights. The DC source metadata element is not used. Two other elements incorporated are Collection and Ranking metadata.

Network: Where can one Access the Digital Library

Network (Where) shows the sites or geographical locations and the interconnections between activities within the digital library enterprise. It illustrates the network-related aspect of the digital libraries in terms of the physical locations of members in the digital library which spread over a geographical area. The planner provides the big picture of the digital library as a centralised system with the control for the whole structure at the Faculty of Computer Science and Information Technology University of Malaya (FCSIT UM) as the developer of the digital library system. FCSIT UM group manages the centralised database server. School A is the content collaborator and joint owner of the system and other potential future collaborators such as School B, Education Departments, Ministry of Education, as well as other repositories, would be able to utilise the application server running locally to fetch the required data from the database server.

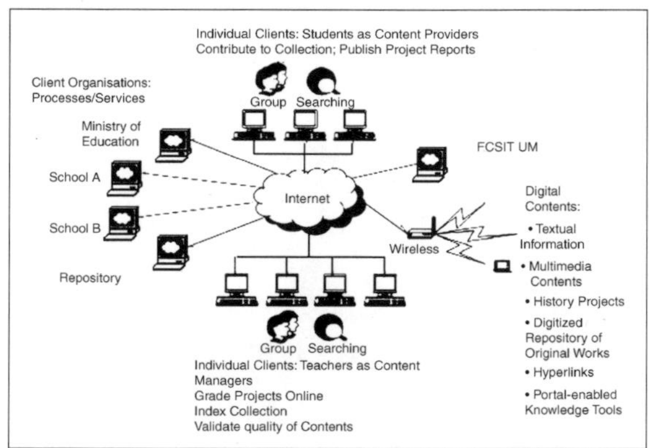

Fig. The Physical Network of the Collaborative Digital Library.

The owner is interested in the conceptual model of "Where" which includes the location of access and place where the primary stakeholders, namely the students and teachers use the digital library. It illustrates the collaborative digital library deployment expressed in term of location of access and computing facilities and network. The school community may access the collaborative digital library system from any 10 locations in the school, as all computers there are connected to the network.

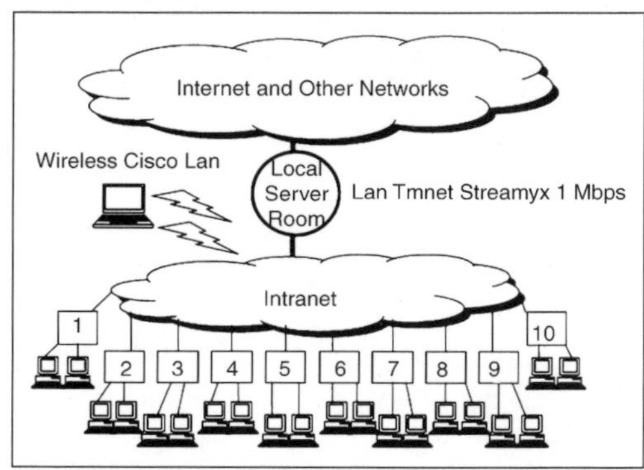

Fig. The School's Network Diagram Positioning the Location of Access for the Digital Library.

From the designer's perspective, the Network Column presents the logical model of the network component of the collaborative digital library which depicts the types of systems facilities and controlling software at the nodes and lines such as processors/operating systems, database and lines/line operation systems.

The notional distributed systems architecture shows servers supporting the digital library services served from the regional (FCSIT) and local data center environment to the school's three primary locations of access. It is referred to as a notional architecture Since, the extent of the ability to remotely serve specific applications in both the baseline state and the target state remains to be established.

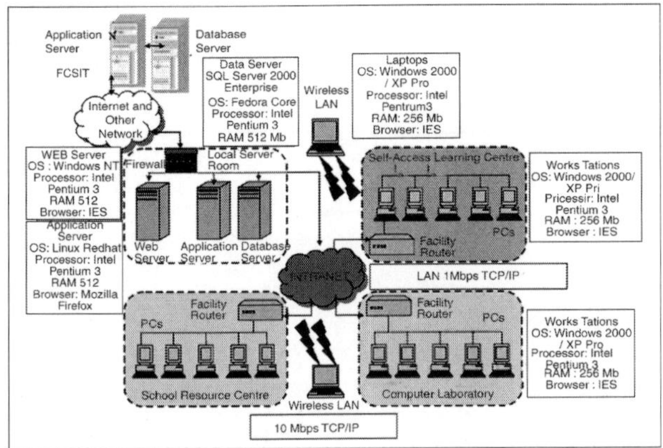

Fig. The Digital Library Notional Distributed Systems Architecture.

Time: When can one use the Digital Library (When do things Happen)

The last column, "When" represents time, or the events to which the digital library responds in relation to time. This is useful for designing schedules, the processing architecture, the control architecture and timing systems. It is difficult to describe or address this column in isolation from the others, especially Column 2 (Process). At the strategic level, the planner describes Time as the business cycle and overall business events. As has been delineated in the digital library goals and objectives (Motivation Column), the digital library provides round-the-clock access. As the Internet is a 24/7 medium, the digital library is available 24 hours a day, 7 days a week. In the detailed model of owner's perspective, the Time Column defines when activities or processes are to happen.

Based on the findings of the case study regarding the school's approach in using the digital library, the chronology of events (such as teacher's notification and requirement of the project, students choose topic, gather information, create report, obtain teacher's feedback, edit and submit report) indicating the processes that take place in the digital library environment populates owner's view of the Time Column. The designer defines the business events or the processes in the digital library, which cause specific data transformations and entity state changes to take place. The business events populate the designer's view of the Time Column of the Zachman Framework used.

People: Who Interacts with/within the Digital Library

Who (People) column represents the stakeholders or the people within the digital library enterprise to which the digital library assigns responsibility for work. Thus, this component concerns the identification of the digital library users, their information needs, their usage of the Internet and online digital resources and their roles in the enterprise. The design of the enterprise has to do with the allocation of work and the structure of authority and responsibility.

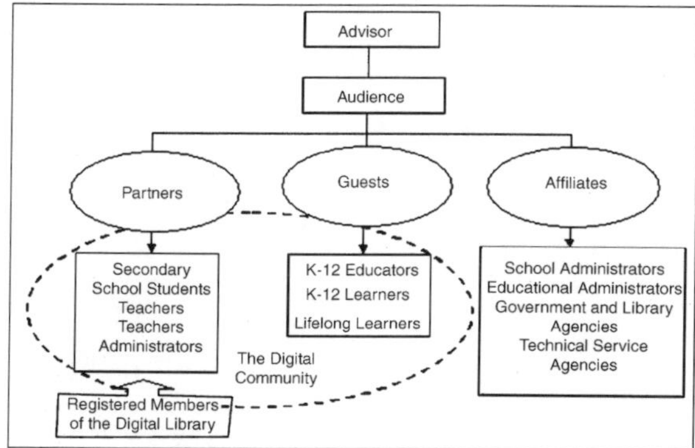

Fig. The Digital Library Organisational Structure (Planner's View of People).

This column also deals with human-machine interfaces and relationships between the people and the work they perform. In Row 1, the planner identifies the audience and the digital library organisation. There are three types of audiences within the collaborative digital library enterprise, categorised as partners, guests and affiliate members. The planner identified these groups of people in the form of digital library organisational structure.

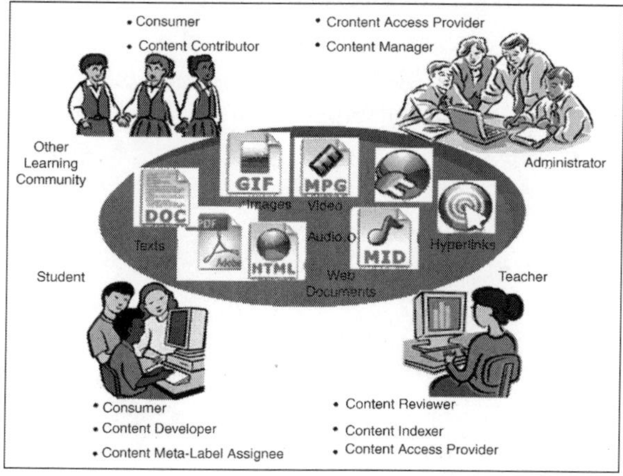

Fig. The Digital Library Actor-Roles Diagram (Owner's View of People).

The digital community follows certain rules and their members play different roles, as consumers, content developers or providers, content access providers and content manager.

Here, the digital library community includes people as well as computers, agents, network connections, files and operating systems, user interfaces, communication links, and protocols, which either use or support the digital library services. The communities of autonomous agents and computers instantiate functions upon requests by the actors of the digital library.

To operate, these agents and computers need structures of vocabulary and protocols. They act by sending streams of queries and retrieving streams of results. The digital library system uses the three-tier client-server architecture.

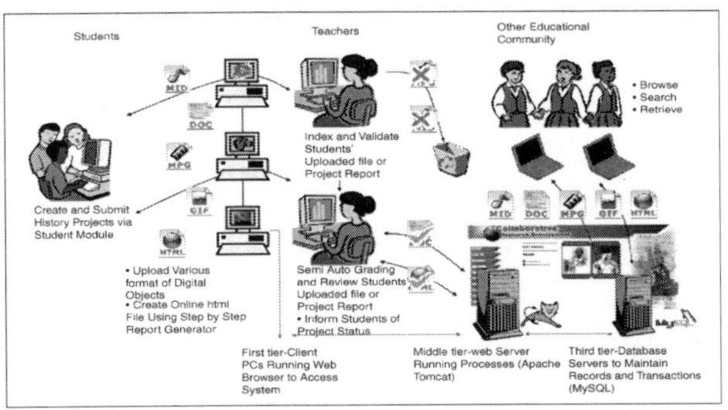

Fig. Actors and Their Roles Depicted in the Digital Library Three-Tier Client-Server Architecture (Designer's View of People).

The client tier comprises computers with web browsers such as Internet Explorer, Netscape Navigator, Mozilla Firefox and Opera. User interfaces are provided for clients to process their application and manipulate their data. All application programmes reside in the middle-tier (web server). The web server processes the request from the client and then returns required result in web page format. It processes data request by linking to a database server (such as authenticating and validating users that login into the system). It is also linked to transaction server, especially when clients are uploading files to the web server. The third tier consists of the database server and transaction for maintaining data records.

Function: What Happens in the Digital Library

How (functions) defines the functions or activities the digital library enterprise is concerned about relative to each perspective. In Row 1, the planner describes the students' research activities that take place, which encompass the entire information seeking process (from recognising the need for information to finding, using and presenting it) and the submission and evaluation of the information in the form of project report. This is presented in the form of rich pictures. Basically, the students do solitary information seeking, have spontaneous interactions with other people such as parents, siblings and friends and ask for help, and work with information in a group. The description of the activities when conducting history projects are then transformed into the online activities the students and teachers would be able to perform in the collaborative digital library. Figure presents the workflows and processes the collaborative digital library enterprise should conduct. These processes are also in line with the owner's plan to use the digital library for school project. The function component refers to the activities students perform in their research, such as choosing topic, searching for information, organising resources, writing, presenting, submitting and teachers grading of project work.

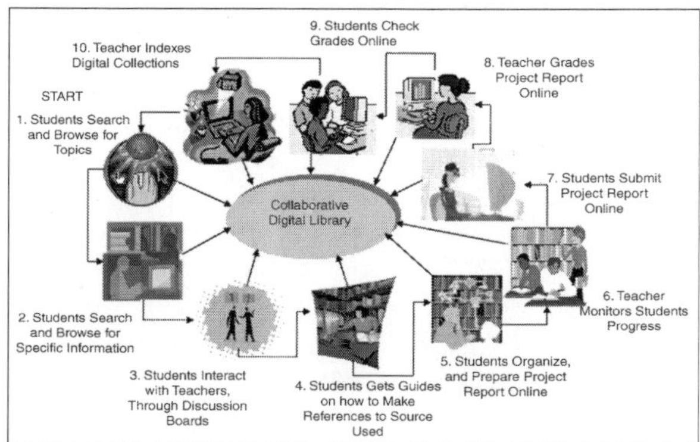

Fig. Activities Performed in the Collaborative Digital Library.

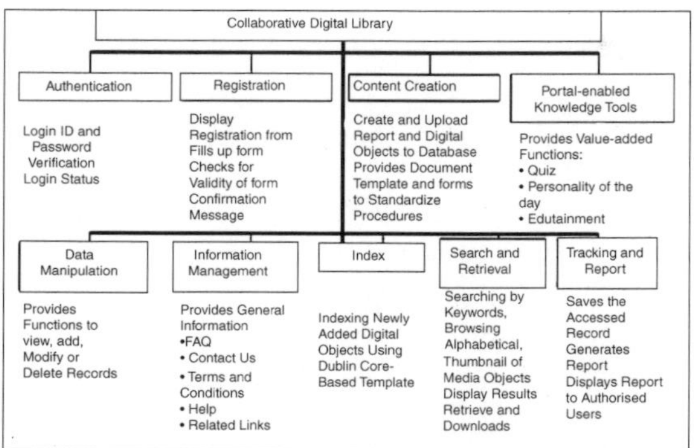

Fig. Conceptual Model of Services in the Digital Library.

Using data from analysis of the activities culled from the research, formulation of behavioural objectives of the digital library as well as from the analysis of digital library functional requirements, the planner develops the user requirement expressed in terms of functions and present it as services in a contiguous structured chart, The structured chart is comprehensible to the owner as the conceptual model of the digital library services. This structured chart populates Row 2 of the Function Column and describes the process of translating the objectives of the digital library enterprise into successively more detailed definitions of its services. Feedback from the stakeholders on the potential features of a service and digital library design implication derived from the analysis of the case study have helped to ascertain the main features required by the collaborative digital library.

In Row 3, the designer portrays the digital services in terms of data transforming processes, described exclusively in terms of definition of programme modules and how they interact with each other. The three system modules, namely administrators (including teachers), students and guests, provide different access types for different level of users. Along with this are specific definitions of security requirements, in terms of who (which role) is permitted access to what function, in the form of structured charts and detailed description of the modules menu.

ZACHMAN FRAMEWORK FOR ENTERPRISE ARCHITECTURE

The Zachman Framework is a logical structure for classifying and organising the descriptive representations of the enterprise that are significant to the management of the enterprise, as well as to the development of the enterprise' systems.

The framework uses a grid model to provide a logical structure for classifying and organising the descriptive representation of an enterprise, in six different dimensions, and each dimension can be perceived in five different perspectives. In this framework, the architecture is described across two independent aspects, the rows represent the views of five different types of stakeholders and the columns represent six different aspects of the architecture.

The points of intersection between the rows and the columns form cells. Each of these cells holds important information of the enterprise that needs to be understood and explicitly declared. The Zachman Framework's enterprise design model is presented in figure.

The Zachman Framework for Enterprise Architecture is found suitable to investigate the initial requirements and define the digital library organisation, processes, technology and information flows, as well as ground the design of digital libraries for the following reasons:

- The framework helps to explicitly show the many perspectives that need to be addressed by the digital library. It requires the planner, owner and designer of the digital library to involve the stakeholders to ensure that it meets their needs and will be used. It holistically controls the approach to investigate the user requirements and guides the data gathering techniques.
- The framework requires the involvement of stakeholders, not just the enterprise architects and developers. and ideally this practice is what digital library designers and developers should follow. This aligns with the need to involve stakeholders in digital library design and development.

- The framework is robust enough. It explicitly shows and requires the designer to consider all aspects of the digital library design.
- The framework is generic in nature and can be applied perfectly to digital library organisation. As such it is a flexible framework and it does not impose a method or restrict any user to a set of pre-defined artifacts.

This chapter shows, through a case study, how the three tiers of Zachman Framework - the contextual or planner's perspectives, the conceptual or the owner's perspectives and the logical or the designer's perspectives– are used to design a digital library.

The first two rows or layers are referred to as the Business Architecture for they describe the functions a business performs and the information it uses. The third row refers to the information and the application architecture. The planner is concerned with positioning the digital library in the context of its environment.

This is when the planner enquires about the demographics of the stakeholders, ICT individual differences, their readiness to participate and collaborate, their awareness of the concept of digital libraries and their perception of the digital library initiative.

The owner is interested in the digital library's deliverable and how it will be used. The designer is concerned with how the digital library is to perform its functions.

This involves investigating the resources that are used, the user behaviour of seeking for resources, the experience of searching, the relevance perceived and the problems encountered.

The possible sets of constructs or artifacts to represent the cell content for each cell in the top three rows or layers of the Zachman Framework are presented in table.What How Where Who When Why SCOPE (Contextual) Planner List of things important to the business List of processes the business perform List of location in which the business operate List of people involved in the business List of events significant to the business List of business goals and objectives SCOPE (Contextual) Planner BUSINESS (Conceptual)

Owner Semantic Model Business Process Model Business Logistic Model Work flow model Master Schedule Business Plan BUSINESS (Conceptual) Owner SYSTEM (Logical) Designer Logical Data Model Application Architecture Distributed System Architecture Human Interface Architecture Processing Structure Business Data Model SYSTEM (Logical) Designer TECHNOLOGY (Physical) Builder DETAILED PRESENTA-TION (Out-of-context view) FUNCTIONING ENTERPRISE–The prototype Data Function Network People Time Motivation FUNCTIONING ENTERPRISE–The prototype table. Zachman Framework at the Contextual, Conceptual and Logical Systems Architecture.

LINKING DIGITAL LIBRARY RESOURCES TO RELATED RESOURCES

This section emphasizes the ability of knowledge organization systems to link digital library resources to other related resources. The basis for this linking is the identification of information within a digital resource that can be extracted and used to search and locate information within a KOS. The KOS may then be used to expand codes to more explanatory full text, to provide more descriptive records, or to link entity names to resources of physical specimens.

EXPANDING CODES TO FULL TEXT

Practitioners of a discipline use coding schemes to facilitate communication within that discipline. It is often helpful to connect these coding schemes to the full names for which the code stands. The examples provided here include links between databank registration codes and the biological sequence data, and between industrial codes and the full name that the code represents.

Linking Sequence Numbers to Biosequence Databanks

The lengthy biochemical and genetic sequences that molecular biologists, biotechnologists, and geneticists identify each day are kept in databanks. Several databanks have been developed, for example, to cover protein sequences, nucleotides, and cell lines. One of the largest databanks contains information on the mapping of the human genome. As molecular biologists began to discover these sequences, they reported them in scientific journals. Difficulties in composing, proofreading, and printing the text soon arose.

Through an ad hoc standards process, major biomedical publishers agreed to require the inclusion of codes or databank numbers for these sequences in articles when they are published. In addition, the sequence itself must be registered in a databank before the paper can be published. Some of the most frequently referenced databanks are listed on the Web site of the National Center for Biotechnology Information. They include GenBank and the Research Collaboratory for Structural Bioinformatics Protein Data Bank.

Each sequence number is different, but all begin with a persistent code identifying the databank. How can the link be made between the literature and the databank? Through a search profile, a text analysis programme, or keyword indexing, the text can be analysed and the sequence databank numbers identified. An active link can be embedded. The active link consists of a search strategy to locate that sequence number in the databank where the actual sequence is stored. When the user clicks on the active link, the script is generated and launched from the user's browser.

The Web-enabled database is searched, and the sequence record is returned to the user. Depending on the services provided by the databank site, the user can analyse the sequence using a number of tools provided by the databank or download the sequence for local manipulation. This type of connection exists between the *National Library of Medicine's* (NLM) search service, PubMed, and GenBank at the National Center for Biotechnology Information. If a search in PubMed yields records that have GenBank numbers, the user can automatically search and display the sequence records from GenBank.

Linking Individual Industrial Codes to the Full Scheme

In business, classification schemes serve to communicate important facts about a company or product. These codes are generally controlled by a government, professional, trade, or international standards organization. They often serve as shorthand for users interested in material in a particular area of industry or a specific business sector. Perhaps the most familiar scheme is the SIC code, which was last updated in 1987. The SIC codes have been used by the U.S. government, economists, financial markets, regulators, and procurement offices to identify manufacturing, agriculture, and service sectors of the economy.

In 1997, a new scheme was approved for use within the United States. The North American Industrial Classification System was developed with Canada and Mexico as a means of providing an agreed-upon scheme for the collection, reporting, and analysis of information about the economy by sector, both within and across borders. Information about NAICS is available from the Web site of the U.S. Census Bureau. The digital library can provide related information by using the authority files for the coding schemes as a linked authority file.

If a company or economic sector mentioned in the digital library's collection can be linked to an SIC or NAICS code, the code can be searched against the official tables of definitions maintained by the U.S. Census Bureau. These files provide definitions of the codes and place each code in the classification scheme with other economic sectors. The digital library's content can be further enhanced by making a link between the SIC and NAICS codes. If the digital library resource has the SIC code, it can be extracted and searched against the Census Bureau's *1997 NAICS and 1987 SIC Correspondence Tables.* The table returns the corresponding code from the alternate scheme.

LINKING TO DESCRIPTIVE RECORDS

Linking the name of an entity, such as a personal name, organization, or location, to additional information about that entity was one of the first uses of hyperlinking. Knowledge organization systems such as dictionaries, glossaries, and classification schemes can be used to link the entities in one resource to richer descriptions of that entity in another resource. This is particularly helpful for users who are new to a topic and in cases where the additional information can make the user's task more efficient. The examples that follow are from three disciplines. The first example links organism names to records that not only describe the species more fully but also put it in the context of the overall classification scheme for living organisms. The second example links chemical names to descriptive records and molecular structures. In the third example, proper names are linked to the biographies for the person.

Linking Organism Names to Taxonomic Records

Genus-species names are the Latin names for organisms–*e.g.*, plants, animals, and microorganisms. Taxonomists, who study and classify living organisms, create records for each of these organisms. Generally, these records are linked relationally to the other organisms in a hierarchy. Beyond the organism name and the information that it and its placement in the hierarchy convey, taxonomic records use other elements to describe the organism. These may include distribution patterns, the authority for naming and classification, and the date the organism was identified.

Scientists base the information on specimens that are retained because they serve as the physical evidence of the description. Natural history museums, private collections, and individual scientists number, or code, the specimens in their collections. Sometimes specimens are supported by photo-graphs or line drawings, which may be digitized. By using a taxonomic authority file as an intermediate authority file, one can link a text or an image file containing a name or picture of an organism to additional related information.

By automatically processing the text or embedding a link from the organism name in the text or from the image to the taxonomic authority record, one can extend the knowledge conveyed by the text. The text can include the descriptive and historical information in the taxonomic record and, ultimately, link to a photograph, a drawing, or appropriate video or audio segments. Because of the ambiguity in organism names, many examples of this type are now created manually. However, depending on the extent of the files involved, the ambiguity of the Latin and common names for organisms can be overcome.

An example of a taxonomic intermediate file is the *Integrated Taxonomic Information System* (ITIS). ITIS is a partnership of U.S., Canadian, and Mexican government agencies, private organizations, and taxonomic specialists cooperating to develop an online, scientifically credible list of biological names of North American plants and animals. It is used by many U.S. govern-ment agencies for consistent naming of plants and animals for regulatory and monitoring purposes. To link textual material in a digital library to the ITIS record, the organism name can be identified manually or automatically in the text and submitted as a query to the ITIS database.

When a match is found, ITIS presents the ITIS record, which provides essential information about the organism. The information includes synonymous names, including some common names, and an indication of the placement of the organism in the larger taxonomic classification scheme.

Linking Chemical Names to Molecular Structures

The unique identification for a chemical substance is not its name but its molecular structure. However, chemical names are commonly used in research documents, project plans, catalogs, and directories, all of which may be resources in a digital library. There are competing systems of nomenclature as well as common and commercial synonyms. The ambiguity is resolved by providing links between the chemical names in the text and the molecular structure. This is done through a chemical registry number or code that is connected to a particular chemical name and an authority record that provides additional information about the chemical. This information includes the chemical's synonyms and some of its chemical and physical properties.

Most important in today's research environment is the link from this authority file to a chemical structure file. Structure files, used with the appropriate software, graphically depict the molecular structure. This sophisticated software allows for three-dimensional visualization, rotation, and substitution of the chemical bonds. An example of the use of the chemical registry number to link chemical names with molecular structures can be seen in the work of BIOSIS, the world's largest not-for-profit producer of biological and biomedical databases.

In 1993, BIOSIS began processing its bibliographic citations to automatically identify chemical names. BIOSIS assigns CAS *Registry Numbers* (RNs) to the chemical names identified in this process. In the STN International online system, hosted in the United States by CAS, a user of BIOSIS can select one or more of the records resulting from a search and extract the RN. The extracted RN can be applied against the CAS Registry File, which contains more than 21 million substances, including organics, inorganics, biosequences, metals, and alloys.

The registry file record for the chemical name, including the link to the synonyms for the chemical name and the structure file itself, can then be accessed. With special tools developed by CAS, the structure can be viewed and manipulated. It can be imported into modeling tools that allow the chemist to manipulate the structure and thereby envision new chemicals. Alternatively, the user can start with any database that contains CAS RNs and extract the resulting RNs to perform a search for complementary bibliographic records in the BIOSIS database. Linking chemical names to structures using RNs on a large scale is neither inexpensive nor easy. There are two approaches to identifying chemical names in text.

Some journal articles include the CAS RN for the major chemicals discussed. In this case, an analysis of the text for the terms "RN", "CAS RN", and variations preceding numerics can identify RNs that can be used as a link. Alter-natively, a programme to identify chemical names in text, similar to that developed by BIOSIS, could be devised.

Developing the identification programme, as well as searching chemical databases, is costly; however, if the digital library has license agreements for chemistry databases, this type of linkage may be possible. In addition, many organizations have small chemical files of their own that may include RNs and other information of particular relevance to the organization's research. It may be possible to link to these local databases using methods that are more direct.

Linking Personal Names to Biographical Information

A common type of authority file is the personal name authority, which controls variants of personal names. For example, the *Library of Congress Name Authority File* (LCNAF) is used to control variant personal names for authors, editors, artists, and others. The *Union List of Artist Names* (ULAN), developed by the Getty Vocabulary Programme, is another example. Name authorities serve as tools for catalogers and indexers. They ensure that the proper form of the name, rather than an unapproved variant, is used and bring together all works by or about the person.

A name authority file can also be used to link a biblio-graphic record or document containing the person's name to a variety of other related materials. If the digital library's resource has a standardized form of the name, it can be identified and searched against the authority file to locate variants. The standardized and variant forms can be joined in a search against a variety of other resources that can provide related information. For example, in the case of a digital library of images of artists' works or biographical or critical text, a name authority file such as the ULAN or the LCNAF can act as an intermediate file to provide additional information. The file, which contains integrated variant names, can be searched by the name appearing in the digital library collection. When the record is found, the information about the artist can be displayed, providing a wide range of contextual material for the user. Citations to significant biographical or critical works about the artist, some of which may also be available on the Web, may also be provided in the name authority file. The variant names from a name authority can also be used to locate and provide automatic links from the personal name in the text to a biography, without requiring that the name be presented in the same fashion in the two resources.

One such resource that could be linked to for biographical information is Gale's Biography Resource, which contains more than 142,000 biographies and related citations from more than 1,000 periodicals. However, to produce this kind of link, there must be a mechanism for locating personal names in text. Several programmes can do this type of text analysis; among those that have been developed commercially are NameFinder from the Carnegie Group and the Intelligent Agent from IBM. In addition, variant names can be extracted from the name authority itself, grouped, and run as a search against the text to locate name occurrences.

LINKING ENTITY NAMES TO PHYSICAL SPECIMENS

In some cases, it is possible to go another step and connect entity names in the digital library resources to physical specimens. The curation of physical specimens or artifacts is critical to the advancement of many disciplines. Exhibition catalogs describe the art objects in a particular exhibition. Museum catalogs provide inventories of the art, natural history, or cultural objects held by a particular museum.

These catalogs, increasingly available as computerized databases, are knowledge organization systems that not only provide descriptive records but also point to the location of the object in a museum, an archive, or another collection. For example, in biology, a physical specimen is particularly important when it is the result of the discovery and description of a new organism or of the reclassification of a known organism.

A type specimen is the example collected from the field by a taxonomist to serve as the prime example for the description of the organism and the validation of its taxonomic classification and naming. These specimens are held by natural history collections, and their deposit is required by the rules of various taxonomic societies. As part of the curatorial activity, the collections assign identification codes. While the primary use of identification codes has been to organize the physical collections, numerous projects are under way in the natural history community to digitize photographs of specimens and create database records for the specimens, including their identifiers, and thereby make them more rea dily accessible.

The degree of digitization varies from specialty to specialty. For example, in botany, virtually all significant research herbaria are digitally cataloging their type collections instead of maintaining paper records. Many are also making digital photographs of the type specimens available over the Web. The publication of identification codes in the journal literature is also changing. Historically, identification codes have been presented in the "Materials Used" sections of journal articles. The level of specificity of the identification code has varied, depending on the biological discipline. For example, botanical journals tend to list only the institution and the catalog, while vertebrate journals provide the code to the specimen level.

The current trend is to require lists of specimens that are more detailed. As the lists become longer and the printing costs increase, journal publishers are beginning to request links to independent Web sites maintained by the researchers or their organizations that carry all the specimens used in the study and provide some level of identification.

If the digital library collection contains resources that include the identification codes, these codes can be extracted and matched against the Web-based catalogs or databases. This link can provide users with location and contact information to allow them to access the physical object mentioned in the digital library resource. Curators or registrars of artistic, archaeological, and cultural history collections also assign inventory or accession numbers to items in their collections.

Identification numbers may also be found in scholarly catalogues raisonnés. Links similar to those described for natural history can be made between text related to works of art and the physical work in a particular collection. An article about a work of art can be linked to additional information about the physical specimen by linking the identification number in the text with an online catalog containing the number and additional information about the work.

As museums digitize their collections to establish a presence on the Web or to reduce the handling of the physical objects, KOSs that can link the digital library resources to the physical object are being developed. If there is a museum with a collection that complements that of the digital library, it is worthwhile to discuss ways in which the digital library and digital museum collections may "co-evolve."

3

Knowledge Organization Systems in Library System

The term *knowledge organization systems* are intended to encompass all types of schemes for organizing information and promoting knowledge management. Knowledge organization systems include classification schemes that organize materials at a general level, subject headings that provide more detailed access and authority files that control variant versions of key information. They also include less-traditional schemes, such as semantic networks and ontologies. Because knowledge organization systems are mechanisms for organizing information, they are at the heart of every library, museum, and archive.

Knowledge organization systems are used to organize materials for the purpose of retrieval and to manage a collection. A KOS serves as a bridge between the user's information need and the material in the collection. With it, the user should be able to identify an object of interest without prior knowledge of its existence. Whether through browsing or direct searching, whether through themes on a Web page or a site search engine, the KOS guides the user through a discovery process. In addition, KOSs allow the organizers to answer questions regarding the scope of a collection and what is needed to round it out.

All digital libraries use one or more KOS. Just as in a physical library, the KOS in a digital library provides an overview of the content of the collection and supports retrieval. The scheme may be a traditional KOS relevant to the scope of the material and the expected audience for the digital library, a commercially developed scheme such as the Yahoo or Excite categories, or a locally developed scheme for a corporate intranet.

The decision of what knowledge organization system to use is central to the development of any digital library. The KOS must be applicable, either automatically or by human catalogers, to the resources included in the digital library. Once the material is included in the collection, the KOS must be meaningful to its users. This section outlines the characteristics of KOSs, describes the common types, and discusses their origins and traditional uses.

COMMON CHARACTERISTICS OF KNOWLEDGE ORGANIZATION SYSTEMS

It is often said that humans are inherent organizers. From an early age, children play sorting and matching games. We cope with our ever-changing world by comparing new objects or experiences with those with which we are familiar, identifying patterns and categorizing what is new into our existing frame of reference. The emphasis on developing comprehensive KOS's can be seen in the writings of our earliest philosophers, many of whom continue to influence our view of the world. For example, Aristotle's effort to categorize knowledge into groups is reflected in our language, our education, and our science.

The original classification scheme of the Library of Congress, used between 1800 and 1814, was based on the philosophical works of Sir Francis Bacon and inherited from the English tradition.

Beginning in 1814, the influence of Thomas Jefferson can be seen on the Library of Congress collection. Jefferson, who reclassified the library, reflected a more humanist philosophy. There is no single knowledge classification scheme on which everyone agrees.

Michael Lesk speculates that while a single KOS would be advantageous, it is unlikely that such a system will ever be developed. Culture may constrain the knowledge classification scheme so that what is meaningful to one culture is not necessarily meaningful to another. Therefore, we live in a world of multiple, variant ways to organize knowledge.

Despite their diversity, KOSs have the following common characteristics that are critical to their use in organizing digital libraries:

- The KOS imposes a particular view of the world on a collection and the items in it.
- The same entity can be characterized in different ways, depending on the KOS that is used.
- There must be sufficient commonality between the concept expressed in a KOS and the real-world object to which that concept refers that a knowledgeable person could apply the system with reasonable reliability. Likewise, a person seeking relevant material by using a KOS must be able to connect his or her concept with its representation in the system.

KNOWLEDGE ORGANIZATION SYSTEMS IN DIGITAL LIBRARIES

This section provides general guidelines that may be useful for an organization that wants to use knowledge organization systems to organize a digital library. The framework described is applicable for KOSs of any type or subject.

PLANNING KNOWLEDGE ORGANIZATION SYSTEMS

Analysing User Needs

Of primary importance to any digital library project is an analysis of its users' needs, in terms of content and functionality. Many volumes have already been written about needs assessment, and providing detailed guidance on this subject is beyond the scope of this paper. However, when analysing how a KOS might be used with a particular digital library, it is essential to thoroughly understand the environment of the user.

One must look not only at the needs for organizing the digital library materials but also at possible links between content within and outside the digital library walls. This is particularly important for KOSs that are acting as intermediate authority files, because in such cases the links may not be readily apparent. It is important to consider other views that might be valuable for users and peripheral communities that might benefit from the digital library's content were it accessible to them through a KOS.

Locating Knowledge Organization Systems

Once the user's needs have been analysed, it is necessary to locate KOSs to meet the need. While an alternate system can be built locally, it is preferable to find an existing KOS for several reasons. First, it is costly and time-consuming to build a KOS. Second, KOSs often benefit by having been built over time. Many of the systems described in this report have been built over decades; some existed in paper before digitization. The value of a KOS comes from its acceptance by the user community; sources built by noted authorities such as learned societies, trade associations, or standards groups will be viewed as more trustworthy than those built internally.

Finally, the networked environment has resulted in both an explosion of primary materials, including documents, electronic journals, and Web-based databases, and in an equivalent explosion of KOSs on the Web. There are several ways to identify KOSs that may be of interest. Many users are already aware of KOSs on the Web within their discipline. Developers may also turn to directories, librarians in the field, and reference sources, or they may perform a general search of the Internet.

Planning the Infrastructure

It is necessary to make decisions about the architecture of the KOS in the context of the digital library setting. The physical location of the KOS is important. Will the system be held externally or internally? There are pros and cons to either approach. If the system is available on the Web, it is possible to consider linking to the KOS as an external system. This architecture requires a script or some search query to locate the resource. One must then launch a query against the resource to obtain the piece of information that will serve as the key between the two files. This key could be a *universal resource locator* (URL) or input to another search query.

A query may be necessary if the KOS is stored in a database. The script may transfer log-on information from the digital library system to the external KOS, in order to provide access to the Web-enabled database. In the case of a more direct link, the access may be by URL. However, the use of a URL as the link has the same problem with persistence as does direct access via a URL from a browser. The organization may move the KOS, thereby changing the URL that is being used as the key. It is important to determine how often the URLs in the KOS change, whether there is a means of notification of these changes, and whether it is possible to consider an alternative that would be more persistent.

Schemes such as the Digital Object Identifier and the Persistent URL have been devised to enable resources to be physically moved among servers without having their names changed. Another alternative is the use of other Uniform Resource Identification (URI) schemes and the *Uniform Resource Name* (URN), which can be sent from the newer Web browsers. The benefit of linking to a remote resource is that the resource will always be upto-date. The maintenance of the KOS is in the hands of the owner, not the digital librarian. It may also be more apparent to users that the KOS is not owned by the digital library.

Linking to a remote KOS also has disadvantages. Persistence and unexpected changes in the organization and content of the system may cause problems. The software or telecommunications route between the digital library server and the KOS may be unreliable. In systems requiring fast response time or large amounts of data transfer, and, therefore, high bandwidth, the fact that a connection must be made between the digital library and the external KOS may make the system unacceptable to the user. Alter-natively, the KOS may be obtained from the owner and loaded locally.

In many cases, this requires licensing that may not be required when the KOS is accessed remotely, because a copy of the whole resource is being provided to the digital library. Loading a KOS locally also requires that one consider issues such as maintenance, local system administration, and disk storage. If the KOS uses special software, such as a database management system, loading the KOS locally will require a copy of that software, which may require additional purchase or licensing. Other considerations are the need for firewalls and interface design.

On the positive side, the KOS is under more local control. Therefore, it may be possible to improve the response time by not accessing the KOS over the Internet. If the KOS is to be used behind the scenes, concerns of speed and integration become more important. If additional modifications need to be made to the KOS to integrate it with the digital library, it will also be necessary to load the KOS locally. If the digital library intends to incorporate numerous secondary KOSs, it is important to consider the degree to which the architecture is scaleable.The National Library of Medicine's UMLS incorporates more than 40 different sources. While its main purpose has been to develop a metathesaurus for moving among these vocabularies, the management of the systems, regardless of the mapping issues, has been a major consideration. Ingest has been a major concern, with the need to develop a system that can handle a variety of input formats-from ASCII text files to highly structured database output.

The architecture must also accommodate the character sets of the incoming sources. This is particularly important if a mark-up language has been used to represent special characters and diacritical marks. Systems that have been developed in Unicode, which extends ASCII to accommodate diacritical marks and non-Roman character sets, cannot be handled by systems that deal only with ASCII or extended ASCII sets. Since many digital library systems are being built as extensions or applications of existing *integrated library systems* (ILS), it is important to consider how the KOSs will integrate with the library system.Unfortunately, many ILS vendors have not considered links to external files or databases in their system designs. In some cases, the vendor may require that the information be stored in the proprietary format of the ILS. The system may require that the files be on the same directory or server as the accessing ILS. The fields that can be linked to the Web or searched may be limited. Outside communi-cations may require Z39.50 client-server connections. With relatively closed systems, ILSs may be a difficult environ-ment in which to implement alternative and non-raditional KOSs.

Digital libraries that are interested in using KOSs should consider this integration when developing requirements for the procurement of a system to support them. Vendors should be encouraged to support relatively open architectures and to consider the extension of traditional library systems to support broader digital library functionality.In addition to these immediate concerns, it is important to consider the incorporation of future KOSs. Initial success may spur the desire for integration of additional KOSs or enhanced functionality for the existing KOS. Success may breed additional requirements and increase the strain on hardware, software, and network architectures.

Maintaining the Knowledge Organization System

For a digital library, an outdated KOS can be more of a hindrance than a benefit. Maintenance, both of content and of the system, should be considered when planning a KOS. This is particularly important if the digital library is to be self-supporting or revenue generating. Version control of the KOS is extremely important.Reloading a new version from the system provider is one way to accommodate changes; however, this may not be acceptable if the locally held version differs substantially from that held by the system's provider. If there has been significant transformation or processing of the original KOS, it may be difficult, or impossible, to reload the original and recreate the changes that have been made.

A transaction-based approach, whereby only changes are transferred between the KOS provider and the library, is also possible; however, this requires that the system provider have the infrastructure, both machine and human, to produce these transactions. It also requires that the changes to the original KOS be identifiable in order to create change transactions. For example, Stuart Nelson of the NLM's UMLS Project recently reported that many systems can create annual transaction records to inform the UMLS about the changes that have occurred to the original system.However, the changes are often not indicated with enough detail to support automatic change transactions in the UMLS. If a change date, for example, is recorded only at the level of the concept record, it is impossible to tell whether the term has changed or if the relationship between this concept and another concept has changed. Since the UMLS splits the incoming terminology and its relationships into a variety of files, it is often difficult to tell how the UMLS files must be change based on the changes made during the maintenance of the original KOS.

Presenting the Knowledge Organization System to the User

In addition to deciding which KOS should be used and what functions it should serve, the digital library will need to determine how to present the KOS to its users. A KOS may be exposed to the user or made relatively transparent. The KOS can be exposed to the user in different ways. Material can be grouped into KOS-related themes or categories on the digital library's Web site.

The KOS may be used at a higher level to identify specific portals for different uses or users. If the content of the digital library includes metadata records, the KOS may be displayed as index terms on the records or in its entirety as a navigation aid to searching. In other cases, the KOS may be transparent. For example, a thesaurus can be used behind the scenes to extend the user's search to include synonyms, to connect the digital library's resources to other information and resources, or to filter or rank the information obtained.

IMPLEMENTING KNOWLEDGE ORGANIZATION SYSTEMS

Acquisition and Intellectual Property Issues

It is critical to properly handle the acquisition of knowledge organization systems. The first question is whether the KOS is under copyright. If so, the copyright holder should be contacted concerning the KOS. It is important to ensure that the apparent contact is the official one. Many references have been reprinted or put on the Web without proper acknowled-gment of the real owner.

Once the contact has been made, there are several points for discussion:

- If the provider maintains the KOS, how will the digital library find out about any changes that may be made in it? Is there a notification mechanism in place? How frequently must the information be updated to be of benefit to the digital library's users? Will the maintenance be self-evident, or must the agreement include notification requirements? What will the owner do if the maintenance can no longer be performed?
- What will happen if the provider discontinues the product or sells or transfers it to someone else?
- What uses can the digital library make of the KOS under the proposed agreement? As with other licensing, it is advisable to aim for the broadest permissions and the longest term possible. At a minimum, the library should be able to renegotiate the terms of the agreement relatively easily.
- In a networked environment, it is beneficial to develop mechanisms for linking to online versions rather than to maintain a local copy of the resource. This ensures that what is presented is up-todate, and acknowledges more clearly the ownership of the KOS. However, there are numerous factors to consider. Will the KOS be used on an intranet or behind a firewall, where access to the outside or information coming into the organization might be prohibited? Does the KOS service use "cookies" or require knowledge of the user's Internet provider address? Does it require a user ID and password?
- If the KOS is to be accessed remotely, are there service issues? Is it likely to be accessed with bandwidth, model, and computer speeds that are adequate for outside connections of this type? Is the use of such a critical nature that unreliable service on the part of the KOS or the Internet connection will cause the digital library itself to be viewed as less useful? Does the KOS require a specialized search engine or search query formulation? Can the digital library system properly display the results, or would the results be better displayed through the KOS system? Will the resulting information be used in its native form or must it be extracted or transformed? If the KOS is to be loaded locally, in what formats can the content be received?
- If the KOS is not available electronically, can it be digitized? Is the owner interested in a cooperative venture, and are the human and financial resources for such an effort available?

Making the Link

There are two parts to establishing the link between the digital library and the KOS. The first is locating the key anchor information in the digital library's resource. The second involves the look up against the target file. The creation of this link may be more or less automatic, depending on the particular situation. The characterization of this activity is meant to be general and to allow both "on-thefly" links and embedded links.

Regardless of what function the KOS is going to serve in the digital library, the essential information contained in the digital library resource from which the link is to be made must be identified. The mechanism for doing this depends on the type of object from which the link is being made and on the information that is expected to be identified in the digital library's resource. The first step is to review any metadata related to the digital library resource. Do the metadata carry the term that is needed to make the link? If this information is included, the level at which the metadata are assigned should be reviewed.

If the metadata indicate the subject matter of the specific resource in which the user will be interested, the metadata can be used to make the links. However, in some cases, the terms that appear in the title or description at the resource level may not be indicative of the subject at the individual item level. Automatically making a link on the basis of the content description for an entire book may misrepresent the content of a chapter. Whether or not the metadata can be used will depend on the amount and type of information given in the metadata and the level at which the metadata are assigned.

If a text resource in the digital library provides no appropriate metadata, the procedure for identifying the key information may involve text analysis. A programme to perform simple string searching or a search engine that can preserve hit locations can be used if the text string has distinguishing characteristics, such as a database acronym, or a specific structure, such as a latitude and longitude coordinate. If the text string has no such cues, text mining or more complex textanalysis tools may be necessary. These tools use a variety of semantic and syntactic algorithms to locate key information.

There have been significant advances in commercially available text-mining tools, such as IBM's Intelligent Agent, which includes specific algorithms for identification of names of places and persons. The second step of the linking activity is to make the connection to the KOS. The methods for doing this vary, depending on whether the system is being loaded locally or is referenced remotely. If the system is loaded locally, it is possible to perform a significant amount of processing to match the two files, assuming that computer resources of this type are available to the digital library organization. If the system is only available remotely over the Web, the interaction will require knowledge of scripting and various Web-based access techniques.

Scripting should be considered in both local and remote approaches, since the more integrated the linking is with the resource, the more maintenance may be required if there are changes in either the resource or the KOS. Regardless of the approach that is taken, making the link requires an analysis of both the information in the original digital library material and the corresponding information in the KOS. If the KOS is being used as an intermediate file to bridge between the digital library's resource and another resource, it is also important to understand the data and the process whereby the search is performed and information returned from the target resource. If the KOS must return a value to the original digital library resource, the data and process must be evaluated in a bidirectional sense.

Choosing the linking mechanism is equally important. The link may be fixed or "on-the-fly." In the case of a fixed link, a specific URL is embedded at the link point in the digital library material. However, as stated before, problems of persistence are inherent in this approach. Alternatively, a URN can be used. The URN requires the creation of a namespace on the point of the target file, and the search is to this namespace rather than to a specific URL. Persistent locators and *digital object identifiers* (DOIs) can also solve this problem. These schemes are sufficient if the material is an HTML document. Content in databases is more difficult to retrieve.

The National Library of Medicine now supports the searching of a variety of its databases through its *Internet Grateful Med* (IGM) URL function. IGM users can create URLs that will actually perform searches against the databases. Information on the syntax for creating such a URL is provided on the NLM Web site. While the intent is that the search URL will be bookmarked by an individual user, the same concept can be used for creating an active link at the anchor point for the link. With additional scripting, the creation of the term *pneumonia* can be automatically replaced with an active link that picks up the term where the link has been made.

KNOWLEDGE ORGANIZATION SYSTEMS ON THE WEB

As online databases moved to the Web, they began to provide their products, including vocabulary aids, in this environment. *Portable document format* (PDF) versions of printed vocabulary aids are common, since PDF can be easily produced from a Postscript file and it retains the look of the printed product. With Adobe's tools for indexing and searching, the PDF file can provide some level of support for linking. Many of these aids, however, remain in the form of HTML files only–there is no database structure to easily support the linking and searching.

In some cases, the full structure of the KOS is not made available on the Web; the only format for a Web-based thesaurus may be an alphabetical list of terms that does not enable the user to navigate easily the hierarchical structure. As unique ways of using these resources are developed, it is hoped that more KOS providers will be encouraged to provide their systems in formats that are conducive to such networked uses. Some of the requirements for such electronic KOSs were identified at a workshop entitled "Electronic Thesauri: Planning for a Standard" and sponsored by NISO. While the focus of this meeting was digital thesauri, consideration was also given to other KOSs in digital form.

The identified requirements include persistent identifi-cation at the concept level, the need for a simple protocol for the distributed querying and response from a KOS, and the development of a standard set of metadata attributes for describing a remote KOS.

To facilitate the search and display of information from a previously unknown KOS, the system must have unique and persistent identifiers for each of the concepts in the system. For example, the California Environmental Resources Evaluation System and the U.S. Geological Survey have developed a system for remote querying and response. It requires that each concept in the thesaurus have a unique identifier.

In the case of the previously described ITIS, which is accessed remotely by the CERES system, the ITIS record number is used as the identifier. Other unique identifiers could include the DOI, or a classification notation that has been made unique by appending the scheme name or the URL to the notation. The second requirement is a protocol for the distributed querying and response of KOSs. This is particularly critical for highly structured systems such as thesauri, semantic networks, and ontologies. Work has been done in this area within the Z39.50 community.

A profile has been proposed by the Zthes Working Group to tailor the Z39.50 protocol to operate on thesauri that follow the Z39.19 standard. A similar effort is under way at the CERES Project. Instead of a Z39.50-based protocol, CERES has developed a structure that is based on the *Resource Description Framework* (RDF) and the HTTP protocol of standard browsers.

The RDF's concept of containers is a natural for managing the hierarchical structure of complex systems such as thesauri. The structure proposed by CERES is likely to be encoded using XML, a mark-up format that lends itself to structured information. This protocol for linking distributed vocabularies will support both searching and cataloging.

The user will be presented with remote vocabularies that can be displayed and navigated by a local client. The third major finding from the NISO workshop was the need for a metadata content standard for the description of KOSs. Such a standard is key to provision of knowledge organization services over the Internet. The metadata identify the Web resource as a KOS and provide important information to allow an application to use it remotely without prior knowledge of its content or structure.

A draft set of attributes for describing KOSs available in a networked environment has been developed by a task group of the *Network Knowledge Organization Systems* (NKOS) Working Group, an ad hoc group of terminology experts from organizations that are interested in issues related to the use and interoperability of KOSs over the Internet. The draft attributes are based on work originally done by Linda Hill and Michael Raugh. The attributes describe the KOS so that content from the system can be transferred over the Internet and handled by a remote browser or client application. The attributes include the depth of hierarchy, the types of relationships included, the subject, storage format, copyright and rights management, and contact information.

To facilitate the transfer of information, the attribute set also includes information on character set and file size. To facilitate the acquisition and licensing of the KOSs, the draft content description includes point of contact information.

During discussions about the metadata content standard, workshop attendees identified three methods for storing the metadata for a KOS. First, the metadata could be stored with the KOS, as metadata elements for that resource. Second, the metadata could be stored in a physically separate knowledge organization registry.

The third possibility is a hybrid approach, where a minimal set of metadata elements is contained in a central registry. The more detailed information would be stored with the KOS itself. There is significant interest in the use of KOSs to organize and search material on the Internet. It is hoped that this interest will result in knowledge organization services that will make these sources more readily accessible to a variety of software applications and to a variety of users. As services and enabled software proliferate, it will be easier to integrate these KOSs into digital libraries.

TYPES OF KNOWLEDGE ORGANIZATION SYSTEMS

A review of some typical knowledge organization systems shows their scope and applicability to a variety of digital library settings. While there are specific definitions for many of these KOSs in the computer science and information science literature, and even in standards documents, there is debate over these definitions.

Terms are often used, particularly in the popular press and in the book trade, in non-standard ways. Reflecting the scope of this practice, a recent *National Information Standards Organization* (NISO) work shop on electronic thesauri emphasized the need to improve the definitions of "terminology relating to terminology".

The descriptions given here provide an overview of possible systems for organizing digital libraries. The descriptions are based on characteristics such as structure and complexity, relationships among terms, and historical function. The list is not comprehensive; nor are the definitions of these terms contained in specific standards documents. They are grouped into three general categories: term lists, which emphasize lists of terms often with definitions; classifications and categories, which emphasize the creation of subject sets; and relationship lists, which emphasize the connections between terms and concepts.

Term Lists

Authority Files

Authority files are lists of terms that are used to control the variant names for an entity or the domain value for a particular field. Examples include names for countries, individuals, and organizations. Non-preferred terms may be linked to the preferred versions. This type of KOS generally does not include a deep organization or complex structure.The presentation may be alphabetical or organized by a shallow classification scheme. A limited hierarchy may be applied to allow for simple navigation, particularly when the authority file is being accessed manually or is extremely large. Examples of authority files include the Library of Congress Name Authority File and the Getty Geographic Authority File.

Glossaries

A glossary is a list of terms, usually with definitions. The terms may be from a specific subject field or from a particular work. The terms are defined within a specific environment and rarely include variant meanings. Examples include the *Environmental Protection Agency* (EPA) Terms of the Environment.

Dictionaries

Dictionaries are alphabetical lists of words and their definitions. Variant senses are provided where applicable. Dictionaries are more general in scope than are glossaries. They may also provide information about the origin of a word, variants and multiple meanings across disciplines. While a dictionary may also provide synonyms and through the definitions, related words, there is no explicit hierarchical structure or attempt to group them by concept.

Gazetteers

A gazetteer is a list of place names. Traditional gazetteers have been published as books or have appeared as indexes to atlases. Each entry may also be identified by feature type, such as river, city, or school. An example is the U.S. Code of Geo-graphic Names. Geospatially referenced gazetteers provide coordinates for locating the place on the earth's surface. The term *gazetteer* has several other meanings, including an announcement publication such as a patent or legal gazetteer. These gazetteers are often organized using classification schemes or subject categories.

Classifications and Categories

Subject Headings

This scheme type provides a set of controlled terms to represent the subjects of items in a collection. Subject heading lists can be extensive and cover a broad range of subjects; however, the subject heading list's structure is generally very shallow, with a limited hierarchical structure. In use, subject headings tend to be coordinated, with rules for how they can be joined to provide concepts that are more specific.

Examples include:

- The Medical Subject Headings (MeSH); and
- The Library of Congress Subject Headings (LCSH).

Classification Schemes, Taxonomies, and Categorization Schemes

These terms are often used interchangeably. Although there may be subtle differences from example to example, these types of KOSs all provide ways to separate entities into "buckets" or broad topic levels. Some examples provide a hierarchical arrangement of numeric or alphabetic notation to represent broad topics. These types of KOSs may not follow the rules for hierarchy required in the ANSI NISO Thesaurus Standard and they lack the explicit relationships presented in a thesaurus.

Examples of classification schemes include:

- The Library of Congress Classification Schedules,
- The Dewey Decimal Classification, and
- The Universal Decimal Classification.

Subject categories are often used to group thesaurus terms in broad topic sets that lie outside the hierarchical scheme of the thesaurus. Taxonomies are increasingly being used in object-oriented design and knowledge management systems to indicate any grouping of objects based on a particular characteristic.

Relationship Lists

Thesauri

Thesauri are based on concepts and they show relation-ships among terms. Relationships commonly expressed in a thesaurus include hierarchy, equivalence and association or relatedness.

These relationships are generally represented by the notation:

- BT (broader term),
- NT (narrower term),
- SY (synonym), and
- RT (associative or related term).

Associative relationships may be more detailed in some schemes. For example, the *Unified Medical Language System* (UMLS) from the National Library of Medicine has defined more than 40 relationships, many of which are associative. Preferred terms for indexing and retrieval are identified. Entry terms point to the preferred terms to be used for each concept. There are standards for the development of monolingual thesauri and multilingual thesauri.

In these standards, the definition of a thesaurus is fairly narrow.Standard relationships are assumed, as is the identification of preferred terms, and there are rules for creating relation-ships among terms. The definition of a thesaurus in these standards is often at variance with schemes that are tradi-tionally called thesauri. Many thesauri do not follow all the rules of the standard but are still generally thought of as thesauri. Another type of thesaurus, such as the *Roget's Thesaurus*, represents only equivalence. Many thesauri are large; they may include more than 50,000 terms. Most were developed for a specific discipline or a specific product or family of products. Examples include the Food and Agricultural Organization's *Aquatic Sciences and Fisheries Thesaurus* and the *National Aeronautic and Space Administration (NASA) Thesaurus* for aeronautics and aerospace-related topics.

Semantic Networks

With the advent of natural language processing, there have been significant developments in semantic networks. These KOSs structure concepts and terms not as hierarchies but as a network or a web. Concepts are thought of as nodes, and relationships branch out from them. The relationships generally go beyond the standard BT, NT, and RT. They may include specific whole-part, cause-effect, or parent-child relationships. The most noted semantic network is Princeton University's WordNet, which is now used in a variety of search engines.

Ontologies

Ontology is the newest label to be attached to some knowledge organization systems. The knowledge-management community is developing ontologies as specific concept models. They can represent complex relationships among objects, and include the rules and axioms missing from semantic networks. Ontologies that describe knowledge in a specific area are often connected with systems for data mining and knowledge management. All of these examples of knowledge organization systems, which vary in complexity, structure, and function, can provide organization and increased access to digital libraries.

THE ORIGIN AND USE OF KNOWLEDGE ORGANIZATION SYSTEMS

In the physical library, classification schemes such as *Library of Congress* (LC), Dewey Decimal System, and the Universal Decimal Classification reflect, among other things, the need to store a single item at a single location on a shelf. To provide multiple access points beyond the limits of a single physical location, subject headings are applied. Libraries use subject heading schemes such as LCSH, Sears, or other specialized schemes developed for specific content or specific collections. At the level of specific content, libraries have used authority files to control variant forms of personal, organizational, and geographic names. However, KOSs can be found in settings other than libraries.

An awareness of the KOSs available from alternative sources is valuable when considering the development of digital libraries for a specific audience.

Abstracting and Indexing Services

Abstracting and indexing (AandI) services developed as an outgrowth of traditional bibliographies and the explosion of journal literature. In the sciences, the development of AandI services was spurred by the post-World War I concerns about inadequate access to scientific information. In the 1950s, investment in AandI services was fueled by the Cold War and Sputnik. Abstracting and indexing services in the humanities, such as the Bibliography of the History of Art or the *Modern Languages Association* (MLA) Bibliography, generally took a different growth path than did their scientific and technical counterparts, but they also quickly became important resources for scholarship in the online environment.

The scope of AandI services varies from broad discipline-oriented services to narrowly defined aspects of the literature and subdisciplines. Special KOSs, such as thesauri and subject categories, were developed to support AandI services and their specific products and audiences. These organizations applied increasingly complex schemes to provide subject access to the literature in a variety of subjects.

By the 1960s, AandI services were moving from the provision of printonly products to print and online services through large online vendors such as Dialog. Later, the products were distributed on CDROM and now, increasingly, on the Web. In many cases, the KOSs migrated from print to electronic media following the products they supported. While increased computing power, more sophisticated search engines, and more independent end-user searching have led to changes in some KOSs, most have retained their importance, even in the Web environment.

For many years, the KOSs related to AandI services were applied only by catalogers and indexers trained in using the KOS indexing for a particular product or products. The primary users of KOSs were librarians and other professional searchers. However, the proliferation of electronic data, the explosion of electronic publishing, and increasing concerns about the difficulty of locating information have led to a renewed interest in these KOSs for use not only by professionals but also by end users.

Publishers

As publishers have migrated to electronic composition systems, they have become increasingly involved in the production of AandI products. Large journal publishers such as Academic Press and Elsevier have developed their own systems to provide bibliographic records linked to the full text of documents. As the content of online journals has grown, it has become necessary to move from systems that provide browsing by table of contents and journal issue to systems that support searching by both free text and by KOS. Electronic journals have resulted in additional KOSs, particularly classification and categorization schemes. For example, Elsevier's Web site has a subject categorization scheme to provide access to individual Web sites of its more than 2000 titles.

Trade, Professional, and Governmental Organizations

A variety of authority files and classification schemes are used to support business and commerce. They range from the *Standard Industrial Classification* (SIC) code and the *North American Industrial Classification System* (NAICS), used in procurement and government statistics, to disease codes used to communicate patient illnesses and treatments among physicians, hospitals, and insurance companies. As more organizations develop Web sites, additional KOSs are being developed to support them.

Internal Projects

Organizations are among the most prolific creators and users of KOSs. Developers of corporate intranets and knowledge management systems have discovered hundreds of specific classification schemes, glossaries, categorization schemes, and other vocabularies in use within organizations. Many of these are geared towards specific tasks and are, therefore, very narrow both in subject scope and target audience. However, for these audiences, they can also be rich sources of information. For example, the *Department of Energy* (DOE), *Environmental Management Science Programme* (EMSP) and the Office of Scientific and Technical Information are developing a digital library to support EMSP programme managers.

Programme managers and researchers have developed "needs categories" and "science categories" to organize the *Environmental Science Network* (ESN). The categories are used primarily to support the process of grant submission and award; however, the ESN also uses them to provide access to related material from within DOE and from other distributed databases from the EPA, the Department of Defence, and NASA. Vocabulary is currently being organized around these categories for use with a Web mining tool that will provide highly relevant Web resources for project managers in specific areas.

ROLE OF LIBRARIES IN MODERN KNOWLEDGE SOCIETY

In the modern knowledge society libraries have a new role and there are various types of library models. In the modern society, where the use of electronic services and Web-based information sources constantly increases, libraries are managed in a more democratic way, have more flexible communication system and work organisation, and their service development is based on the quality and user-orientation of services. In the modern knowledge society libraries have a new role and there are various types of library models.

These are as follows:

- Traditional library as a memory institution
- Library as a learning and research centre
- Library as a cultural and communication centre
- Electronic library
- Digital library
- Virtual library as library without walls

Libraries had been performed many important roles in the past agrarian and industrial societies. But those roles were limited in scope. In the 21st century, libraries have to perform pivotal roles in disseminating and sharing the culture of knowledge. In this age of knowledge libraries should be repositories of all of the knowledge and information accumulated by human kind.

They will have to store all kinds and forms of material and information and disseminate beyond the geographical boundaries. Today's advanced information technology is enabling libraries to accomplish this immense task. Exchange of knowledge has always been the most important objectives of libraries. Various systems have been developed to share and exchange the records of human knowledge. Universal Bibliographic Control and Universal Availability of Publications are two major Programmes of IFLA (International Federation of Library Associations and Institutions) to exchange knowledge world over.

OCLC is the world leading library network in USA for sharing intellectual knowledge among academic community in all over the world. But libraries in the 21st century should fulfill more dynamic role. They should exchange knowledge and information with users inside and outside their country, thus going beyond their traditional reference and lending services. This would possible when libraries agreed to expand their roles beyond the geographical boundaries by using sate of art technologies. The modern libraries certainly can not be passive repository for books and other printed materials. The opposite requirements of storing increasing collection in various forms and of maintaining easy access to most part of it can only be balanced by deploying information and communication technologies. Libraries should upgrade their services by digitising their resources for online use. These services should be accessible to anyone, regardless of time or location, through digital communication devices. Libraries can play significant role in providing a good education and knowledge of high quality. Individuals around the world, no matter how poor they may be, can access whatever knowledge and information they need by visiting libraries via the internet, such as the library of congress.

PROBLEMS AND OPPORTUNITIES FACING LIBRARIES IN INDIA

Library and information services are fundamental to the goals of creating, disseminating, optimally utilising and preserving knowledge. They are instrumental in transforming an unequal society into an egalitarian, progressive knowledge-based society. It is well known that in India most of the libraries function in the government sector.

These are in academic and research institutions and under the public library system, which is again under the state and central governments. At present, education being a state subject and coming under the purview of different apex agencies, there is no common direction or coordination among them. It is imperative that all libraries (public, academic, research and special) change gear and develop at an accelerated pace. Developments in information communication technology (ICT) have enabled libraries to provide access to all, and also bridge the gap between the local, the national and the global. Yet the Library and Information Services (LIS) sector in India has not kept pace with the paradigmatic changes taking place in society.

There are a few libraries which are using state of art technologies to disseminate knowledge to their respective user community. There is lack of cooperation among the libraries of different organisations and which cause the lack of union catalogues at national level.

The national library failed even to do this immense task. One of the major problems faced by LIS sector in India is lack of bibliographic control at national level which causes duplication in research. A considerable number of libraries had not been developed bibliographic databases of their documents for putting them on network. To summarise, the major constraints faced by the libraries which militate against effective dissemination and use of information are:

- A considerable percentage of the population is illiterate or functionally literate making libraries of minimal use to them.
- Poor resource allocation for infrastructure improvement and collection development for public libraries.
- Lack of sufficient sanctioned posts, forcing most services to be operated by voluntary Non-professional staff, which damages information organisation and services.
- Lack of national policies promoting ICT as a tool for development of library systems and services.
- Lack of adequate trained manpower in the use of IT.
- Lack of funds for acquiring necessary hardware and software facilities.
- Resistance on the part of library staff to change from their traditional practices to the use of IT.

Despite the problems, Library and Information Services (LIS) sector in India has got remarkable achievements. Efforts had been made to set up networks at local, regional and national level to deploy information and communication technologies and to build electronic information sources. Besides INFLIBNET at the national level to support university and college libraries, a number of other national networks and various library networks have also been developed including NICNET (National Informatics Centers Network), ERNET (Education and Research Network), CALIBNET (Calcutta Library Network), DELNET (Developing Library Network), etc.

A number of educational institutions are members of such networks. These networks, especially INFLIBNET and DELNET, are engaged in compiling union catalogs, creating various databases of experts, providing training to library staff, ILL, online facilities, reference service, assistance in retrospective conversion, ,etc. To overcome the problem of financial crunch and the rising costs of journals, librarians have formed consortia to subscribe all the required journals and databases. Some special libraries and research organisations have established consortia known as FORSA (Forum for Resource Sharing in Astronomy) to share electronic access to journal literature.

NISCAIR (National Institutes of Science Communication and Information Resources), one of CSIR labs, has formed a consortium for CSIR labs for accessing e-journals and databases. In order to solve the problem of universities and college libraries, UGC launched a major initiative called UGC-INFONET that provides high speed Internet connections so as to have electronic access to professional literature including research journals, abstracts, review publications, and databases from all areas in science and technology, as well as in social sciences and humanities.

The Ministry of Human Resource Development (MHRD) has set up the "Indian National Digital Library in Science and Technology (INDEST) Consortium" for the subscription to electronic resources for 38 academic institutions, including the Indian Institute of Sciences, Indian Institute of Technology, Regional Engineering Colleges, Indian Institute of Managements, and about 60 centrally-funded/aided government institutions through the consortium. For the improvement of quality of library and information services through the systematic acquisition, organisation and dissemination of knowledge, various library associations have been set up at national and state level.

They annually organised conferences, seminars and training Programmes to trained and update library professionals with latest development in LIS. Recently libraries and research organisations realise the importance of digital libraries and they started the work of digitisation of important documents. NISCAIR and the Department of Indian Systems of Medicine and Homoeopathy (ISMandH) have entered into an agreement for establishing a Traditional Knowledge Digital Library (TKDL) on Ayurveda. TKDL will be available in English, German, French, Spanish and Japanese Since, these languages account for more than 98 per cent of the international patent applications.

TKDL in the first phase targets Ayurveda. But as a whole it would encompass, in addition to Ayurveda, Siddha, Unani, Yoga, Naturopathy and Folklore medicine. The Indian Institute of Science (IISc), Carnegie Mellon

University (CMU), the International Institute of Information Technology, Hyderabad (IIITH) and many other academic, religious and government organisations, totaling about 21 'Content Creation Centers', have become partners in the Digital Library of India (DLI) initiative for the digitisation and preservation of Indian heritage present in the form of books, manuscripts, art and music.

Each centre brings its own unique collection of literature into the digital library. DLI has a vision to build a universal digital library of world knowledge. One million books have already been available through this project. India perhaps has one of the oldest and largest collections of Manuscripts in the world. These manuscripts are in different languages and scripts; written on different materials such as birch bark, palm leaf, cloth, paper ,etc. They are in the custody of libraries, museums, monasteries, mutts and individuals.

A significant proportion is not preserved scientifically. Experts estimate that almost all palm leaf manuscripts may perish due to wear and tear over next 50 to 100 years. In this regard the National Mission for Manuscripts has taken a step to save the most valuable, intellectual property of our cultural inheritance. The missions has started a pilot project for digitising the manuscripts in five states across India covering five caches of manuscripts and for the same four digitising agencies have been selected.

Importance of open access archives, institutional repositories and open access journals has been realised by the library and information professionals in India. This movement has been accelerated by the availability of open source software namely DSpace, EPrints, Greenstone, ,etc., Indian Institute of Science, Bangalore, INFLIBNET Centre, Ahmedabad and Documentation Research and Training Centre (DRTC), Bangalore are the leading institutions who made this movement a great success. Among the top 25 publishing countries, India ranks 12th for the overall number of journals, but drops to 18th for journals with online content. At present there are more than 150 open access journals in India.

The open access journals in India are mainly initiated by six journal publishers, namely, Indian Academy of Sciences, Indian National Science Academy, Indian Medlars Centre of National Informatics Centre, Medknow Publications, indianjournals. com and Kamla-Raj Enterprises. The Indian Institute of Science was the first in the country to set up and interoperable institutional archive ePrints@IIScr. The archive now has more than 7000 records, with over 90 per cent having full text. Presently there are 25 institutional archives in India which are registered in the Registry of Open Access Repositories (ROAR). An open access statement is likely to be ready by this year. The CSIR also has a plan to setup a national digital repository of research literature. NISCAIR has already started to work on the project known as National Science Digital Library. National knowledge Commission is also formulating similar open access policies and guidelines for the higher education and R and D sectors to improve access to research literature and disseminate research literature to the global communities. The National Knowledge Commission has submitted its report to the government on how to redefine the information services sector. The report of Knowledge Commission on library sector suggests that "Every state should establish a registry and archives of knowledge based digital resources which should be made accessible to all".

ORGANISATIONAL STRUCTURES AND INFORMATION IN LIBRARY

An organisational structure is a means to incorporate various functions in order to pursue some predetermined objectives. Organisational structures also provide the lines along which information flows. Researchers have described two ways to organise libraries. They are:

1. Specialisation; and
2. Coordination and integration.

Coordination and integration simply means bringing together all individual efforts to achieve particular objectives. Specialisation, however, can be interpreted in two approaches: departmentalisation and hierarchy. Departmentalisation means the organisation is structured horizontally by identifying and grouping similar or related required activities or tasks into departments, for example, function, activities, geography, subjects, form of material, etc.

There are two main approaches to departmentalisation within academic libraries, function and subject, and they are matters of continual debate. The first approach is a structure dominated by administrative function. The subject divisional library is the alternative approach to the strictly functional. The staff are split by subject, with services and processing entirely subordinate.

- The introduction of computers into academic libraries is a major reason why the debate between functionalism and subject organisation has been by-passed.

One consequence of automation has been that:

- Technology has reduced the time necessary to carry out one of the most tedious part's of librarian's work, record creation and manipulation.

The second method of specialisation in organisations is the creation of a vertical hierarchy, with the individuals located on the top of organisation having more authority than those at successively lower levels.

- 'Such structures are often also represented diagrammatically as a family-tree, depicting line management responsibilities above and below. And any given structure can be either functional or subject-orientated.'

The merits of a hierarchical structure have been questioned by researcher; he points out several problems, such as:

- 'Reporting lines tends to be long, and the responsibility of any individual very limited. Many staff rarely come into contact with staff more than one or two grades higher, with the result that communication is often poor and it is hard for staff below a senior level to have any sense of involve-ment in the organisation.'

In place of a hierarchical structure, researcher proposed a 'flat' structure as one possibility for libraries in the near future. In examining the rapid change and different climate that are being encountered by libraries, The 'flat' management structure as having:

- Fewer middle managers, and more reliance on the two extremes–the senior administrators and lower level staff–to make decisions.

It could be speculated that the implications for the development of Management Information Systems (MIS) in libraries with 'flat' management structures may be comparable to the general problems of introducing MIS in small organisations:

- Larger organisations have found greater success with MIS use than smaller ones. Libraries, even the largest, are relatively small organisations and much planning is required to initiate and gain acceptance of MIS. There will be more resistance in small organisations than in very large ones since the likelihood of a lesser degree of bureaucratisation and traditional line and staff authority divisions are in place in such operations. The perception of the MIS as crystallising these divisions may offset their initial acceptance.

MANAGEMENT INFORMATION SYSTEMS

Researcher has defined a Management Information System as:

- The process and structure used by an organisation to identify, collect, evaluate, transfer, and utilise information in order to fulfil its objectives. It is a system that provides management with information to make decisions, evaluate alternatives, measure performance, and detect situations requiring corrective action.

The implementation of performance assessment in academic libraries is an essential part of good management practice. Although she had reservations about the current Management Information Systems in university libraries because, for example, few academic libraries had produced a statement of their objectives, she still believed that Management Information Systems could contribute to effective management of library activities.

The four main objectives for Management Information systems have been defined as:

1. To facilitate the decision making process in the library by providing the managers with accurate, timely, and selective information that assists them in determining a specific course of action.

2. To provide for the objective performance measurement and assessment of selected relevant areas of the library. The areas are to be determined during strategic planning.
3. To provide pertinent information about the library's internal and external environments.
4. To provide information on alternative strategies and contingency plans.

The purposes can only be implemented if people look upon Management Information Systems as an integral part of the framework of management in the academic library and not as a peripheral system which has been installed for the benefit of an individual or a single department.

- There may be subsystems within the larger system, which may be branch libraries, or departmental divisions such as cataloguing, acquisitions or circulation, but they must still be seen as integrated parts of the whole, and must function as such. In the systems approach, however, the library organisation must be seen as an organic whole, with information as its lifeblood and in which each part of the system is integrated by the flow of information throughout.

An integrated Management Information System is very important because it can be used to provide supporting information to determine:

- *Efficiency*: is the library doing things right.
- *Effectiveness*: is the library doing the right things.
- *Competitiveness*: is the library heading in a direction which is consistent with the environment.

Any discussion of the Management Information System must lead to consideration of the inputs data, processing data and the outputs data. Inputs to the management information system consist of both internally and externally generated library data. External information covers factors such as legislation, politics, trends in society, changes in technology, user demand, and comparative statistics for other, similar institutions. Internal data is that derived from administrative routines and transactional information. Administrative routines include those related to personnel, finance, acquisition, cataloguing, processing of materials, binding, building services, maintenance services, etc.

Output measures will include data of circulation, general user satisfaction, etc. All service points will need to be monitored so that internal performance comparisons can be made and the contribution of each service point are the overall objectives of the organisation assessed. In term of library managers' needs, a variety of inputs is evidently needed. It may be necessary to process information in different ways for different levels of decision-making needs, and different types of output reports will be needed to meet those different needs.

Selection of appropriate data elements for inclusion in a Management Information System assumes that:

- Clear goals and measurable objectives have been developed for the library,
- For each data element there is rationale for how it will be used or in what combinations with other data elements it can be used to determine success towards the accomplishment of objectives, overall library effectiveness, or performance measures for specific library services/operations, and
- The library can, in fact, collect reliable and valid data for a particular data element.'

The data in a management information system also needs to be processed to turn it into meaningful information for library management. For this reason, management information systems require an appropriate data processing system. Data processing is the capture, storage and processing of data for the purpose of transforming it into information useful for decision making.

In recent years, data processing for management information systems in business and industry has increasingly been undertaken by computers:

- A modem MIS will always rely to some extent on computer technology, although a computer is not a requirement. The reality of the 1980's would indicate that a computer is a necessity for the most sophisticated systems.

In libraries, in contrast, the development of the use of computer has been:

- Modular, in the sense that it is based on a single library operation such as acquisitions, serials, control or cataloguing. The more general applications of management information lay hidden, as it is often seen only as a departmental resource.

This need not necessarily have been so. An early prediction of the advantages of information produced by computers was made in 1979 by Tague, who suggested that computers should produce information for control at both macro and micro level in libraries.

However, in 1986, Brophy, having analysed eight large computer systems used in British libraries, noted that:

- Automated library systems seem to be primarily about control at the micro level. Moreover, they produced management information which was relatively crude, highly structured and very much a system by-product.

The needs of individual managers tended to be overlooked, especially when the design of MIS was in the hands of computer personnel.

- Too often, management information has been produced as an afterthought following computerisation. Most computerised issue systems, for example, were never designed to produce management information although librarians have often struggled over the data generated by these systems in an attempt to derive some meaningful information about issue patterns.

Technological changes have helped to ease this problem. As opposed to the use of mainframe and mini-computers, 'the advent of the microcomputer now provides an alternative to the dependence on large-scale centralised computer systems. Computer power can now be deployed cheaply to different parts of an organisation to allow for local processing of data.'

Computers should be easily able to provide four types of report: periodic reports, exception reports, on demand reports, and predictive reports. Periodic reports provide routine, statistical information in detailed or summarised form. Exception reports highlight areas requiring managerial attention and would focus on those that have been overlooked. On demand reports provide a response to a particular non-standard question. Predictive reports give forecasts and provide comparisons based on statistical manipulation of data.

The principal requirement of the outputs of academic library management information systems is that they should be of interest to:

- The relevant committee - the members wish to know how the library service is performing and whether the institution, is getting value for money.
- The chief financial officer - his role is primarily custodial, and he wants to be assured that there is no overspending and that money is used for the purpose intended.
- The chief librarian - who wants to know how services under his control are performing in accordance with plans, targets and budgets.
- The managers of individual sections or services–who want to have data on the operations and performance with plans, targets and budgets.
- Outside organisations requesting library perfor-mance data on a regular basis.

In these ways, the outputs of management information systems become information for decision making.

In general, management information is:

- 'The right information in the right form at the right time, so enabling the manager effectively and effici-ently to do his/her job.'

The value or quality of management information is determined by three factors. They are:

1. The content of information: Information is the substance of communication, but to be information rather than data or noise, it must be meaningful, relevant and new to the receiver.
2. The form or presentation of the information: Information should be presented in a style and format readily understandable by the manager. This means that the producer of information must be aware of the recipient's knowledge of technical terms, numeracy/literacy levels, his individual characteristics, the characteristics of the group

with which he works and so on. These and other factors help the information producer to form an idea of the perception level of the manager and increase the likelihood of producing understandable information capable of being used which, it will be recalled, is the only way information can create value.

3. The timing of its presentation: Information which is produced must be communicated to the manager in time to be used. Delays in data gathering, processing or communication can transform potentially vital information into worthless waste paper.

In the planning process, information should support the decision making process. Since one of the major problems facing academic libraries is the impact of changes in available financial support, the Colleges of Further and Higher Education Group (CoFHE) of the Library Association has been considering the categories of management information required for making decisions concerning the budget.

They concluded that these are:

- Information about the institutional identity of the library.
- Information about the target group.
- Information about the collection resources.
- Information about the financial resources.
- Information about library personnel.
- Information about facilities and equipment.
- Information about various programmes and functions.

CoFHE also considered the requirements for collecting management information, and suggested the following guidelines:

- The information sought must be worth the costs of collecting it - direct and indirect.
- Consider sources of information already available within the institution before setting up mechanisms to collect it.
- Keep the collection of information relevant, i.e., remember the purpose - 'to support the budget request.'
- Remember to consider qualitative and quantitative data as both can be relevant.

MANAGEMENT INFORMATION SYSTEM VS. DECISION SUPPORT SYSTEM

Researcher identified four major problem areas of management information systems. They are:

1. Output is undiscriminating.
2. The information is not analysed for a purpose.
3. The system is not user-friendly.
4. The information which is given by MIS may not be acceptable.

Decision support systems can be seen as an extension of the idea of management information systems to provide a wide range of information in a more flexible and interactive way. They are designed to support decision making needs of management rather than act a useful by-product of transaction processing systems.

The special feature of a decision support system is that it solves a major problem of management information systems, *i.e.*, the poor communication between the system and the users, library managers. Decision support systems have interface outputs which are more live than those of management information systems.

The main interfaces in decision support systems are:

- Regular reports which provide information on parts of the system, which are predetermined by the system's users.
- Event-centred reports in which a report is generated only when a predetermined event has occurred. This will usually be the result of an exceptional condition, which is signalled by the system.
- *Ad hoc* reports which are generated in response to a stimulus by the system user to report on a condition which is not normally monitored.
- A query language which enables the user to interface directly with the system and to test changes in conditions experimentally. This is usually performed with 'goal-seeking' and 'what if techniques.

Beside the interface output, a decision support system also provides the report formats which may be required by the system's user, ranging from simple one-off designs to sophisticated presentations for senior managers. They are:

- *Standard reports* containing details prompted by the system user but in a format determined by standard software.
- *Tailored reports* containing information determined by the user and in a format designed by the user.
- *Tabulations* enabling the user to examine a range of statistical data rapidly, in either a standard or tailored format.
- *Spreadsheet format* allowing the user to transfer data from the system into a separate format which can be manipulated in a statistical layout.
- *Graphic presentations* providing a method of transmitting a trend analysis rapidly, and in a user-friendly manner.

Like management information systems, the data input into decision support systems can be external or internal data concerning the library. The three levels of influence on decision making can be isolated:

- Information from the library's operations.
- Information from the parent organisation.
- Information at the national and regional level.

The differences between a management information system and a decision support system lie not only their features, but also in their users. Management information systems tend to be used by lower and middle management because of their ability to assist in making structured decisions. In contrast, decision support systems tend to be more useful to top management because they can help with decisions on unstructured issues. Where they exist, decision support systems appear to be mainly used at the strategic management level.

DECISION-MAKING, ORGANISATIONAL STRUCTURES, AND INFORMATION NEEDS

Whether organisations are large or small, there is managerial stratification. The tasks of top management are development of the organisation's domain, management of the interface with external environments and establishment of the organisation's administrative climate; middle management develop rules, procedures and policies for day-to-day operations; and technical management sees that services are rendered and policies carried out.

In a conference on Management Information Systems, researcher identified the library staff with each of these management levels as follows:

- Senior/top managers (*e.g.*, deputies and chiefs).
- Middle managers (*e.g.*, heads of major divisions).
- Line/technical managers (*e.g.*, service desk super-intendents).
- 'some individuals will straddle more than one category. Deputies, for example, will be concerned with middle management and senior management. Furthermore the model is generalised, and it is true that in smaller libraries such stratification may break down since everyone is doing a bit of everything!'

Decision-making has been defined as:

- the formulation of alternative courses of action to meet the situation under consideration and in the choice between these alternatives after an evaluation of the effectiveness in achieving the decision maker's objectives. One of the most important factors is information from which an appreciation of the decision can be made.

There are three stages in decision making:

- Intelligence;
- Design, and
- Choice.

The intelligence stage encompasses collection, classification, processing, and presentation of the data necessary for the later stages of the decision making process. During the design stage, the decision maker outlines alternative solutions, each of which involves a set of actions to be taken. He usually uses quantitative techniques and design tools such as are common in management sciences and system analysis. The data gathered in the previous stage is now examined in statistical and other models to forecast possible outcomes for each alternative. In the choice stage, the decision maker is faced with various alternatives. One alternative must be selected, which becomes the formal decision and consequently generates actions to be taken.

This may seem deceptively easy, but in reality there are many difficulties that usually make choice a complex stage. It becomes clear that decision making is the conversion of information into action. The intended actions are planning, organising, directing and controlling of activities to achieve objectives.

However, decision-making at different managerial levels is not necessarily an identical process, and there are clear implications for the type of management information required.

- The degree of structure is dependent on the degree of predictability of the variables involved in a given decision. Unstructured decisions have few predictable variables; structured ones have many . . . Unstructured decisions are usually made at the strategic planning level and semi-structured decisions at the operational management level. The most structured decisions are reached at the operational control level.

Library managers might, therefore, be supposed to need access to the information which is appropriate to their level of decision making.

The relationship between the needs for information in all three levels of library management is:

- These levels and their various concerns obviously overlap, and in some cases may be undertaken by the same person, especially in smaller libraries. Nevertheless, the distinction remains a generally valid one, in terms of information need. At operational and some middle levels, formal information, systemati-cally provided in short time comparisons, forms the bulk of what is required. Higher up the pyramid, unstructured information, much of it external, is a more significant consideration; also the more senior librarians will only want snapshot or selective sets of data derived, for example, from operational systems and the university budget.
- There are two kinds of management information, the formal and the informal. Both of them derived from external and internal sources to the academic library but informal management information are mostly found externally such as from the users and the administrators who govern budgets.

INFORMATION NEEDS AND PERFORMANCE MEASUREMENT

Information which is reliable, accurate, timely and well presented will always help library managers to make decisions. Moreover:

- Systematic procedures are needed for allocating resources in line with objectives and ways must be found for monitoring and controlling these resources.

Performance assessment is the systematic measurement of the extent to which a library has achieved its objectives in a certain period of time. Performance assessment can be applied in libraries, in the contemporary British terminology, to: service input cost measures, service output measures, service effectiveness measures, and service domain measures. Internally, performance assessment is concerned with making the library work efficiently and effectively. Externally, it can be used by library managers to justify the budget to the parent body. Without performance assessment it is difficult to determine how well the library is progressing. The term 'performance assessment' encompasses both performance indicator and performance measure. Performance indicators:

- Provide objective data on the extensiveness and effectiveness of library services. They quantify library performance in terms of goals achieved and services delivered... but to guide resource allocation.

Four types of performance indicators have been defined. They are: (i) operational performance indicators, (ii) effectiveness indicators, (iii) cost-effectiveness indicators and (iv) impact indicators. Researcher also observed that performance indicators are intended to improve decision making and service performance, aid public accountability and help define and evaluate policies. If performance indicators are seriously used and real consequences follow from the judgements based on them, then all concerned should be aware that the chosen performance indicators will come to be taken by the staff to be representative of the objectives of the library.

The relationship between performance measures and performance indicators is that they: 'can not be interpreted in the same way. Though the indicators are calculated from direct measures, there are some important factors, such as higher order effects, the particular aims of the library, or certain attributes of what is being measured, which can not be brought into the calculation. Therefore, however carefully it is arrived at, a performance indicator can not be seen as an absolute measure of performance, but as guide which needs to be considered in relation to local conditions and other indicators.'

4

Methodology of Achieving Organisational Changes in Library System

INTRODUCTION

Recent years were for the libraries a period of faster, greater and more dramatic changes than has ever before been experienced. The omnipresence of the new technologies, the ever-increasing cooperation, the globalization as premises of the evolution towards the *Global Information Society,* the emphasis on quality, the diminution of the financial resources are the main agents imposing the change of libraries. Implementing the necessary changes for the academic libraries is no easy job as it requires a differentiation between changes to ensure the coherence of actions within the available resources.

It is also important to use planning and control methods that contribute to reduce the span of the change process and to optimize the use of resources. Finally, it requires suitable structures, staff training and overcoming the resistance to change. All these respects are subjects of change management–a distinct discipline whose key-aspects-in point of increasing the success and the efficiency of organisational changes–we present. The concept of organisational change, as defined by the management theories, is a significant, extended, important change that affects the entire organisation or parts of it.

Such changes do not occur naturally, they are changes whose implementation is the task of the management team. The methodology of achieving these changes is one of the main issues of change management and it is treated in very different ways by management theoreticians. The best known approach is the one proposed by Kurt Lewin and E. H. Schein that identifies three essential stages in the process of organisational changes, stages somewhat similar to chemical processes: unfreezing–the trial to create the reasons for change; moving/implementing change–identifying solutions adequate to circumstance and applying them; freezing–a new equilibrium is crystallizing. From the point of view of implementing changes in the university library, the methodology presented by Popescu, M. has the advantage of a pragmatic approach that defines two major stages of the process of starting and implementing change: identifying the need of change and achieving change. Identifying the need of change aims to establish the favourable changes that may add value to the organisation.

In the authors' opinion the important changes must be implemented from a strategic point of view; this means that, when establishing the changes that must be done and their order, the mission and the strategic objectives of the organisation are kept in mind.

This way one can avoid the risk of starting complex and expensive processes that can not be financially supported or that have little or no effects upon the performances of the organisation. Several studies discussing changes in libraries develop the above idea.

Thus, Troll, A.D. underlines that the evaluation activity usually carried out in libraries is not enough in order to plan changes: without knowing the external and the internal context and the library's strategy, such an evaluation is of no help in understanding what changes are relevant and can assure the accomplishment of the library's mission. It's necessary to define clearly the strategic objectives and the main lines of change that sustain planning changes in the library.

To complete this idea we state that, once the strategy is elaborated it has to be communicated; making public and discussing the mission, the policy and the general objectives of the library are means of communication through which the top management acknowledges everyone concerned its view on the future of the library and obtains their support. Communicating, informing and involving the staff are elements that contribute to overcome the resistance to change which is normal in the case of any major change. The bigger the changes, the greater the resistance to change and ignoring this is the source of many failures as shown in many studies on this topic.

Achieving change, the second stage, is a complex process having clearly stated beginning and ending points and, between, a sequence of three activities:

- The preliminary study or the planning–it's goal is to define change, to evaluate the achieving conditions and the expected results;
- Projecting the change–it refers to defining solutions and including them in specific documents;
- Implementing and checking the results–it is a stage that, paradoxically, often raises difficulties because of the resistance to change.

These three activities are intricately interconnected: change is achieved progressively, but the process is not linear, solutions adopted in one stage are often rectified in a following one. The amount of innovation the solutions bear, the fact that change by definition involves contouring and implementing new solutions–what causes it to seem unique and risky–the important quantity of resources involved, the participation of many specialists and actors from different structures are characteristic elements that render complex and difficult the achieving of organisational changes.

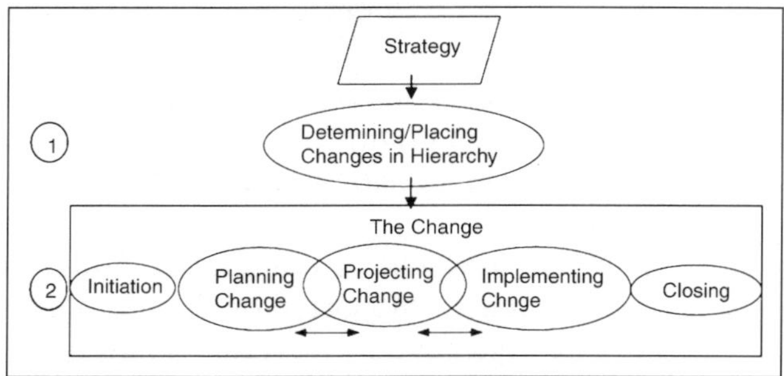

Fig. Stages of the Process of Achievement Organisational Changes

The solution is to approach them as projects, in the manner proper to project management. The scheme in figure synthesizes the methodology for accomplishing the organisational changes, whose application ensures: on one hand–the coherence of the actions, through relating to the strategy of the organisation, on the other hand, advantages determined by approaching the change as project, by using the project as 'vehicle for the change', which means, implicitly, applying the principles and methods specific to project management.

LIBRARY OF TRANSILVANIA UNIVERSITY

The case study realised at the Library of Transilvania University of Brasov sets out to analyse the changes made during the last decade within the university library, from the perspective of the change management, to present the change priorities inscribed in the library strategy along the years to follow and to identify the key factors on whom there depends the success of the change projects. *Transilvania* University of Brasov is an institution of higher education and research, which enjoys high prestige on the local, national and international level.

It is an extended university, with 16 faculties–8 are of technical profile and 8 of university profile, with more than 22.000 students at the university degree, master's degree and doctorate cycles, full time and distance learning. In the context of globalization, of Romania's integration within the EU, the University achieved important changes in all fields of activity and structures, in view of harmonizing with the new requirements and in view of assuring the quality of the services of education and research.

The Library is a structure of *Transilvania* University of Brasov, an entity without its own judicial personality, subordinated to the top management of the university. The mission of the university library is to ensure the documentary and information basis necessary for the education process, to enhance and to communicate them, as well as other services, to the benefit of the information users, facilitating the diversified and rapid access to all categories of sources. The documentary patrimony of the Library of *Transilvania* University of Brasov includes: books, serial publications, manuscripts, cartographic documents, printed musical documents, audio-visual documents, graphic documents, electronic documents etc. The collections of the Library are constituted and developed through acquisition, transfer, national and international exchange, donations and sponsorship. The endowment is ensured through financing from the university management, as well as through transfers, donations and sponsorship.

The organisation and the functioning of the Library observe the provisions of the specific legislation elaborated on the national level, as well as the internal regulations of the university.

The Library has its own strategies and plans of activity whose approval by the Senate of the University ensures the integration in the general strategy of the institution. Like the university it is part of, the library achieved a series of changes in order to improve its performance.

For instance:

- The relocation of the library became a strategic objective during the year 2005 after the finalization of a building with another initial destination. The placement of the Library in this building ensured the concentration of the activities and the amelioration of the working environment, however the adaptation costs were high, without ensuring the perfect compliance with the needs of the library;
- The automation of the processes of document management and communication is likewise questionable under the aspect of the adopted solutions, taking into consideration that the used software requires expensive hardware resources, and the results with respect to the performance of the processes were not up to the expectations;
- The efficacy of the actions undertaken within the library for the access to digital information may be appreciated as reduced, because of the lack of correlation between the equipments in the structure of the informatics system, as well as of the insufficient training with respect to the users' access to these resources. These resources did not benefit from an adequate promotion among the users who, to a too great extent, ignore their informative value and even their existence;
- The modernization of the evaluation system is slowed down by the lack of an adequate evaluation model and also by the generalized delay of the automated means for collecting and processing the data, and the efficiency of the evaluation is also affected by the persistence of the non-trained and disinterested staff in accomplishing this activity.
- The endowment with sufficient, stable and qualified staff is hindered by the still low number of librarians with specialized studies from the geographical area, by the unattractive level of the wages, by the

rooting in certain posts of non-efficient employees, refractory to the new.

The outlined deficiencies are, at least in part, determined by the manner in which change management was implemented in the university library, both as regards planning the changes and settling the solutions, and as regards their implementation. It is to be observed especially the neglecting of the social aspects with respect to the staff's training, the resistance to change etc.–as factors which have negatively influenced the efficacy and the efficiency of the change processes.The university library will continue the process of the qualitative transformations during the following period, but in different ways. The aim is at using efficiently the strategy, as management instrument and at developing mechanisms that should allow the continuous control and improvement of the library performance through systematic actions. To this purpose, in a first stage there was carried out the diagnostic analysis of the management system of the library, whose conclusions are presented as follows, synthesized in strengths and weaknesses.

STRENGTHS

- There is a strategy of the library, harmonized with that of the university. The mission of the library and the system of values are published on the site. The objectives are realistic, measurable; the accent is laid on improving the performance, in order to contribute to ensuring the quality of the educational and research services carried out by the university. There was set as priority axis of research the implementation of a system of quality management, through which there is created the framework for the continuous improvement of the quality.
- The university and library management has the capability to professionally approach the changes, evinces competences as regards the ample perspective and its concretization in valid strategies of development, the settling of the plans for further action and the provision with the resources necessary for accom-plishing the change projects, the optimization of the structure, the implementation of modern methods of management.
- Human resources: the library has 52 employees, among which 32 with higher education and 11 with higher education in the field. The staff benefited from training and of mobility exchanges in the country and abroad.

WEAKNESSES

- *Control of the Performance*: The library achieves the assessment of the performance every year; however the criteria and the indicators which are used do not reflect the qualitative aspects of the activity, the effects of the library services upon the educational and scientific research processes. There is no management system that should measure the costs of the services/activities realised by the library.

- *Control of the Processes:* There has begun to be implemented the management through processes, however the action is in an incipient phase of analysis and description of the key processes through procedures.
- *Human Resources*: Staff's evaluation is done in compliance with the law, however the insufficient resources used in this process make the evaluation not always relevant. The participation of the staff in solving the problems is unequal and the rewarding system is non-stimulating.
- *Organisational Culture:* There is no culture of the quality, there are insufficiently promoted values such as team work, staff's implication, opening towards change.

Taking into account the submitted situation, the priority axes for the development of the capability of the library to continuously improve its performance are the following:

- *People:* The continuation of the process of staff training in quality management, with accent on achieving behavioural changes, on raising the degree of implication in solving the problems and on team work.
- *Users:* Orientation towards the customers, definition of the requirements and evaluation of their satisfaction. This implies in the first place the improvement of the system evaluating the library performance, through the introduction of criteria and indicators that should better reflect the effects upon the quality of the educational and research processes. The control will be also extended upon the costs of the services and of the activities realised by the library.
- *Processes:* Development and implementation of instruments and also of working and control procedures that should ensure the optimization of the processes and their continuous improvement.

The achievement of the change processes will be coordinated by the Management Council of the library. Both the initiation of the projects and their unfolding will be largely promoted in the framework of the library, for obtaining the feedback and for attracting the people in realizing the changes. The financing of the projects will be done from its own funds, but there will be likewise accessed funds from the Operational Programmes.

CONCLUSIONS

The existence during the last decades of the university libraries has been characterized by ample changes, a process that will continue. The achievement of the changes is an issue of the management library, whose results may be considerably improved through a professional approach, based on the methods of the change management. The case study developed by the authors presents the first sequences of the change programme that will be achieved during the years to follow at the library of *Transilvania* University of Brasov, with reference to the methodology of change elaboration and implementation.

GERMAN LANGUAGE AND LITERATURE, UNIVERSITY OF TARTU

BRIEF HISTORY OF THE UNIVERSITY OF TARTU

I will start my presentation with a small overview of the University of Tartu as our library is a part of the university and it is not possible to observe them apart. The University of Tartu is the oldest university in Estonia and one of the oldest in the Northern countries. On 30 June 1632, King Gustav II Adolf of Sweden signed the Foundation Decree of *Academia Dorpatensis*, which marks the beginning of our university's history.

We can distinguish five periods when we speak about the history of the University of Tartu:

- The Swedish period 1632-1710
- The Imperial Tartu University 1802-1918
- 1919-1940 Tartu University in the Republic of Estonia
- 1944-1989 Tartu State University
- 1991-Tartu University in the newly independent Republic of Estonia

I only describe three of them as the important ones for my presentation. The first, the so-called 'Swedish period', is important while it turned a small provincial town to the university town. The Town Council was interested in having the university here to restore its former prosperity. Tallinn and Riga were big and important centres and not at all interested in the university and the noisy and hectic young men-students.

Sweden in its turn wanted to:

- Strengthen the Lutheran religion in the former Catholic country;
- Strengthen the presence of the Swedish kingdom.

The students were mostly Swedes and Finns. We are proud that our university is so old but in fact the university, established during the Swedish period, was not one of the best reconized universities in Europe. The university in Tartu functioned with the Faculties of Philosophy, Law, Theology, and Medicine, enjoying the privileges similar to those granted to the University of Uppsala.

The University of Tartu was closed in 1710 after the Swedish army had surrendered to the Russian forces after the defeat in the Northern War. The second period of the history of the university was 1802-1918 'reopening of the university'. This period can be characterized as the prosperity of the university. The Baltic Germans needed the university to educate their children. After the French Revolution studying abroad was not allowed. Russia also needed its own university. So in Tartu the European science and the Russian state met. The Germans wanted to have a small Heidelberg or Göttingen and somehow they succeeded in it.

The official language at the university was German and the religion was Lutheran. The 19th century was the period of prosperity of the university, the scientists K. E. von Baer, J. W. Struve and many others show us the level of scientific research in Tartu at that time. The teaching of Germanic languages also goes back to this period and has long traditions. Already in 1865 the Department for German Language at the University of Tartu was established. The first professor at the department was Leo Meyer, a linguist from Göttingen who stayed in Dorpat for 33 years. The number of students increased every day, Rutiku and Kegelmann.

OVERVIEW OF THE FOUNDATION OF GERMAN LIBRARY

I concentrate my attention on the fifth period which begins in 1991 while at that time our library was established. After the collapse of the Soviet Union the situation in our country was changing. We had to build up new society, a new educational system. The example of our library illustrates the developments in Estonia very well. In many areas we had to start from scratch. When learning foreign languages, it is natural that the dictionaries, lexicons and scientific literature are at students' disposal, but in Tartu it was not so.

The first German DAAD–Professor in Tartu–Claus Sommer-hage–started establishing a library. Among the many names the DAAD-Lecturer Claus Sommerhage should be emphasized. In 1992-1997 Dr. Claus Sommerhage was Guest Professor at the Department for German Language and Literature, 1997-1999 Extraordinary Professor. He innovated new curricula in teaching German literature, especially Modern German Literature.

Since his coming only the overview courses had been taught. He started with analytical literature seminars, Rutiku and Kegelmann. The most important thing he did for the department was establishing our library. He knew that without a library teaching literature was impossible. As Sommerhage had said we had a couple of copies of the novel Aula by Hermann Kant on our shelves. He was right. He started looking for funds in Germany and Switzerland, he used his own connections and personal charm. Without intensive support of the German and Swiss funds our library would not exist today.

FINANCING, PROGRAMMES, FUNDS

Our library is unique because until 2003 there was no budget for it. Nevertheless, it was increasing with every day. At the beginning many books were donated to our library. Tartu is an old university town and professors and lecturers had their own very good libraries. Many professors and lecturers decided to give their German books to our library. The theatre 'Vanemuine' liquidated its library in 1999 and we received all their books in the German language. From there we have our 23-volume complete works of Dostoevsky from 1922 which is considered to be the best Dostoevsky translation since then.

The oldest book in our library dates back to 1780. We also received books from our German friends. More than 15 years Professor Norbert Nail from the University of Marburg equipped us with every kind of books and journals about the German language and linguistics. Since 2001 our library is in the project of Gebert Rüf Fund-the Swiss Baltic Net for the Swiss Libraries and Swiss Literature in the Baltic States. We can order German Swiss literature every year for 1000 ChFr. The sum is not big but very valuable for our library. The project also coordinates the work of Schweizer Lesezimmer in the Baltic States.

We meet every year in Lithuania, Latvia or Estonia to present our annual work and discuss our problems. These meetings are always useful and interesting. This time the meeting takes place in Vilnius In 2005-2007 our library was involved in the programme 'Menschen und Bücher', an initiative of the Goethe Institute for Central and Eastern Europe.

For our library it was a great privilege to be involved in the programme because our financial resources have always been limited. This time we could order books necessary for us and all our lecturers were involved in the ordering process. So we could efficiently enrich our library and every lecturer could order books for his or her course. The budget was 15,000 EUR and we could also invite a German author to Tartu.

DEPARTMENT LIBRARIES AT THE UNIVERSITY OF TARTU

Since 2003 the University Library has pursued the policy of supporting department libraries. Until then the status of a small department library was obscure. At the Department for German Language and Literature the library policy was always clear. We needed a well equipped library for students and lecturers, we were for the open access. Since 2002 our books are in the library system INNOPAC, which makes every process with books very easy and transparent. Sometimes the department libraries are in a bad state, the books are available for very few readers but our policy was different from the very beginning. When we do have a book, people must know about it, they must have access to it.

IMPORTANCE TO THE STUDENTS AND LECTURERS

One of the priorities of our library is its closeness to students and lecturers. We are informed of every need very quickly and for the students it is comfortable that everything about one subject is concentrated at one place. Since 1999 the

Department for German Language and Literature has its own rooms in the former printing-house in the centre of the town, opposite the university main building. The renovation of the building had been contributed by different foreign embassies. It houses Departments for German, French, Spanish and Scandinavian Languages and is called 'Paabel'.

For our library it gave a possibility to expose all the books better, to create a real library system, to create a room where people like to work. The rooms for the German library in this new building are next to the seminar rooms. The students can use library early in the morning and between the lectures and seminars during the day. Our users are the students of the Department for German Language and Literature, the students of the Language Centre of the University, the Master's course students who study translation and interpretation. Every reader who possesses the university library card is welcome in our library. Closeness also means that we always consider the requests of the students.In the last years when we received our budget, we have ordered books for the students who need them for writing their Bachelor's or Master's theses. The priority of our library is to be of high scientific quality. This is the direction Claus Sommerhage gave to our library and we still hold on to it. It is sometimes difficult because of our insufficient financing, but we always choose books carefully, ask advice from our German patrons and friends, try to be informed of the newest scientific literature. So we can affirm that our library has been created by professionals and it fulfils its tasks.

One of our main tasks is to support the study process. At the Department for German Language and Literature the main research areas are linguistics, sociolinguistics, contact and text linguistics as well the Swiss literature and the German literature by women writers and the Baltic-German literature. Some subject areas in our library are very well presented, for example German linguistics, literary science, German history, German language history. In the last years the collection of our dictionaries and lexicons is almost ideal.

As translation and interpretation are taught at our university, the collection of these books is almost excellent. We also have a good collection of German language textbooks. We have a sufficient number of copies thanks to 'LUKKA'– EU supporting programme. At our department teaching of modern Swiss literature has long traditions. Associated Professor Eve Pormeister has taught it already for 20 years and even wrote her Doctoral thesis on this subject. She has connections with the Embassy of Switzerland, Swiss Funds, Pro Helvetia. Her special interest is the reason why Swiss literature is so well presented in our library.

PLEASANT MEETING PLACE, NICE INTERIOR

Last but not least, in a small department library, the milieu plays a big role. There are people who never go to the main library of the university. They do not like too big bleak rooms without cosy corners, with too many strange people. Our library is a kind of a social gathering place for the students who study the same subject, have the same problems and pleasures. The nice and comfortable interior plays an important role here.

As our rooms have interesting architecture, it is possible to establish exhibitions and that is what we regularly do. The last exhibition is from our student who studies art as her minor. She was happy to have an opportunity to show her paintings to her friends and fellow-students. We all can enjoy her colourful and interesting works.

ORGANIZATION OF AMERICAN LIBRARY ASSOCIATION

The American Library Association (ALA) is a non-profit organization based in the United States that promotes libraries and library education internationally. It is the oldest and largest library association in the world, with more than 62,000 members.

HISTORY

Founded by Justin Winsor, Charles Ammi Cutter, Samuel S. Green, James L. Whitney, Melvil Dewey, Fred B. Perkins and Thomas W. Bicknell in 1876 in Philadelphia and chartered in 1879 in Massachusetts, its head office is now in Chicago. During the Centennial Exposition in Philadelphia in 1876, 103 librarians, 90 men and 13 women, responded to a call for a "Convention of Librarians" to be held October 4–6 at the Historical Society of Pennsylvania. At the end of the meeting, "the register was passed around for all to sign who wished to become charter members," making October 6, 1876 to be ALA's birthday.

In attendance were 90 men and 13 women, among them Justin Winsor, Charles Ammi Cutter, Melvil Dewey, and Richard Rogers Bowker. Attendees came from as far west as Chicago and from England. The aim of the Association, in that resolution, was "to enable librarians to do their present work more easily and at less expense." The Association has worked throughout its history to define, extend, protect and advocate for equity of access to information. Library activists in the 1930s pressured the American Library Association to be more responsive to issues put forth by young members involved with issues such as peace, segregation, library unions and intellectual freedom.

In 1931, the Junior Members Round Table (JMRT) was formed to provide a voice for the younger members of the ALA, but much of what they had to say resurfaced in the social responsibility movement to come years later. During this period, the first Library Bill of Rights (LBR) was drafted by Forrest Spaulding to set a standard against censorship and was adopted by the ALA in 1939. This has been recognized as the moment defining modern librarianship as a profession committed to intellectual freedom and the right to read over government dictates.

The ALA formed the Staff Organization's Round Table in 1936 and the Library Unions Round Table in 1940. The ALA appointed a committee to study censorship and recommend policy after the banning of *The Grapes of Wrath* and the implementation of the LBR. The committee reported in 1940 that intellectual freedom and professionalism were linked and recommended a permanent committee – Committee on Intellectual Freedom. The ALA made revisions to strengthen the LBR in June 1948, approved the Statement on Labeling in 1951 to discourage labeling material as subversive, and adopted the Freedom to Read Statement and the Overseas Library Statement in 1953.

In 1961, the ALA took a stand regarding service to African Americans and others, advocating for equal library service for all. An amendment was passed to the LBR in 1961 that made clear that an individual's library use should not be denied or abridged because of race, religion, national origin, or political views. Some communities decided to close their doors rather than desegregate. In 1963, the ALA commissioned a study, *Access to Public Libraries*, which found direct and indirect discrimination in American libraries.

In 1967 some librarians protested against a pro-Vietnam War speech given by General Maxwell D. Taylor at the annual ALA conference in San Francisco; the former president of Sarah Lawrence College, Harold Taylor, spoke to the Middle-Atlantic Regional Library Conference about socially responsible professionalism; and less than one year later a group of librarians proposed that the ALA schedule a new round table programme discussion on the social responsibilities of librarians at its next annual conference in Kansas City.

This group called themselves the Organizing Committee for the ALA Round Table on Social Responsibilities of Libraries. This group drew in many other under-represented groups in the ALA who lacked power, including the Congress for Change in 1969. This formation of the committee was approved in 1969 and would change its name to the Social Responsibilities Round Table (SRRT) in 1971). After its inception, the Round Table of Social Responsibilities began to press ALA leadership to address issues such as library unions, working conditions, wages, and intellectual freedom. The Freedom to Read Foundation was created by ALA's Executive Board in 1969.The Black Caucus of the ALA and the Office for Literacy and Outreach were set up in 1970. In June 1990, the ALA approved "Policy on Library Services to the Poor" and in 1996 the Task Force on Hunger Homelessness, and Poverty was formed to resurrect and promote the ALA guidelines on library services to the poor. The ALA archival materials, non-current records, are currently held in the University of Illinois archives. These materials can only be used at the University of Illinois.

MEMBERSHIP

ALA membership is open to any person or organization, though most of its members are libraries or librarians. Most members live and work in the United States, with international members comprising 3.5per cent of total membership.

GOVERNING STRUCTURE

The ALA is governed by an elected council and an executive board. Since 2002, Keith Michael Fiels has been the ALA executive director (CEO). Policies and programmes are administered by various committees and round tables. One of the organization's most visible tasks is overseen by the Office for Accreditation, which formally reviews and authorizes American and Canadian academic institutions that offer degree programmes in library and information science. The ALA's current President is Molly Raphael. Notable past presidents of the ALA include Theresa Elmendorf, its first female president, Clara Stanton Jones, its first African-American president, Loriene Roy, its first Native American president, Michael Gorman, and Roberta Stevens..

ACTIVITIES

The official purpose of the association is "to promote library service and librarianship." Members may join one or more of eleven membership divisions that deal with specialized topics such as academic, school, or public libraries, technical or reference services, and library administration. Members may also join any of seventeen round tables that are grouped around more specific interests and issues than the broader set of ALA divisions.

Notable Divisions

- ALA Editions (book publishing).
- American Association of School Librarians (AASL).
- Association for Library Collections and Technical Services (ALCTS).
- Association for Library Service to Children (ALSC).
- Association of College and Research Libraries (ACRL).
- Library Information Technology Association (LITA).
- Public Library Association (PLA).
- Reference and User Services Association (RUSA).
- Young Adult Library Services Association (YALSA).

Notable Offices

- Office of Intellectual Freedom (OIF).
- Office for Accreditation (OA).
- Office for Literacy and Outreach Services (OLOS).
- Office for Information Technology Policy (OITP).

Notable Sub-organizations

In 1970, the ALA founded the first lesbian, gay, bisexual and transgender professional organization, called the "Task Force on Gay Liberation", now known as the GLBT Round Table. On July 23rd, 1976, the Committee on the Status of Women in Librarianship was established as a Council Committee of the ALA on recommendation of the Ad Hoc Committee with the same name and of the Committee on Organization.

The Committee on the Status of Women in Librarianship works to "officially represent the diversity of women's interest within ALA and to ensure that the Association considers the rights of the majority in the library field; to promote and initiate the collection, analysis, dissemination, and coordi-nation of information on the status of women in librarianship; to coordinate the activities of ALA units which consider questions of special relevance for women; to identify lags, gaps, and possible discrimination in resources and programmes relating to women; in cooperation with other ALA units, to help develop and evaluate tools, guidelines, and programmes designed to enhance the opportunities and the image of women in the library profession, thus raising the level of consciousness concerning women; to establish contacts with committees on women within other professional groups and to officially represent ALA concerns at interdisciplinary meetings on women's equality; and to provide Council and Membership with reports needed for establishment of policies and actions related to the status of women in librarianship; and to monitor ALA units to ensure consideration of the rights of women."

In 1979 the Committee on the Status of Women in Librarianship received the Bailey K. Howard-World Book Encyclopaedia-ALA Goal Award to develop a profile of ALA personal members, known as the COSWL Study. In 1980 the Committee on the Status of Women in Librarianship was awarded the J. Morris Jones-World Book Encyclopaedia-ALA Goals Award with the OLPR Advisory Committee to undertake a special project on equal pay for work of equal value.

National Outreach

The ALA is affiliated with regional, state, and student chapters across the country. It organizes conferences, participates in library standards development, and publishes a number of books and periodicals. The ALA publishes the magazines *American Libraries* and *Booklist*. Along with other organizations, it sponsors the annual Banned Books Week the last week of September. Young Adult Library Services Association (YALSA) also sponsors Teen Read Week, the third week of each October, and Teen Tech Week, the second week of each March.

Awards and Honours

The ALA annually confers numerous book and media awards, primarily through its children's and young adult divisions. The children's division ALSC administers the Caldecott Medal, Newbery Medal, Batchelder Award, Belpré Awards, Geisel Award, and Sibert Medal, all annual book awards; the Odyssey Award for best audiobook and the (U.S.) Carnegie Medal and for best video. There are also two ALSC lifetime recognitions, the Wilder Medal and the Arbuthnot Lecture.

The young-adult division YALSA administers the Margaret Edwards Award for significant and lasting contribution to YA literature, a lifetime recognition of one author annually, and some annual awards that recognize particular works: the Michael L. Printz Award for a YA book judged on literary merit alone, the William C. Morris Award for an author's first YA book, the new "YALSA Award for Excellence in Non-fiction for Young Adults", and the "Alex Award" list of ten adult books having special appeal for teens. Jointly with the children's division ALSC there is the Odyssey Award for excellence in audiobook production.

The award for YA non-fiction was inaugurated in 2012, defined by ages 12 to 18 and publication year November 2010 to October 2011. The first winner was *'The Notorious Benedict Arnold: A True Story of Adventure, Heroism and Treachery* by Steve Sheinkin and four other finalists were named. Beside the Alex Awards, ALA disseminates some annual lists of "Notable" and "Best" books. The annual awards roster includes the John Cotton Dana Award for excellence in library public relations.From 2006 the ALA annually selects a class of Emerging Leaders, typically comprising about 100 librarians and library school students. This minor distinction is a form of organizational outreach to new librarians. The Emerging Leaders are allocated to project groups tasked with developing solutions to specified problems within ALA divisions. The class meets at the ALA Midwinter and Annual Meetings, commonly January and June. Project teams may present posters of their completed projects at the Annual.

Conferences

The ALA and its divisions hold numerous conferences throughout the year. The two largest conferences are the annual conference and the midwinter meeting.

The latter is typically held in January and focused on internal business, while the annual conference is typically held in June and focused on exhibits and presentations. The ALA annual conference is notable for being one of the largest professional conferences in existence, typically drawing over 25,000 attendees.

POLITICAL POSITIONS

The ALA advocates positions on United States political issues that it believes are related to libraries and librarianship. For court cases that touch on issues about which the organization holds positions, the ALA often files amici curiae briefs, voluntarily offering information on some aspect of the case to assist the court in deciding a matter before it. The ALA has an office in Washington, D.C., that lobbies Congress on issues relating to libraries, information and communication. It also provides materials to libraries that may include information on how to apply for grants, how to comply with the law, and how to oppose a law.

Intellectual Freedom

The primary documented expressions of the ALA's intellectual freedom principles are the Freedom to Read Statement and the Library Bill of Rights; the Library Bill of Rights urges libraries to "challenge censorship in the fulfillment of their responsibility to provide information and enlightenment." The ALA Code of Ethics also calls on librarians to "uphold the principles of intellectual freedom and resist all efforts to censor library resources."

The ALA maintains an Office for Intellectual Freedom (OIF) headed by Barbara M. Jones, former University Librarian for Wesleyan University and internationally known intellectual freedom advocate and author. She is the second director of the Office for Intellectual Freedom, succeeding Judith Krug, who headed the office for four decades. OIF is charged with "implementing ALA policies concerning the concept of intellectual freedom," that the ALA defines as "the right of every individual to both seek and receive information from all points of view without restriction.

It provides for free access to all expressions of ideas through which any and all sides of a question, cause or movement may be explored." Its goal is "to educate librarians and the general public about the nature and importance of intellectual freedom in libraries." The OIF compiles lists of challenged books as reported in the media and submitted to them by librarians across the country. In 1999, radio personality Laura Schlessinger campaigned publicly against the ALA's intellectual freedom policy, specifically in regard to the ALA's refusal to remove a link on its web site to a specific sex-education site for teens.

Sharon Presley said, however, that Schlessinger "distorted and misrepresented the ALA stand to make it sound like the ALA was saying porno for 'children' is O.K." In 2002, the ALA filed suit with library users and the ACLU against the United States Children's Internet Protection Act (CIPA), which required libraries receiving federal E-rate discounts for Internet access to install a "technology protection measure" to prevent children from accessing "visual depictions that are obscene, child pornography, or harmful to minors."

At trial, the federal district court struck down the law as unconstitutional. The government appealed this decision, and on June 23, 2003, the Supreme Court of the United States upheld the law as constitutional as a condition imposed on institutions in exchange for government funding. In upholding the law, the Supreme Court, adopting the interpretation urged by the U.S. Solicitor General at oral argument, made it clear that the constitutionality of CIPA would be upheld only "if, as the Government represents, a librarian will unblock filtered material or disable the Internet software filter without significant delay on an adult user's request."

Privacy

In 2003, the ALA passed a resolution opposing the USA PATRIOT Act, which called sections of the law "a present danger to the constitutional rights and privacy rights of library users". Since then, the ALA and its members have sought to change the law by working with members of Congress and educating their communities and the press about the law's potential to violate the privacy rights of library users.

ALA has also participated as an *amicus curiae* in lawsuits filed by individuals challenging the constitutionality of the USA PATRIOT Act, including a lawsuit filed by four Connecticut librarians after the library consortium they managed was served with a National Security Letter seeking information about library users. After several months of litigation, the lawsuit was dismissed when the FBI decided to withdraw the National Security Letter.

In 2007 the "Connecticut Four" were honoured by the ALA with the Paul Howard Award for Courage for their challenge to the National Security Letter and gag order provision of the USA PATRIOT Act. In 2006, the ALA sold humourous "radical militant librarian" buttons for librarians to wear in support of the ALA's stances on intellectual freedom, privacy, and civil liberties.

Inspiration for the button's design came from documents obtained from the FBI by the Electronic Privacy Information Center (EPIC) through a Freedom of Information Act (FOIA) request. The request revealed a series of e-mails in which FBI agents complained about the "radical, militant librarians" while criticizing the reluctance of FBI management to use the secret warrants authorized under Section 215 of the USA PATRIOT Act.

Copyright

The ALA "supports efforts to amend the Digital Millennium Copyright Act (DMCA) and urges the courts to restore the balance in copyright law, ensure fair use and protect and extend the public domain". It supports changing copyright law to eliminate damages when using orphan works without permission; is wary of digital rights management; and, in ALA v. FCC, successfully sued the Federal Communications Commission to prevent regulation that would enforce next-generation digital televisions to contain rights-management hardware.

It has joined the Information Access Alliance to promote open access to research. The Copyright Advisory Network of the Association's Office for Information Technology Policy provides copyright resources to libraries and the communities they serve.

ACQUISITIONS AND THE PARENT ORGANISATION

There are entities within the parent organisation to which acquisitions connect more closely than do other library departments:

PURCHASING DEPARTMENTS

Libraries are rarely in a position to conduct financial transactions directly with their suppliers. Usually they must work through the parent organisation's purchasing and payment bureaucracy. Maintaining smooth relations demands understanding of each other's way, and, on the library's part, an understanding of the parent organisation's rules of doing business and a willing-ness to follow them.

The librarian should seek to:

- Be allowed to order from publishers, vendors or bookstore directly, and to be able to issue official purchase orders that do not require prior approval from the purchasing department;
- Seek authority for making payments directly to the supplier without going through the financial department;
- Win the right not to go through a periodic bidding process;
- Not to be forced to break purchases into separate small units so as not to exceed a single-purchase ceiling imposed by the parent organisation;
- Demand a renewal of blanket requisitions at the beginning of each year for major vendors.

ACCOUNTING DEPARTMENTS

The library needs to pay its suppliers as quickly as possible, which sometimes entitles them to earn a discount. If this is not met, apart from losing the discounts, the librarian is the one to whom suppliers complain. The problem may lie with the size and practices of the parent organisation which interject delays of excessive verification between approval of payment and sending the cheque, or because of work overload. The delays may arise from the automated systems which do not interface between departments.

To ensure successful interaction involves the internal auditors before buying or designing the library automated system without any compromise, and ensure efficient linkage between systems.

Data consistency is imperative for a successful interface between automated systems. The librarian has also to be aware of the audit trail: orders must be authorized, allocation and transfer of funds must be authorized, and invoices are as well. Now, the usual practice is to accept as sufficient the financial information recorded on the item's machine-readable record in the library system.

This demands not only that specific fields be available for audit-related information, but that records be maintained for as long as the parent organisation's accounting practices require.

Applicable control mechanisms for keeping data safe may include segregating various functions and using different passwords to access each function, requiring authorization for tran-sactions, and maintaining a log of all record updating activities. Libraries may want a way to double-check the accuracy of the financial reports, they protect themselves by running their own funding system whether automated or manual ledger entries.

COMPUTING FACILITIES

Some libraries have their own systems. The acquisitions demands for interconnectivity and interfacing with outside computer systems. Since acquisitions deals in commercial transactions, it needs convenient access to the commercial world's systems.

CAMPUS BOOK STORES

Such stores usually supply titles for the individual needs of the population of parent organisation on the campus. The library may use them for urgently needed replacements. Such stores in hospitals do not store materials of interest to the library.

AUTOMATION OF ACQUISITIONS ACTIVITIES

Here, the impact of automation on acquisitions in particular will be discussed. This impact has been explicit in three areas:

- *Creation and Updating of Bibliographic Record*: The bibliographic record connects the various divisions of the library and its users. As soon as the manual files disappear, and a single machine-readable record takes their place, a record will be equally accessible to all staff and users. A complete, accurate record will not cause unwanted duplication, and will state which items have been ordered and received, and will stand as a reliable base on which to add further information. Public services and users will know what is on the shelf, what is on order, and what is waiting for processing.
- *Creation and Updating of the Financial Record:* A good book fund accounting system provides built-in verifications and safeguards to prevent many errors. An automated accounting system saves staff time, improves relations with suppliers and enables a wide range of management reports.
- *Data Transmission and Exchange Pertaining to Both*: Electronic data transfer in place of rekeying has the greatest potential for cutting error rates and increasing both speed and efficiency in technical processing. Internal connection will enable the automatic data transfer between the library and the accounting department. External connection to bibliographic utilities and vendor systems can be used to download bibliographic information and send orders, claims, and payments with a minimum investment of human effort.

ACQUISITION OF SERIALS

The Anglo-American cataloguing rules, second edition defines a serial as:

- A publication in any medium issued in successive parts bearing numeric or chronological designations and intended to be continued indefinitely. Serials include periodicals; newspapers; annuals, the journals, proceedings, memoirs, transactions, etc. of societies; and numbered monographic series. Series is a group of separate items related to one another by the fact that each item bears, in addition to its own title proper, a collective title applying to the group as a whole. The individual items may or may not be numbered.

The indefinite continuation of a serial is important from the acquisitions point of view, as it continues arriving, which necessitates updating its record.

BENEFITS OF LIBRARY ORGANIZATION BY THE SERVICES WITH TQM

"Sirkin" suggests some ways a library might use the principles of TQM to enhance library services:

- Create service broachers and information kits.
- Conduct a user survey about library services.
- Improve signage.
- Change hours of operation.
- Provide a more convenient material return.
- Simplify checkout of material.
- Use flexibility in staff assignment.
- Co-operate with local government.
- Ask vendors to give products demonstration.
- Give new staff a through orientation.
- Create inter departmental library advisory groups.
- Improve the physical layout of the library.
- Track complaints.
- Develop an active outreach programme.
- Open satellite offices.
- Publicize new or changes services.
- Develop user and staff training materials
- Target services o specific groups.
- Offer electronic document delivery.
- Follow the mission statement.

While TQM clearly has positive aspects implementing it can have potential challenges "Jurow" ad "barnnard" identify four barriers to the adoption of TQM in libraries:

- *Vocabulary:* Objections to terms such as "total" "quality and "management" which imply that high standards are not already being met.
- *Commitment:* TQM takes several years to implement and requires a long term commitment by library managers
- *Process:* Our culture tends to be impatient and we try to solve problems quickly, contrary to TQM ' careful process analysis; and
- *Professionalization:* Professional can be resist to turning over their

practices and services to what they perceive as the "uniformed whims of the customer."

"Sitckin"also notes that it is not possible to satisfy everyone's demands; choices will need to be made.

WHY LIBRARIES SHOULD ADOPT TQM

Libraries are among the most ancient social and cultural institutions in existence. Ancient libraries as well as modern ones have one thing in common: all of them have a body of information recorded on of them have a body of information could be retrieved when needed. The accessibility of information requires good organizational ability from those who are structure of the organization where desired information is retrieved and made accessible efficiently and in a timely manner to the users. Creation and maintenance of such a structure requires an effective management process that facilitates work towards the goal. Today technology has changed our social and economic life. In the workplace methodologies change people work at home or on the web with flexible time table, and more and more virtual communities are emerging in different fields. The most important stakeholders in the library are customers, providers of subsidies, staff and other libraries. These stakeholders are interested for various reasons, in the introduction of TQM. The introduction of TQM makes great demands on the staff.

The following factors in particular need to be taken into account:

- TQM involves a process of change and therefore requires of staff that they be ready to play a constructive role in that process.
- TQM requires a basic re-orientation from the media stock towards customer and markets. For TQM a result oriented approach, not the input of resources, is of vital importance.
- A strongly hierarchical organization with fragmented responsibilities is not well suited to the introduction of TQM since all staff needs to feel a responsibility for influencing quality.
- The effort necessary for implementing TQM is at the same time rewarding for both staff and the institution: Improvement of the institution in which they work, a strengthening of that institutions position, and more opportunity of staff to influence their own work.

The management of quality in libraries, as a management method that allows the improvement of performance, has been the object of interest for the managers of these services. In this context, that permits the reality of the information service is essential to better adequate and quality proposals.

FINAL COMMENTS

Quality can be described right time as well as doing it right the first time and doing it right each time.

It requires continuous improvement. In this context of the library, it can be described as:-

- Q – Quest for excellence of knowledge
- U – Understanding the user's demand.
- L – Leadership quality for librarian.
- I – Involving all staffs.
- T – Team spirit for achieving common goal.
- Y – Yardstick to measure progress.

There are various aspects of dimensions of quality that are utilized by a user to evaluate library service:

- *Performance*: Performance of library services according to the user's need.
- *Features*: Special features of library, that appeals to users.
- *Access*: Approachability to library and easy access to document.
- *Competence*: Possession of special skills and knowledge required performing the library services in the changing content.
- *Responsiveness*: Whole-heartedly endeavour to provide services as soon as possible.
- *Courtesy*: Respects, politeness as tidy appearance of library staff.
- *Communication*: Listening carefully to the users educating and informing them in the language in which they can understand easily.
- *Reliability*: Providing reliable information thus making users free from doubt and confusion.
- *Credibility*: Trust worthiness, belief having the user's best interest at heart.
- *Tangibles*: The physical evidence of various services, tools, equipments, and latest information technologies.
- *Availability*: Unlimited access to the library.
- *Maintainability*: Restoration of service immediately if it has failed at any juncture.

ORGANISING A NATIONAL DATA INFRASTRUCTURE

In 1994 the Federal Geographic Data Committee (FGDC) recommended that a National Spatial Data Infrastructure (NSDI) be organised. The NSDI would be an "umbrella of policies, standards, and procedures under which organisations and technologies interact to foster more efficient use, management, and production of geospatial data". The NSDI was conceptualised as fostering more cooperation and interaction between different organisations from the public and private sector.

The recommendation was a response to alterations in the traditional flows of data across the government based on new convergences of information, computer technology, and communication. A significant component of the data being used in government transactions and commercial transactions was digital geospatial data. The FGDC considered digital geospatial data as being critical to solving many "environmental, economic, and social problems." The FGDC had also recognised that "the use of GIS technologies for the digital analysis of spatial problems had become pervasive". With the integration of GIS and increased use of geospatial data into problem-solving operations, a major goal of the NSDI was to make "an environment to respond to the current need of digital geospatial data."

The FGDC envisioned building the framework around the procedures, technology, and guidelines that enhance integration, sharing, and use of these data, and the institutional relationships and business practices that encourage the maintenance and use of data. The framework would represent the best available data for an area, and be certified, standardised, and described according to a common standard. Today, the FGDC standards provide a foundation on which organisations can build by adding their own detail and compiling other data sets.

MEETING DIGITAL GEOSPATIAL DATA NEEDS

The FGDC reported that many billions of dollars are spent by organisations on an annual basis in both the public and private sector in attempts to manage digital geospatial data. With digital geospatial data becoming a valuable asset within the business practices of many public and private sector organisations, most organisations can only afford to collect or purchase only a small portion of information they require. Often only the most basic digital geospatial data is acquired by organisations, usually a dataset that pertains to a specific geographic area or that has some unique attribute characteristics.

The datasets are often incompatible with other datasets, due to differences in software platforms. Researchers at the FGDC found that data collected by differing organisations may be similar in geographic extent use different geographic bases and standards. Hence, many of the resources organisations spend on geographic information systems (GIS) go towards duplicating other organisations' data collection efforts. The same geographic data themes for an area are collected again and again, at great expense.A data framework would improve the ability for organisations to share data. The framework would provide a basic geographic data in a common format and an accessible environment that anyone can use and to which anyone can contribute. In this environment, users can perform cross-jurisdictional and cross-organisational analyses and operations, and organisations can funnel their resources into applications, rather than duplicating data production efforts. Researchers at the FGDC further noted in their findings that geographic data users from many disciplines have a recurring need for a few themes of basic data: geodetic control, orthoimagery, elevation, transportation, hydrography, governmental units, and cadastral information. Many organisations produce and use such data every day.

The framework provides basic information for these data themes. By attaching their own geographic data, which can cover innumerable subjects and themes, to the common data in the framework, users can build their applications more easily and at less cost. The seven data themes provide basic data that can be used in applications, a base to which users can add or attach geographic details and attributes, a reference source for accurately registering and compiling participants' own data sets, and a reference map for displaying the locations and the results of an analysis of other data. Researchers at the FGDC envision the information framework to be an evolving data resource to which geographic data producers can contribute.

Integral components of the information network incorporate procedures, guidelines, and technology to enable participants to build, integrate, maintain, distribute, and use framework data. These elements ensure that users can depend on accurate, detailed data that can be certified and integrated into the framework to create a trustworthy data source; users can update their data holdings from the framework data; and users can attach additional information to the framework. These procedures would ensure the standardisation of datasets and enable the efficient transfer of digital geospatial data across the Internet. The FGDC envisions the information framework integrating data from all types of organisations in both the public and private sector. The framework environment is designed to be responsive to the needs of the geographic data community in terms of data creation and maintenance, and provides unrestricted access to data.

A COOPERATIVE INFORMATION NETWORK

The FGDC also envisions organisations building the information framework by coordinating data development activities. Organisations can coordinate framework data along two dimensions. "The first dimension emphasises opportunities for organisations with similar needs. An example is a metropolitan area in which local governments, their customers, state and federal agencies with facilities in the area, utilities, and others require high-resolution spatial data for their operations. In this case the framework provides a starting point for sharing the commonly needed geographic base information and allows each organisation to add the unique information it requires to meet its business needs".

The second dimension emphasises opportunities for organisations needing different amounts of detail for an area. For example, a local government, a regional transportation planning organisation, and a state transportation agency may require road data for an area, but at different levels of geography. For efficient data sharing the organisations would have to share the results of their individual efforts and would benefit from using a common geographic base and generalised data created from this base.

The framework provides a starting point for a base and the data generalised from it, "providing the organisations with contemporary and consistent data for decision making and helping them avoid confusion caused by differences in the vintages, common attributes, and other characteristics of the base data". The framework is being developed by this entire community, with organisations from all areas playing roles. For some, the framework will supply the data they need to build applications.

Others will contribute data, and some may provide services to maintain and distribute data. Some organisations will play several roles in framework development, operation, and use. An essential community partner in the information network can be libraries.

Librarians have the skills and experience needed to help the information network to facilitate digital geospatial data and to aid in its search and mining procedures. Some researchers have advocated the 'geolibrary' as a possible model for a library to facilitate digital geospatial data.

DIGITAL GEOLIBRARIES AND DIGITAL COLLECTIONS

One approach used by librarians in making digital geospatial data available to their users is to incorporate Web-based mapping functions with their library geospatial information holdings. Such efforts combine the locational aspects of the metadata descriptions of the geospatial data in the catalog with the mapping capabilities of GIS software. In building Web-based functions into their geospatial collections, some libraries have termed their collection a 'digital geolibrary.'

Different perspectives about geolibraries have been discussed in the scholarly geography and information science literature such as from Boxall and Goodchild. Goodchild refers to a geolibrary as being comprised of georeferenced information that can be accessed by a geographic footprint. Likewise, in his discussion of geolibraries, Boxall notes that their scope extends beyond the traditional map library if the construct of a geolibrary is based upon the idea that information has a geographic footprint.

His discussion references earlier research that explains georeferenced information as including such things as photographs, videos, music, and literature that can be given a locational variable that defines a footprint. The collection areas of geolibraries extend beyond the traditional scope of map libraries and archives to include almost all information contained within libraries.

He later mentions that it can include information outside of libraries as well. This is the theoretical basis for what we now view as geolibraries. Boxall discusses that a significant focus of geolibraries is on digital information and metadata, as well as the distributed nature of the libraries and 'collections.' He adds that '...Distributed geolibraries provide a useful framework for discussion of the issues of dissemination associated with the National Spatial Data Infrastructure (NSDI)". The vision is readily extendible to a global context.

Boxall feels any discussion of “Digital Earth’ (DE), the ‘Global Spatial Data Infrastructure’ (GSDI), and ‘Distributed Geolibraries’ should be framed around the broadest definitions of information and infrastructures; namely to include and focus upon the people, technology and organisations which give rise to and sustain such infrastructures’.

An early significant effort at establishing a digital spatial library was the Alexandria Digital Library at the University of California Santa Barbara. The Alexandria Digital Library was one of six federally funded library projects. The U.S. National Science Foundation founded it in early 1994. The Library’s collection and services focus on georeferenced information: maps, images, data sets, and other information sources with links to geographic locations. Much of the information in the collection was primarily of the University’s service area, or Southern California.

A key aspect of the collection is the ability to perform data queries and retrieve results by geography location. The basic means of describing and finding information is with a geographic footprint. A footprint depicts the location on the surface of the earth associated with either an object in the collection such as a map, remote sensed image, or aerial photograph, or with a user’s query. The footprint may be represented as a point or polygon, with latitude and longitude coordinates. As a user queries the collection through a user interface, the user creates a footprint or an interactive map to indicate the area of interest.

The query area is matched with the object footprints in the metadata to retrieve relevant objects about the query area. This approach to query structure allows the user to choose arbitrary query areas and is not limited to geographic areas with place names. The objects in the collection that fall within a particular query area do not have to have the names associated with them that the user enters for a text based query. By translating a user’s textbased query into a footprint query for a certain geographic area, the user can retrieve all types of information about a location such as remote sensed images, data sets, aerial photographs, and textual information. The catalog for the Alexandria Digital Library is configured for searches that will retrieve objects that are either in an online format or physical location as a map.

Using the Alexandria Digital Library as a model, the Idaho Geospatial Data Center was started in 1996 by a team of geographers, geologists, and librarians. The aim of the team was the establishment of digital library of public domain geographic data for the state of Idaho. As a theoretical and practical foundation for their digital spatial collection, which they termed a ‘geolibrary,’ the team used a set of parameters as defined by Goodchild. Goodchild defined a geolibrary’s components as including a browser or specialised software application running on the user’s computer and providing access to the geolibrary through a computer network. A geolibrary also includes a ‘basemap’ or geographic frame of reference for the browser’s queries.

A basemap would provide an image of an area corresponding to the geographical extent of geolibrary collection. The basemap would depend on the scale of the search being performed from a large geographic area, such as a state, or a smaller location, as a city block. A gazetteer or index that would link place names to a map would also be included. A large collection of collection catalogs would be maintained on distributed computer servers. The servers would be accessed over a network with the browser, using basic server-client architecture.

A geolibrary would ideally provide open access to many types of information with geographic referenced queries regardless of the storage media Using a grant from the Idaho Board of Education's Technology Incentive Programme, the team built a geographic digital data repository or the Idaho GeoSpatial Data Center (IGDC). The library contained a number of digital geospatial datasets that was searchable through a flexible browsing tool. The collection contained a number of public domain information such as Digital Line Graphs and Digital Raster Graphics from the United States Geological Survey and U.S. Bureau of the Census TIGER boundary files for the state of Idaho. The site provided an interactive visual analysis of selected demographic/economic data for Idaho counties.

The site also contained interactive links to other Idaho and national spatial data repositories. A key aspect of the IGDC's collection was the development of the GeoLibrary's browser, which was implemented using MicroSoft Visual Basic 5.0 and ESRI MapObjects technology. The interface of the browser consisted of three panels resembling the Microsoft Outlook user interface. A first panel, a map panel, would be used to explore the geographic coverage of the geolibrary and to select an area of interest.

A second panel in the interface was where the query would be performed. The final panel is where the query results would be displayed for analysis and to download spatial data. In many ways, librarians are well aware of the ideas outlined in the discussion on the concepts and components for digital data infrastructure. Library collections and services in electronic form, such as a digital library, integrate many aspects of the client-server architecture in providing access to materials in an online distributed environment. Digital libraries have in them collections of digital information objects of various formats in an ordered database defined by descriptive data standards.

Organised in a regular manner, the database is searchable using query applications via a user interface, usually through an online catalog. Information is compartmentalised in short descriptions using metadata tags to ease search and retrieval applications. The overall structure is guided by administrative oversight that takes into account the needs of the various users involved in the community. Researchers, such as Goodchild, envision an intersection of the concepts of the digital library and that of the spatial data infrastructure in a sort of 'geolibrary'.

Researcher envisions a geolibrary as a library filled with "georeferenced information that can have a geographic footprint.' Including multimedia, images, and music that could be assigned a location attribute, geolibraries would thus extend beyond the scope of a traditional map library and provide new services and resources for users to discover. The survey of the characteristics of spatial data databases and related infrastructure indicate the involvement of many different factors in assembling a data infrastructure. However, in addition to data providers, databases, metadata, data networks, technology, and institutional arrangements, there is also a significant in organisational and human resource factors.

Researchers offer six talking points that are essential to consider in building a spatial data infrastructure. These include technology, policies and standards, human resources, institutional arrangements, spatial data and metadata, and data networks. They suggest that spatial data infrastructure should not recreate the wheel in its technology development. It would be prudent to look at what information technology has accomplished to date, and then integrate that knowledge with GIS expertise, regardless of the difficulties involved. Integration of existing technology also applies to standards and policies. Standards enhance communication and development with a common language and concepts, leading to guidelines that affect architecture, processes, methods, or policies.

There should be a common consensus of minimal guidelines that can accommodate those working with geospatial data, retrieval, and discovery. User-guided development is also critical when examining the human resources side of GIS information and technology. Further, the use of qualified researchers and developers is essential. To create institutional frameworks, agreements have to be certified to establish national, regional, and global spatial data infrastructure. These spatial data infrastructures should be created over the geographic data, stored in the spatial databases, and their description in rich, descriptive metadata. Finally, open systems and ease of access is of strategic importance to ensure quality and accuracy from remote systems.

The need for data description standards for digital geospatial data is especially apparent in the proliferation of WebGis applications in the wake of spatial data distribution enabling initiatives, such as the NSDI. WebGIS (also known as Internet GIS) describes a type of geographic information system. WebGIS basically consists of client, server, and network model, wherein the client is integrated in a Web browser. While creating many opportunities for librarians in making available unique geospatial datasets, the tremendous growth in WebGIS has created many challenges for libraries in trying to incorporate digital geospatial data in their services and legal considerations in the use of distributed data.

WEB GIS AND LIBRARIES

In recent years the number and scope of WebGIS applications has grown tremendously. In their survey of WebGIS applications, Researchers discuss a wide number of interactive mapping sites available on the Internet. They note that many users of the Internet have already experienced using WebGIS software tools through interactive mapping tools available on the Internet. Such sites include: Yahoo Maps, National Map, and GoogleEarth Other WebGIS applications that are available on the Internet give access to a varying amount of specialised geospatial data.

Many local government Web sites for city and county governments across the United States offer interactive mapping sites such as the City of Albuquerque and City of Durham for users to access technical data about their municipalities. These mapping sites give access to socioeconomic, demographic, and planning data. Many government sites use ESRI software products such as ArcGIS and ArcWEB services to facilitate data searches for information.

Other WebGIS applicatiosn include environmental planning, agricultural planning wetlands management, archaeological research, health planning research, transportation planning, citizen political participation and education planning. Other developments in WebGIS include different data visualisations to offer unique perspectives on information for analytical purposes, such as three-dimensional modeling and combinations of software such as multimedia and WebGIS to offer comprehensive views of geospatial data A net effect of the increasingly popularity of WebGIS. The popularity of WebGIS applications among the public has led to unequal data distribution across the Internet, since bandwidth is constrained.

In their study of WebGIS, Yang identify two issues related to improving access to digital geospatial data on the Interent. The first issue concerns the sharing of and interoperability for heterogeneous data among different systems, different communities, and different users. The second issue is a quality of service issue, that of how to improve the system performance so data are delivered to the users within a reasonable time span. In regards to the first issue, the authors identify international organisational efforts at creating accepted conventions in data descriptive standards in regards to interoperability and data access. The strides being made by the aforementioned organisations and agreement between international geospatial data producers and providers is creating an environment wherein libraries have access to geospatial Web Services, such as ESRI's Geography Network and Geosptatial One Stop. Web service Internet sites essentially provide access to GIS data, software, educational and mapping, or related services.

For libraries, the services can give access to current and large amounts of geospatial data are usually available in a timely manner. In his study of how academic libraries can integrate digital geospatial data into their collections and services, Morris provides a good overview of the issues involved in trying to facilitate Web Service data in an academic library. Some drawbacks of attempting to integrate Web services into a library environment can include lingering technical issues like linking data resources, developing sustainable licensing models, and negotiating access rights to digital geospatial data.

IT'S ROLE IN MANAGING ORGANISATIONAL CHANGE

IT AND ENVIRONMENT - GOALS-STRUCTURE

Researcher defined environment as those factors which not only are outside the system's control but which determine in part how the system performs.

Uncertainty is the difference between the amount of information required to perform the task and the amount of information already possessed by the organisation:

- *Proposition* 1: Turbulent environment drives organisations to use IT for monitoring the preferences of the environment. System theorists have recognised the importance of 'feedback' for the survival of the system and for maintaining a 'steady state' or 'homeostasis'. Organisations are purposive systems that learn of the impending threats by scanning. Scanning is the process by which the organisation acquires information for decision making. The modes of scanning are primarily determined by the external environmental stimuli and are determined by the magnitude and by the direction of the discrepancy between the goal and its realisation. While surveillance is useful for information-gathering process, search is oriented towards finding a satisfactory solution to a specific problem. Complex systems require complex controllers. IT will provide the 'complex controller" to the increasingly complex organisation. The information systems of an organisation need to evolve to remain consistent with the changing organisational structure. Referring to the obscurity of causal laws of turbulence, Aldrich argued that scanning could provide the firm with the desired 'competitive edge.'
- *Proposition* 2: Turbulent environment drives organisations to use IT for translating the information on environmental preferences into goals. Continuously changing environment requires organisations to continuously reassess their goals. Effective structuring requires a consistency among the design parameters and contingency factors have demonstrated that organisations' goals can be generated by external forces, such as other groups seeking to use the organisation to further their own ends.
- *Proposition* 3: Turbulent environment drives organisations to use IT to align their structure with environmental preferences. The very efforts of the organisation to maintain a constant external environment produce changes in organisational structure. Scott argued that organisational structure and goals are driven by the preferences in

the environment. The structure is determined by the information-processing capacity requirements of the organisation which in turn are governed by the IT being used. Aldrich, Perrow, Walker and Woodward have attributed structural differences to the organisation's technology. Mintzberg had suggested that the organisation's environment and technology are the independent variables that determine the structural variables of the organisation. Fowles, in his narrative on the history of organisational communications technologies contends that the phenomenal expansion of organisations can be largely attributed to advances in the technologies of organisational communication. Yates argued that in absence of technological communication organisations could have evolved differently. Preliminary econometric analyses of the overall U.S., economy for the period 1975-1985 further confirms that the increased use of IT is correlated with decreases in firm size and vertical integration.

IT AND ORGANIC STRUCTURE

- *Proposition* 4: Turbulent environment drives organisations to make more use of IT for increasing their 'organic' characteristics. 'Organic' firms are better equipped to sustain themselves in turbulent environment. A dynamic environment will drive the structure to an organic state despite other forces; the more complex the environment, the more decentralised the structure. Introduction of IT at the 'operating core' level transforms a bureaucratic administrative structure into an organic one. Effectively, automation of routine tasks eliminates the source of many of the social conflicts throughout the organisation. Law of requisite variety implies that the rate of change of organisational systems must correspond to the rate of change of environmental systems, *i.e.*, organisations with complex environmental interactions would develop complex structures like adhocracies or networks. Adhocracy is suitable for a dynamic and complex environment, when the firm has sophisticated technical systems and the focus is upon consistently offering differentiated products for retaining the customers. Future organisations would be 'networks' characterised by adhocracies with flexible systems of projects and teams brought together quickly to accomplish specific tasks. Some existing organisations have already 'farmed out' their operations by establishing them as separate organisations or contracting them out to other organisations.
- *Proposition 4a:* Turbulent environment drives organisations to use IT for empowering workers at all levels. Growing availability of telecommunications has offered technologies like distributed systems and client-server architecture that facilitate the process of

empowerment of the lower levels. In the 'informated' organisation, workers would be 'empowered' by virtue of access to necessary information to perform higher-level tasks. Ramstrom has argued that tactical decisions relating to 'soft' information would be delegated to the 'grass-roots' where there is easy access to relevant information concerning the immediate environment, at the same time providing these levels with the information generated within the system by means of 'cheap' internal information systems.

- *Proposition 4b:* Turbulent environment drives organisations to use IT for increasing the spans of control. Information technologies, by facilitating the standardisation of coordination would facilitate larger spans of control or work units which would be characterised by extensive lateral communication and self- contained authority structures.
- *Proposition 4c:* Turbulent environment drives organisations to use IT for increasing lateral communications. Selective use of lateral decision processes for situations involving task uncertainty increase the information processing capacity of the organisation. Bringing the points of decision down to the points of action reduces the information overload on the managers. Since specification of 'procedures' in complex situations creates inefficiencies, organisations in turbulent environments would use more IT resource for delegating the decision-making to workers. Increased use of groupware for lateral coordination will spell the demise of middle management.

IT AND DIFFERENTIATION - INTEGRATION

- *Proposition* 5: Turbulent environment drives organisations to reduce their 'dimensions' by focusing on core competencies by leveraging their use of IT.
- *Proposition 5a:* Turbulent environment drives organisations to use IT to reduce differentiation and integration to focus on increased specialisation. Organisations structure themselves to minimize coordination costs and group together similar activities to achieve the benefits of process specialisation. Environmental uncertainty or 'task predictability' is the basic independent variable influencing the design of the organisation. Faced with increased uncertainty, organisations can reduce the need for information processing by decreasing the 'diversity of outputs'. Reduced differentiation and integration of activities would decrease the coordination effort involved thus reducing the information processing requirements. Reduced coordination costs with IT would result in the substitution of IT for human coordination. Greater specialisation would be achieved by focusing on few core competencies.

IT'S ROLE IN MANAGING ORGANISATIONAL INTERDEPENDENCIES

- *Proposition* 6: Turbulent environment drives organisations to actively seek Inter-organisational relations to leverage their core competencies. Cooperation, especially in the international context, will be necessary to gain a competitive advantage in the future. To survive in an increasingly competitive environment, firms would form alliances that would bring together their core competencies to create the 'best of all" products.
- *Proposition 6a:* Turbulent environment drives organisations to reduce environmental complexity and uncertainty by seeking interdependencies with other organisations in the environment.
- *Proposition 6b:* Turbulent environment drives organisations to use more IT - effort to establish coordinating mechanisms with other firms.

To survive in the fast-changing environment the 'adaptive organisation" would be more like a shifting 'constellation' that has 'linkages' with independent and semi- autonomous organisations. Use of inter organisational linkages such as EDI would enable new forms of organisations and reduce the coordination costs of increasingly market-driven organisations. Increasingly, electronic linkages are becoming the necessary condition of doing businesses with larger firms.

Using an analogy to the study of community chests conducted by Litwak and Hylton, we observe that in the increasingly global competition, the firms are competing for the common customers' 'fund' and the increase in one firm's revenue would come at the expense of other firm's loss. Coordination, being a function of interdependency, should grow in periods of increased competition for 'funds.'

THE IT PARADOX

- *Proposition* 7: Increasingly turbulent environment would feed the need for further advancements in IT which would further increase turbulence.

Business needs are incessantly driving the demands for increased capabilities of IT. In turn, increasingly advanced IT is being utilised in more and more sophisticated ways by the businesses to outdo competition. IT, which is being deployed as a solution to the increased complexity and uncertainty of the environment, has paradoxically contributed to the situation by 'compressing time and distance.' In absence of the present day advances in IT, would we be talking of globalisation or time based competition? Perhaps, not.

The pace of complexity is increasing fast. Hopefully, the advances in technology would be able to keep up with the environmental changes. Turbulence refers not to chaos in the environment, but to an increasing causal interconnection that renders environments obscure to local observers. Thus how can IT help organisations in responding to the challenges of an increasingly complex and uncertain environment?

How can IT help the organisations achieve the 'flexible' organisation structure? We provide academic libraries as a living educational example that has been impacted by the strong trend of convergence of the technological advancements.

CHANGE MANAGEMENT STANDARDS

- All substantive changes to the IT Environment must adhere to the XX change Management process. A substantive change has the potential to affect the ability of users and systems to interact with each other.
- All changes must conform to the published guidelines that dictate the 'look and feel' of the XX web environment.
- All web page content changes must have the approval of the web page owner prior to change implementation.
- All changes to the production systems within IT will have a corresponding set of documentation that describes the change, the business reason for the change and the disposition of the change. This includes emergency and exception changes.
- The risk and/or impact ratings of the requested change will determine which of the four phases of the change workflow will be required to promote the change into production. For 'minor' changes only Analysis and Implementation will be required.
- Anyone with a valid XX Notes access will be able to enter a change into the Change Request process. Only authorised approvers will be able to accept a change request into the Change Management process.

STATUS OF CHANGES

The following status codes are used to reflect the status of a change request:

- *Open* – The change has been received and accepted but has not been assigned.
- *In-Progress* – The change has been received, acknowledged and assigned. Work is in progress to fulfill the change request.
- *Approved* – The business and technical assessments have been completed and the change has been approved and committed to the change scheduler.
- *Rejected* – The change has been rejected and will be routed back to the Request for Service process and sent back to the customer with an explanation and a recommended course of action.
- *Closed* – The change request has been closed.
- *Canceled* – The change request has been canceled.

TYPES OF CHANGES

The Change Management Procedure applies to all types of changes related to the XX IT environment.

The following is a description of each of the types of changes that can take place and the rules that apply to each:

- *Application Changes:* Changes to any application code that is running on or linked to by any hardware or software in the XX IT environment. These changes are typically made to enhance the function or performance of or to fix a known error in the IT application environment. These changes cannot be implemented without approval of the owner of the application and cannot be requested by any programmer other than the one assigned to the programme. Assignment of Risk Category Level of the change is to be a joint effort of both the owner and the Change Implementer.
- *Hardware Changes:* All XX IT and IT support equipment installations, discontinuances and relocations are controlled by the Change Management Procedure. This activity can be requested by anyone but must have the approval of the Operations Manager.
- *Visual Image Changes:* Changes to the 'artistic' presentation of web pages are not required to make entries into the Change Management system. Changes to 'Active' areas of the web page are required to use the XX Change Management procedure.
- *Software Changes:* The criteria for entering a software change into the Change process are based upon the effect that the changes may have on the IT support resources. If the changes affect the system, users or the support staff there is a requirement to enter it into the Change process. If the change is made for the exclusive benefit of the requester and if failure could not affect anyone else, that change would be exempt from the Change Process. For example, a change made by a programmer affecting a procedure or a programme under development on a test application requires no entry. However, when stand-alone test time is required on a production system, a change request form is required.
  - Typically, software changes would include changes to the Operating System, Vendor supplied Programme Products, e.g., Visual Studio, Java, etc., or common application support modules. However, during the last two and first five workdays of each month changes are restricted to emergency and critical necessities as determined by the Director of Information Technology.
- *Network Changes:* All installations, discontin-uances and all relocations of equipment used for IT teleprocessing communications are entered into the change process. This includes all routers, switches and

telephone lines as well as Personal Computers if they are connected to the network.

- *Environmental Changes:* Environmental changes normally involve the facilities associated with the IT Installation. These facility changes include items such as air conditioning, chilled water, raised flooring, security, motor generators, electricity, plumbing and the telephony system for voice and data. For example, when there is a planned weekend power outage initiated by the local power company this information is submitted to the Change Management Process a minimum of two weeks prior to the scheduled outage and communicated to management, staff and the user community.
- *Documentation Changes:* All procedural changes to the standard operating procedures will be implemented through the Change process. Also, all permanent deviations from the published schedule time for running of production applications will be communicated through the Change Management system.

CHANGE LEVELS

The following guidelines for definition of Change risk levels are provided for consideration during the planning cycle. It must be clearly understood that these requirements are the minimum for each of the defined levels. The Requester may wish to plan additional lead times, documentation or reviews to insure that targets can be met and planned implementation schedules can be achieved. All changes are tracked, correlated and used for management reporting, statistics, trending, etc., to identify when and where additional resources should be provided.

For any change that fails, the Change Requester must enter an explanation in the comments section of the Change Record for that change and notify the Change Coordinator. The Change Coordinator will then close the change with the appropriate close status. If the change is to be attempted at a later time, the Change Requester should re-enter the change with the new date. Changes that cause a Platform outage will be reviewed at a Quality Measurement Meeting.

LEVEL E CHANGES

Emergency changes are those changes that are vital in order to ensure that IT's committed service levels are maintained. An Emergency change should not be used in order to bypass the appropriate lead-time for a change that has been entered into the system.

Exception changes are those changes that are a result of a business need and must be installed prior to the required lead-time. These types of changes proceed to the implementation phase when the requester's manager and the

Director of Information Technology acknowledge that an Emergency or an Exception situation exists and authorise the modification planned. These changes will be post-reviewed to assure successful implementation, along with identification of any external impacts or new requirements. Post-review will also evaluate the reason for the Level E change request and try to determine a way of eliminating this requirement in the future. The post-review will also evaluate if, in fact, the change addressed a real or a perceived emergency condition. In all cases, the review must determine if additional action is required, what that action should be and who will be responsible for the action. Documentation requirements for Emergency changes are the same as any change. The Requester is responsible for meeting all requirements for the change documentation within one week of the implementation.

For non-application changes:

- Is the change needed to restore immediate service to the end user.
- Is the change necessary to fix an existing problem immediately.
- Is this a change that must be installed immediately but the need for it was not recognised early enough to be approved through the regular process.

For application changes:

- Must this change be done immediately to fix problems for jobs that ABENDed during the previous night or are required to run in order to bring up on-line systems.

What Types of Management Approval is Required for Level E Changes

Approval required by:

- Director of Information Technology or her designee.
- Change Management Process Owner or his designee.
- Manager of the user department requesting the change.

Depending on the scope and impact of the proposed change, approval by one or more of the following individuals may be required.

- Operations Manager.
- Application Development Manager.
- Network and Technical Services Manager.

LEVEL 4 CHANGES

A Level 4 Change would have a major impact on IT services if a problem occurs during install. The install time is lengthy and the backout is very difficult or impossible. Level 4 Change Requests are to be entered into the Change Management Data Base at least thirty business days prior to the planned implementation date. The Requester or representative for a Level 1 change is required to attend the Change Communication meeting immediately prior to implementation so that any questions or concerns may be addressed.

Whenever a Level 4 change must be expedited to address a critical timing situation, a special meeting must be held. To expedite a Level 4 change, all parties that may be affected by this change must be present or represented at the special meeting.

It is the responsibility of the change requester to arrange the meeting and assure attendance by the required groups or individuals. If the required groups or individuals cannot be assembled, the change cannot be expedited and an escalation will be required.

How do you know that the Change Falls Under Level 4

For non-application changes:

- From the end user's eyes, is it possible for the change to have a major impact on services if problems occur.
- Is the change visible to all end users.
- Is this a high-risk change.
- Is this the first time this change has been done.
- Is the change difficult or impossible to backout.
- Is it extremely difficult to install the change.
- Does the change involve a lengthy install time.

For application changes:

- Would failure of the job being changed stop the flow of all jobs for critical files or an application system.

What Types of Management Approval is Required for Level 4 Changes

Approval required by:

- Change Review Board.
- Manager of user department requesting change.

Depending on the scope and impact of the proposed change, approval by one or more of the following individuals may be required.

- Operations Manager.
- Application Development Manager.
- Network and Technical Services Manager.

LEVEL 3 CHANGES

A Level 3 Change may impact a large number of end users. It is a high-risk change that requires a significant effort to backout. Level 3 Change Requests must be entered into the Change Management database fifteen business days prior to implementation.

All Level 3 changes will be communicated via the Change Management reporting system.

The requester or representative for a Level 3 change is required to attend the Change Communication Meeting immediately prior to implementation so that any questions or concerns may be addressed.

How do you know that the Change Falls Under Level 3

For non-application changes:

- Will the change be visible to a large number of end users.
- Is this a high-risk change.
- Has the change been done only infrequently?
- Will a significant effort be required to backout the change.
- Is it difficult to install the change.

For application changes:

- Would failure of the job being changed stop the flow of jobs for non-critical files or applications.

What Types of Management Approval is Required for Level 3 Changes

Approval required by:

- Manager of user department requesting change.
- Network and Technical Services Manager.
- Change Review Board.

LEVEL 2 CHANGES

A Level 2 Change is not transparent, but is minimal in risk and impact. It is the responsibility of the Requester to notify any areas of a potential impact. The change is a Level 2 if it requires an IPL of a system, subsystem or the restart of a critical component on a production system. Level 2 Change Requests must be entered into the Change Management database prior to the Scheduled Change Window being requested. The Requester or representative for a Level 2 change is required to attend the Change Communication meeting immediately prior to planned implementation so that any questions or concerns may be addressed. All Level 2 changes will be communicated via the Change Management reporting system and will be tracked and reported by the Change/Problem Coordinator.

Examples of Level 2 changes:

- Single fixes–APAR, PTF, etc.
- Low usage programme product upgrades, installations.
- PARMLIB updates which require an IPL to implement.
- Regular maintenance updates to system or application libraries.
- Hardware Preventative Maintenance.
- Data management to critical volumes.

How do you Know that the Change Falls Under Level 2

For non-application changes:

- Will the change have only minor impact on services provided to the end users if problems occur.
- Will the change be visible only to a small group of end users.
- Is this a moderate risk change.

- Is the change relatively simple to install.
- Has the change been implemented successfully a number of times before.
- Does it require only a moderate effort to backout the change quickly.
- Will it require only an IPL, recycle of major application or reloading of an NCP to implement or backout.

For application changes:

- Is this the first time the job has been installed.
- Must this job be fixed to run tonight.

What Types of Management Approval is Required for Level 2 Changes

Approval required by:

- Manager of user department requesting change.
- Change Review Board.

LEVEL 1 CHANGES

A Level 1 Change has little or no external visibility, no external dependencies or no operator intervention. There is no associated risk or impact with the change, either to the system if the change is incompatible or to the Requester if the change implementation is delayed. The change does not require an IPL or recycle of an application to implement or backout. Level 1 changes are entered into the Change data base and will be communicated daily to any affected areas where impact or interest can be identified outside of the Requester's own area.

How do you Know that the Change Falls Under Level 1

For non-application changes:

- Will the change have only minimal or no impact on services provided to the end users if a problem occurs.
- Is the change familiar or common to those who will implement it.
- Is the change reliable and low risk.
- Is the change easy to backout if a problem occurs.
- Can it be backed out without an IPL, recycle of a major application, or reloading of an NCP.

For application changes:

- Would failure of the job stop just this job.
- Is this a low priority job.

What Types of Management Approval is Required for Level 1 Changes

Approval required by:

- Manager of user department requesting change.
- Change Review Board.

CONCLUSION

The current environment of academic libraries are made complex with the addition of many technological factors such as: electronic bibliographic databases, numerous operating systems, Web browsers, HTML, and other markup languages. Increasing amounts of information like text, video, audio, and graphics are available in an online format. Many print materials are being digitised into electronic format. As a result of the changes in technology, librarians are required to learn about metadata and description for electronic data especially for GIS data. In digital collections, such as the FGDL, cataloging and data access issues are even more significant to librarians.

In comparing spatial data infrastructures and geolibraries Nogueras-Iso offer some discussion about their characteristics that are valid here:

- Spatial data infrastructures have an important political and social component. Government involvement in the creation and maintenance of spatial data has created a hierarchy of local, state, national and regional levels that can affect access to data.
- Standardisation processes in spatial data infrastructures involve not only the organisation of data, but also issues related to the capture and integration of these data. These problems are inherent to digital libraries but are aggravated in the case of geo-referenced data. The wide range of data users can have a significant effect on visualisation and manipulation of data.
- Necessity of interoperability with other digital library systems. As a consequence of the necessity for managing heterogeneous information, spatial data infrastructure services could be developed over the services provided by other digital library systems.

Traditionally, geospatial data has been produced in limited formats, either as a paper map, atlas, or as reproductions of aerial photographs. With the application of data processing capabilities, advances in graphic presentation, and production, digital spatial data presents unique problems in description and classification. The high variability of the subject content of digital spatial data elements, though, may require additional metadata structure for better access by users. Since the 1960s, digital spatial data has been produced in a variety of formats and in a number of carriers. Digital spatial data can include information digitised and recorded by a single researcher or be in the form of large-scale geographic coverage processed and packaged by firms like International Computer Works, Inc. Much digital spatial data is also generated by government agencies at the city, state, and federal level and is issued in a variety of formats like on CD-ROMs with computer files with accompanying attribute data in relational databases.

5

Modern Technology in Library System

ROLE OF LIBRARY

Library plays a very critical role in supporting the academic programmes of the institute. It identifies, evaluates, procures, processes and then makes these learning resources available to the faculty and students for their teaching, learning and research assignments. Thet is why, DR.S.R. Ranganathan, facther of library Science development in India has famously said that the Library is the trinity of Learning Resources, Faculty/Students and the Library Staff.

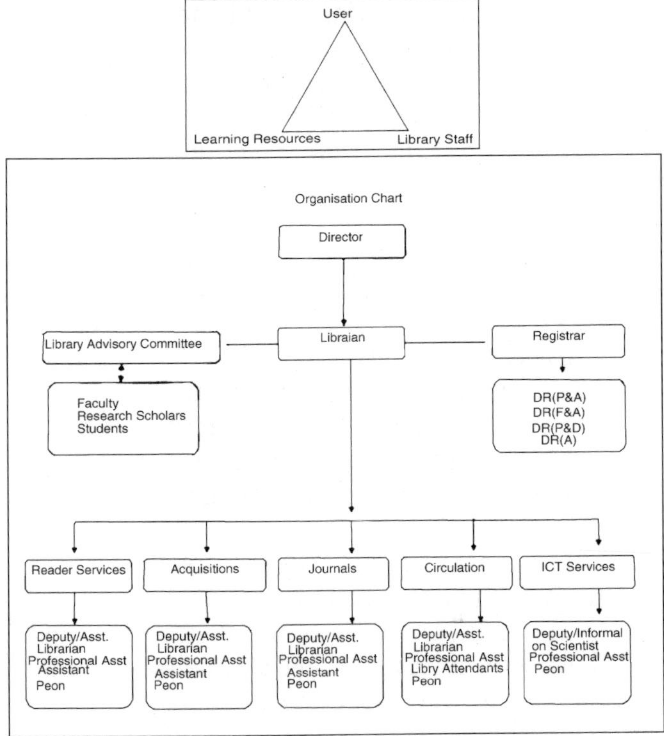

Fig. Organization Chart.

LIBRARY ADVISORY COMMITTEE (LAC)

The function of the Library Advisory Committee is to support the functioning of the library so that it can facilitate the library development plans by advocating the library development activities with the management. The purpose of the Library Advisory Committee is to act as a channel of communication and dialogue between the University Library and its users. The Committee's main objective is to aid in the establishment a bridge between the Library and the academic fraternity and the institute management.

The Library Advisory Committee (LAC) is to be appointed by the Director of the Institution:

- *Composition:*
  - The suggested composition of this Committee is as follows:
    a. *Chairperson:* Director/or any person nominated by the Director will be the chairperson
    b. *Members:* One faculty each from Schools/Independent Centers (Librarian to propose panel names)
    c. *Secretary:* Librarian Shall be the Secretary of LAC
    d. All officers of the Library shall participate in the meeting to provide required inputs
- *Meeting Frequency:* The LAC would meet at least once in every quarter to review the library affairs
- *Tenure*: The committee shall be reconstituted once in two years. Director can recommend a replacement for a member who withdraws from the LAC. No member shall serve the Committee for more than two consecutive terms. For the sake of continuation one third of members from previous committee need to continue
- *Meeting Minutes:* Meeting minutes shall be recorded and circulated to all members for consideration. In the next meeting, the minutes shall be confirmed by the members.
- Terms of Reference for LAC:
  - To provide general direction to the Library
  - To review the functioning of the library with regards to its support to the academic programmes of the institute.
  - To advise the management on matters of policy relating to development of library.
  - To outline the library collection development policy as and when required, for its implementation.
  - To monitor and evaluate, from time to time, trends and developments in information technologies, networking, library automation, library cooperation etc., and to direct the library in their adoption.
  - To suggest ways and means to generate revenue from library resources.

- To formulate action plan for the development of library infrastructure, facilities, products and services.
- Evaluate the suggestions made by the library users
- To formulate the policy for library use and procedure to be framed
- To assist library in providing need based information services
- To review the requirements of the new progra-mmes being introduced and advise library about financial assistance.
- Evaluating the books procurement school wise and allocation of budget accordingly.
- Any other function as assigned by Director

LIBRARY BUDGET/FINANCES

Library budget means the financial allocation to procure documents and provide access to the information resources.The present annual library budget of the library has the following components:

- UGC Plan Grants
- Allocation from Institute Maintenance Grants (Journals)
- School/Centre Grants(Like DRS Projects, etc)
- Programme Specific Grants (Like JTCDM, SRTT Grants, etc.)
- Trust/endowment Grants (Tata Excellence Grants)

Allocation from Projects being Carried Out at TISS

Several projects are being carried out at institute. Most of them depend upon to a great extent on library infrastructure for the learning resources and internet access. However, not all projects have a separate allocation to be given to library for using the library facility. Library will grow only when it is supported by all who make use of its resources. In this case, each project, should earmark at least 8per cent of its total project cost towards library expenditure. And this should be indicated to the library, so that all the learning resources needed by the project and their faculties are procured using their own project funds.Annual Reports, directories, Year Books, India Reference Annuals and those having no archival importance (such as India-a reference annual, Handbook of universities, Swami's handbook, etc.) may be procured under non-capital budget sub head. Budget must have contingency funds for Binding and other stationery needed to process and maintain the Books/Journals.

Library: Different from Stores

As indicated in the GoI. M.F. OM 23(7)- EII(A)/83 dated 7th Feburary 1984, (GFR 116(2)(1) (1978)), "the position of library books, etc., is different from that of stores".The above OM is reproduced below:

- "Librarian subject to the powers delegated under Delegation of Financial powers Rules, 1978, may purchase books, etc., from the reputed and standard book sellers on the prevalent terms and conditions. Tenders need not be called for this purpose."

Resources with Ephemeral Value and those whose Revised Editions are Frequently Published

Annuals, directories, yearbooks, Swamy's handbooks, etc., do not carry long lasting value, and therefore be purchased from contingent expenditure budgets only which also would facilitate easy weeding out of these items. The categorization of the documents for its ephemeral value or otherwise be decided by the library committee.

MODERN DIGITAL LIBRARY SYSTEM

Invenio is an integrated digital library system originally developed at CERN to run the CERN Document Server, currently one of the largest institutional repositories worldwide. It was started over 15 years ago and has been matured through many release cycles. Invenio is a GPL2 Open Source project based on Apache/WSGI + Python + MySQL architecture. Its modular design enables it to serve a wide variety of usages, from a multimedia digital object repository, to a web journal, to a fully functional digital library.

The development strategy used to implement Invenio ensures it is flexible in any layer. Being based on open standards such as MARCXML and OAI-PMH 2.0 its interoperability with other digital libraries is guaranteed. Being originally designed to cope with the CERN requirements for digital object management, Invenio is suitable for middle-to-large scale digital repositories. Records can be of any nature. This presentation will introduce the different features of Invenio, their usage in the CERN context and how other institutions and projects are also driving some of its development.

USAGE

Besides being used to run the CERN Document Server, Invenio has also been chosen by several other big institutions or projects. Among them it is about to be used to serve the SPIRES High Energy Physics information through the recently launched INSPIRE service, that will become the repository of reference for high energy physics.

It is used by the EPFL. ADS has expressed interest to move to an Invenio-based platform, while starting a collaboration at the data level between astrophysics and high energy physics worlds. For example in Spain Invenio is already used by the *Dipòsit Digital de Documents* (DDD) and by the "Repositorio Digital de la Universidad de Zaragoza". Recently the European Commission has chosen Invenio to become part of two important projects D4ScienceII, and OpenAIRE, with the latter having the goal to set up a portal where all the EC funded research project documents will be available.

FEATURES

Let us demonstrate the key Invenio features by following the lifetime of a record in the system, from ingestion to dissemination. As an integrated digital library, Invenio is built to allow the management of digital objects and the meta-data associated with them. Meta-data are stored in the MARCXML format, which has the flexibility to store any kind of information and which can be easily converted, thanks to XML style-sheets to any other meta-data format.

INGESTING RECORDS

Data and Meta-data can enter into Invenio powered repositories through different ways. They can be manually deposited by an author, through custom and fully configurable web interfaces, backed by an equally configurable work-flow architecture, that lets the submission administrator set up any kind of procedure triggered by a deposition. Meta-data and data can as well be harvested regularly from OAI-PMH compatible repositories. Data can also be input into the system from any non-standard format by writing ad-hoc conversion scripts either in XSLT or in the proprietary BibConvert's language. Users also have the possibility to upload records by sending e-mails that will be parsed automatically. The system can be configured to accept submission by robots thanks to the availability of a simple web API.

DIGITAL OBJECT MANIPULATION

Fully fledged tools to integrate and manipulate digital objects are available. In particular Invenio can manage multiple formats for the same document, multiple revisions, automatic conversions between formats, automatic stamping of PDF documents with watermarks, creating icons, automatic text extraction to allow for full-text searching, automatic meta-data extraction and many more. Data consistency is also ensured by MD5 checksum being continuously verified.

INDEXING AND RANKING

All the new records ingested into the system and their modifications are indexed by a very fast indexing engine that has been developed in-house. All the indexing stages are configurable; which metadata fields to index, how to extract tokens, which language is expected in order to apply stemming and removing stop words, and so on. A plug-in based ranking engine takes care of creating special indexes to be used at search time for sorting results based on word similarity, citations, download statistics, and to present citation networks.

CURATING RECORDS

Curators have powerful web-based tools to manipulate records, whilst maintaining change histories, auto-completion of fields based on fully configurable knowledge bases, multi-record modification, assisted duplicate record finding and an efficient AJAX-based record merging tool, and so on. Curators can also exploit flexible tools to perform meta-data compliance checks against configurable rules. Automatic tools are also available to extract citations and references from scientific papers and to extract keywords based on a given ontology, to enrich the available meta-data. Distributed curation activities can be instantiated through integration of Invenio with RT, one of the most famous open source ticketing systems.

DISPLAYING RECORDS

Bibliographic records can be displayed in any format, thanks to an easy and fully-configurable formatting layer, which allows creation of record-based rules to choose which representation of a record to use, while each representation can be fine tuned to fit any particular need. Thus any kind of content can be hosted and properly displayed, such as multimedia documents, books, address book contacts, and so on. Records can be organized in a flexible hierarchical structure using real and virtual collections. Each collection can in turn be customised to choose the look and feel and the kind of features enabled. The whole web appearance of Invenio can be fully customised thanks to an integrated templating system, thus facilitating integration of Invenio into an existing institutional portal. Since Invenio is being developed in an international environment it supports internationalization and comes translated already in 25 different languages.

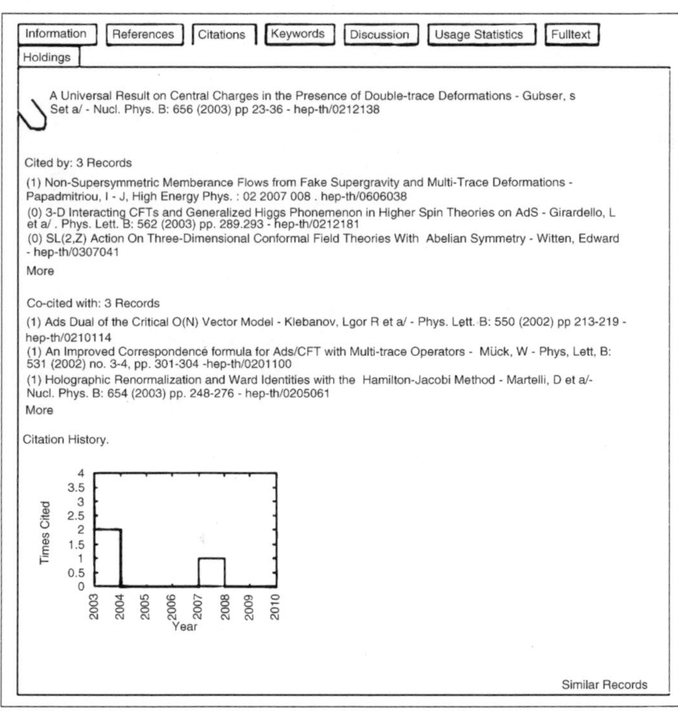

SEARCHING AND BROWSING RECORDS

A powerful search engine resides at the core of Invenio Fig. 3.1. Supporting a Google-like syntax, it can be used to dig into the repositories in a very easy way, while allowing the more experienced users to take advantage of many advanced features such as regular expressions, range queries, selection of meta-data, and many more. Results can be clustered by collections and ranked with respect to word similarity, number of citations, downloads based rankings, and any other pluggable algorithm. Any search query can automatically turned into an RSS feed to add to a personal news aggregator. Thanks to integrated support for MODS and UnAPI standards, search results can be stored in Zotero, a powerful Firefox plug-in useful to organize a personal digital library. The system offers users powerful citation and author analyses.

COLLABORATIVE TOOLS

Invenio integrates several collaborative and typical web 2.0 tools such as baskets, to store and share records or external resources with other users, personal e-mail notification alerts, record commenting and reviewing, internal web-based messaging tools, approval/reviewing work-flows.

EXPORTING RECORDS

Data and meta-data can be exported in several ways, the most important being through OAI-PHM protocol and by means of a pluggable exporting module.

AUTHENTICATION AND AUTHORIZATION

While offering for free local accounts management, Invenio can be integrated with institutional user databases to delegate the authentication phase and to exploit externally available user details. Using the *role based access control* (RBAC) model of Invenio one can define a list of roles, attach users to particular roles, and grant rights to perform actions such as view-restricted-collections based on user group membership, user IP address, and more.

CIRCULATION

Invenio supports the operation of a physical library by integrating a circulation module, as well as by supporting inter library loans. Users can submit loan requests, and follow the request status, the librarians have a web interface to accept/reject loan requests, to send overdue letters, to set up sub-libraries, etc.

CREATING JOURNALS

As an example of an application that has been built on top of the core Invenio, the web journal module lets repository administrators create online web journals with regular issues built from articles stored in the repository itself. A specific appearance can be set up in order to have a layout providing journal-like reading experience. This is currently used today for producing the official CERN Bulletin, which is issued every two weeks.

BOARD AND DIRECTOR'S RESPONSIBILITIES

If there is a mantra for governing boards of library trustees it is: "The board sets policy, the director operates the library with the assistance of staff." What does this really mean, and what are the differences? Because I have worn the hats of both a librarian and a trustee, I was asked to offer some thoughts on this topic.

Sometimes the line between policy and operation is very thin and the differences are subtle. Basically, the board of trustees and the library director must work as a team, just as the director must construct a team with staff. In order to work successfully, it must be a process of two-way communication, consultation and trust building.

BUILDING A BOARD, DIRECTOR, AND STAFF TEAM

In addition to regular board meetings, an annual planning retreat with the director and selected staff is an opportunity to build communications and plan for the library future. Although the library vision and mission statements do not change very often, they should be reviewed along with the library strategic or long-range plan and annual plans. A retreat offers the time to discuss in depth, and to clarify directions, goals and strategies for the coming year.

These meetings are, by law, open public meetings that the public may attend so opportunities for citizen input can be incorporated into the retreat agenda. Indeed, ongoing ways should be found to obtain input from residents of the library community. The board should meet following the retreat and include on its agenda a discussion of appropriate policies and plans for the library.

COMMUNITY INVOLVEMENT

If the trustees and director are to fulfill their responsibilities, both must be active in the community. Both must know the community to develop those policies and practices that bring the best possible library service their community. Any five- or seven-person library board is likely to represent a variety of community connections. These connections can provide avenues to knowing and understanding the community and to advocacy for the library. Trustees have a responsibility to stay informed–to regularly attend board meetings and to read and understand information presented to them about the library and its operation.

They also have a responsibility to actively listen to community residents. It is equally important that they advocate for the library with community residents and with local, state, and federal governmental representatives. In order to do this, trustees will need to answer questions and to explain library policies and practices. They need to work as a team with the library director, because some questions, especially about library practice, are best directed to the library director. The director and staff must also be prepared to explain library policies and actively advocate for the library.

DEVELOPING POLICIES

There are several levels of decision-making involved in policy-making. There are many times when the board will ask the library director to analyse impacts before it establishes a policy, and there will be times when the director will consult the board before proceeding with a specific course of action. Often the director will call the board's attention to need for policy in a specific area and may draft language for the board to consider.

In other instances the board may identify need for a policy and will either ask the director to draft language for board discussion and action or they may jointly develop specific language. Sometimes the director will make decisions related to library operations and will simply inform the board of her or his actions, or perhaps ask for their concurrence for a proposed course of action.

This latter course of action is probably wise in situations where it is not initially clear whether additional policy decisions will need to be made or where the distinction between practice and policy is not entirely clear. Discussion can usually clarify the issues and decisions can be made, often by consensus. Certain kinds of decisions may be delegated to the director.

EXAMPLES OF DIRECTOR AND BOARD ROLES AND RESPONSIBILITIES

Let me elaborate on the respective roles and responsibilities of trustees and director with several examples. Especially in large libraries, some of the tasks or decisions that I've identified as the director's will likely be delegated to managerial or supervisory library staff.

Mission/Roles of the Library in the Community

It is the governing board's responsibility to determine the mission and roles of the library after a planning process that includes a great deal of input from residents of the community, and in coordination with the library director. These fundamental decisions need to be articulated in a mission statement and supported by policy and planning. Once those fundamental decisions are made, it is the board's responsibility to hire a director who is in agreement with and can support the chosen roles.

In the case of the newly formed Stevens County Rural Library District, the roles were actually established before the director was hired and the board needed to assure that the new director supported the roles. A more specific example of how this works: Board policy or the library mission states that the library is to be user friendly and a place where people feel welcome. It is the library director's responsibility to make it happen. It will involve setting expectations regarding attitudes of staff towards the library customers, training for staff, and establishing library practices and procedures that make users feel welcome and satisfy their needs. These are all responsibilities of the director.

Budgets, Contracts, and Grants

The board approves the library budget, as drawn up and recommended by the director, but it is based on goals set by the board. The budget corresponds to the annual work plan for the director and staff. The board may suggest general policy directions for the budget, but the director in consultation with staff decides what is possible within budget constraints, and how best to meet the entire gamut of needs. The director expends money within approved budget parameters and keeps the board informed. While trustees may review and approve vouchers each month, they should not approve individual expenditures. The board should be informed by the director of any major changes needed in the budget and the proposed changes must have board concurrence. Trustees should not be involved in adjustments made to budgets as long as those adjustments are within general budget parameters as approved by the board.

A contract or grant must also correspond to the goals of the library. The board must approve all contracts with contracting cities, consultants, and the like but the contract or grant specifics will be drawn up and recommended by the director. Trustees must certainly be kept informed of potential contracts or grants, and should provide input regarding the content or parameters of impending contracts or grant documents. Whether to apply for a particular grant or enter into a contract with a specific entity may be a policy matter, and thus the board will make the final decision. There may be instances where the board determines that it is appropriate to delegate to the director the responsibility for signing agreements on behalf of the library.

Buildings and Property

The board, in consultation with the director, may determine in policy whether to own buildings or rent space, whether to buy land for buildings, the general locations of new buildings, etc. On the other hand, the board may also establish a broad goal that will guide the director and staff in making these decisions. This broad approval usually happens when there are multiple decisions to be made as a result of a substantial bond issue. The governing board may also set policies such as whether to allocate a certain percentage of a building's cost for art works. The director makes recommendations on these matters and implements the decisions. The director decides, without further board action, on specifics such as colour scheme and décor, furniture, computer system requirements and design of the building. The director will keep the board informed and trustees may offer opinions, but these are operational decisions that should be made by the director.

Personnel

The board establishes overall personnel policies such as guidelines for salary and benefits, hiring practices, and other personnel actions unless the library is part of a city and must follow municipal policy. The director implements personnel policies. Trustees should not become involved unless personnel policy changes are called for. Unless the library is part of a municipal system that maintains authority to hire the director, the board hires the library director and sets salary and benefits. In this process, the board may seek input from library staff and/or community residents, but the ultimate decision rests with the board.

In turn, the director hires library staff and the board is not involved in interviewing or selection. Unless the salary schedule is established by the city, the board approves the salary schedule as drawn up and recommended by the director. It is the director's responsibility to decide where a job classification will be placed on that salary schedule. If library staff belong to a labour union, the library trustees should not take an active part in labour negotiations.

The board might, however, approve the hiring of a consultant to assist the director by carrying out negotiations. When an agreement is reached and recommended by the director, the board will approve the labour contract. The board does an annual performance review for the library director. As a result of the review the board and director should jointly set goals and expectations for the coming year. The annual performance review of the director will be based on how well those goals and expectations have been achieved. The director will carry out annual performance reviews of library staff, set goals for staff performance, and determine staff training needs. The board approves policies for staff training, attendance at conferences, workshops or classes, travel reimbursement and the like, but they are not involved in staff review. Staff development policy statements will likely be drawn up by the director, based on staff needs and available budget, and recommended to the board.

Such "working policies" are really largely procedural and, as such, the responsibility of the director. If underlying policy statements are needed, the director informs the board of the need and recommends content or draws up language for board consideration. Disciplinary actions related to library staff are a responsibility of the library director. Although the board sets disciplinary policy as part of overall personnel policy, unless it is mandated by their city government, board members should not become involved in specific disciplinary actions. Complaints made directly to board members must be referred back to the director for action.The director should always consult the library attorney on any disciplinary actions that may reach the point of hearings before a human rights commission or a lawsuit. Trustees must certainly be kept informed and will probably need to approve expenditures for attorney fees. Disciplinary action or firing of a library director is, of course, a governing board responsibility.

Collections, Hours, and Services

These are "working policies" or operational procedures and largely the responsibility of the library director. The board of trustees sets the goals in its adopted plan and defines strategies for collections, access and services, but it is up to the library director and staff to implement the actions that meet the goals. Although a board member may have a special interest in a particular collection, or personally see a need for certain services, a board member must make it very clear that their personal suggestions are not endorsed by the authority of the board. The director and staff must always remain free to consider board member suggestions, just as they would any citizen suggestions, but staff are ultimately responsible for judging how best to develop the collection and library services.

The board may adopt a goal that addresses the issue of access to the library, thereby setting an expectation for the number of hours open or other services. The director, however, must decide how many and what hours are feasible within the budget, and balance available staff resources with the expertise needed by the facility. The director should keep the board informed of what has been put into practice. A similar process will govern decision about services such as story times for children, computers for public access, outreach services to nursing or retirement homes, and others.

Community Relations and Publicity

The library board might establish a goal stating that the library will support and encourage partnerships and cooperative ventures with community organizations whenever feasible.

The director is then clearly enabled to create working agreements with such organizations. However, this is an example of a situation where the director may appropriately decide that such relationships are good library practice and simply proceed to implement cooperative actions while keeping the board informed.

An example might be that the library agrees to house the materials of a local genealogical or historical society. This action may, or may not, require a formal agreement that the board should approve. The board might establish a goal that says the library will use all means possible to keep residents of the community informed about the library, its services, and activities. The details of how this is to be done and by whom are for the director to decide. However, it is wise for the trustees and director to work together and decide which activities are appropriate for board members to undertake and which are director or staff functions. The words of wisdom are "Just be sure everyone is delivering the same message."

Wrapping Up

The director must do her or his best to carry out the governing board goals and policy directions. It is imperative that the board backs the director's decisions. It is not always crystal clear where policy stops and practice starts. However, we are all in this library business together. People become librarians because they believe in the value of libraries to communities. People become library trustees for the very same reason. By clarifying our respective roles and responsibilities, by building trust and good communication, and by working together as a team, we can all be more effective in bringing the best possible library service to the people of our communities.

GOVERNING AND ADVISORY LIBRARY BOARD RELATIONSHIPS

Library boards exist in political environments, regardless if they are advisory or governing. Relationships between library boards and their appointing authorities can be collegial or fractious, depending upon the issues at hand. A board's effectiveness is influenced by its breadth of representation from key community constituents among its members and its active involvement in community life. In all library settings, success is influenced by a clear understanding of and commitment to the library's mission and an appreciation for the political dynamics.

Contracting or Annexed Cities and Towns

Library boards in cities and towns that contract for library services or are annexed to a rural or intercounty library district are advisory. They are a special interest standing committee whose mission is to advocate for the library for such purposes as building improvements in cities where library services are in city owned facilities. They may also be an advisory committee to the rural or intercounty library district whose role is to provide library personnel, programmes, services, materials and various policies for their use in the city or town.

City or Town Libraries

Library boards in cities that support an independent public library may be advisory to the city or may be responsible for the management of the library. In cities that elected to be an Optional Municipal Code city to broaden the city's power of self-government, the library board is advisory. The public library is considered a department of the city. The breadth of responsibilities of the advisory board may vary according to local tradition and expectation.For instance, policies affecting the public's use of the library–meeting rooms, circulation, collection development, unattended children, rules of conduct– may be delegated to the library board for adoption or may be enacted by the city council as ordinances. In cities that are not an Optional Municipal Code city, the library board is responsible for the management and control of the library. These responsibilities include employing library staff, controlling finances and setting policies for the governance of the library, but they exist within the context of a city.

Library Districts and Regional Libraries

Library boards for rural county, intercounty, island, partial-county library districts and regional libraries are the governing bodies for these municipal corporations. Their responsibilities include levying tax, entering into contracts, employing staff, controlling finances, leasing and purchasing real estate, and setting policies for the governance of the library. Even though county commissioners and/or city councils appoint them, they are not advisory to them. Their responsibility is foremost for the operations and integrity of their library.

TECHNOLOGICAL INNOVATIONS IN IMPROVING LIBRARY SERVICES

Once librarians were considered only the custodians of the library collection, but the change in information media from print to electronic has shown the new sunrise in the life of librarians. The basic aim of a library is to meet the teaching, learning, scholarly-research and other information needs of its faculty, students and research scholars and that too effectively and with efficiency. Medical library and information professionals ensures that health care providers have access to reliable, relevant, accurate, up to date and timely information that enhances the quality of health care.

The migration of information from paper to electronic media has changed the whole nature of research. With the easy availability of office computers and the transformation of media, the popularity and usage of digital and virtual libraries has been increased. World Wide Web has totally changed the meaning of a library. Physical presence has been decreased rapidly with the invention of virtual library. There is a universal assumption that man was born innocent or ignorant and should actively seek knowledge. "Information seeking is thus a natural and necessary mechanism of human existence". Information seeking behaviour is the purposive seeking for information as a consequence of a need to satisfy some goal. In the course of seeking, the individual may interact with manual information systems or with computer-based systems.

Information seeking behaviour involves personal reasons for seeking information, the kinds of information which are being sought and the ways and sources with which needed information is being sought. Information seeking behaviour is expressed in various forms, from reading printed material to research and experimentation. Scholars, students and faculties actively seek current information from the various media available in libraries, *e.g.* Encyclopaedias, journals and more currently, electronic media. In this era of 'E', a sea change can be seen in the information-seeking behaviour of the users of library. In the phase of print media, users had no choice except going to the library and search for the material in books, journals and archives for hours. Search was very time consuming in print phase. Changing needs of users have changed the role of a librarian, which has transformed a librarian into information professional. Librarians have always acted as a link between knowledge source and its users.

In this era of 'E', librarians are playing the role of an electronic middleman. They are now helping the readers in the best possible way by using the latest technology and searching techniques. Users are being connected to the information resources via Internet for hyper-links and for many more options and choices for advance search. The change in the information-seeking behaviour is the result of the invention of E-resources. Readers felt relaxed with this invention and inclination towards these resources was natural.

There are many types of E-resources like Ebooks, E-journals, various open sources, gateways and databases. Chronologically we can divide these resources specifically journals as, in-print journals, on-line journals free with print, only on-line journals, on-line databases. In the era of 'E', readers demand has become significant as they ask for an article or topic in place of a book or journal and at the same time they prefer to search online databases to fulfill their needs. With the invention E-resources quantity and quality of research both have been affected. Different search techniques are undertaken by library users to search and locate relevant information.

To understand how users of libraries search and locate relevant documents, we librarians, need to understand the search techniques and what resources and sources of information they generally use and require. Information professionals and users both suffer from the problem of exhaustive information, from a wide range of sources and shortage of time to find, manage and evaluate.

Sometimes users search internet indiscriminately without knowing the facts. Here librarian plays an important role by making the users aware of the importance of the evaluation of the retrieved information by guiding them, how to retrieve, what to retrieve and how to further use that retrieved information, which is called evaluation of information.

The challenge posed by the information explosion is being successfully met by electronic information sources. Further this information explosion, diversity of user need, financial crunch and impossibility of self-sufficiency has led to the formation of consortia at local, regional, national and international level.

OBJECTIVE

The main objective of this study is to know the changing needs and information-seeking behaviour of the users and further various methods and resources being adopted by the librarians to fulfil these needs, which is the result of various technological innovations. Information seeking is a fluid and situation dependent activity where a seeker's actions are influenced by access to information, perceived quality and trust in the information source. This reminds the necessity of regular study and development of information system and management information services in North Indian Medical Institutes.

This work intends to study followings in libraries as a prototype of North Indian Medical Institutes:

- To examine information seeking behaviour of library users of North Indian Medical Institutes.
- To study the problems faced by the library users of North Indian Medical Institutes while seeking and using information.
- To explore the role of the library consortia's for providing service to the library users.
- To review the use of E-databases in this era of information explosion.

HYPOTHESIS

In this study it is hypothesized that:

- Physical visit to the libraries has been declined.
- Preference of users has been shifted to online documents from print one.
- Lack of knowledge about IT is the main problem the user face in the information searching process.

METHODOLOGY AND SCOPE

There are many ways to get information. The most common research methods are: literature searches, talking with people, focus groups, personal interviews, telephone surveys, mail surveys, e-mail surveys and internet surveys. A survey has been conducted on North Indian Medical Libraries through a questionnaire to know the changes in the information-seeking behaviour and needs of the users in this era of 'E'. So the medical professionals who were enrolled as member in the various medical libraries of Chandigarh and adjoining areas were considered for the study in hand. Further it can be stated that there were about 720 active library users of these libraries, so these users were taken as the subject for the study.

Through the stratified random sampling technique 72. Questionnaire method was used as it can be completed in one of the two basic ways. Firstly, respondents were asked to complete the questionnaire with the researcher not present and thus data was collected from 72 medical professionals, out of which 33 were students and 39 were senior residents, Assistant professor and professors. Secondly, respondents were asked to complete the questionnaire by verbally responding to questions in the presence of the researcher. This variation is called a structured interview and this method was applied on 28 librarians to know their observations.

FINDINGS (USERS)

Visits to the Library

Twenty-nine respondents (40per cent) reported frequently visiting a medical library, 18 (25per cent) rarely visited and 24 (33per cent) never visited; one respondent did not answer this question. Respondents in their first year reported frequent visits to the library more often than those did in their second year. In the overall group, those who never or rarely visited a library indicated that E-resources are not sufficient; documents that they needed were not available or libraries were not needed because of the Internet.

So the main observation regarding visit to the library is that students visit library more frequently in their initial years of college/ institute. Overall group of users prefer to search Internet as they are not satisfied with the available E-resources in their library. They only visit the library after making sure that this required information is available in the library. This service is being provided through WEB OPAC in most of the libraries today. So hypothesis 1 stands proved.

Preference of Information Sources

Most respondents reported performing database searches independently. Among those who did their own searches, MEDLINE and PUBMED was the bestknown and most frequently used database: only 1 of 72 respondents did not know of MEDLINE. HINARI is being used by some users but the main problem with this database is that site is very slow. When asked about criteria for selecting references, the most important feature was free full-text availability with the demand of online database and formation of consortia. Regarding access to the full text, few respondents said they visited a library to check document availability and ordered articles through a library. More than half of respondents preferred electronic tools for literature searching.

Yet most indicated they preferred to print documents rather than read them online. Respondents were further asked about their preferences about the form of the document. An online database is the most preferred format (39per cent) in contrast to the print only format that is the least preferred one (10per cent). This observation directly shows the shift of the preferences of the users from print to the online formats. It is strongly supported by the findings in which online journals and databases have become the most preferred form of document as 75per cent users need only online resources in form or the other. Further users prefer taking print of the required information as they feel discomfort in reading directly from the screen. So hypothesis 2 stands proved.

Problems in Information Seeking

Several problems were identified in the information searching process. Many respondents found difficulties in choosing among the large number of documents retrieved in searches and lack of time was also noted as a problem. Common obstacles in the information-seeking process identified by respondents include lack of time, doubt about the existence of relevant information, retrieval of too much information and difficulties with navigation and searching. Since latest innovations have made the search easier with the latest options like E-mail alerts, send articles etc., but problem in information searching still persists due to the lack of knowledge of I.T. So the hypothesis no. 3 also stands proved.

OBSERVATIONS (LIBRARIANS)

According to the librarians, Internet search engines, E-print services, author Web sites, full-text databases, electronic journals and print resources are all used to some extent by most of the users. Convenience remains the single most important factor for information retrieval. Speed of access, ability to download, print and send articles are top advantages of electronic journals for all groups. All these services and facilities are possible with the application of IT. These observations reaffirm that important opportunities remain for librarians and libraries in providing both access to information resources and educating clinicians in how to effectively utilize such tools. Determining the relevance of a document or source is solely an individual's perspective, so the library or librarian is not a determining factor in differentiating sources.

It would, however, be advantageous for a library to know and have the relevant material available for use. Library users expect their libraries to obtain new electronic resources while simultaneously maintaining or growing traditional print collections until the electronic resources are fully stable. Libraries are expecting to do this with no additional funding. Research has also concluded that information sources like electronic databases are of fundamental importance in a clinical environment giving their direct contribution to decision making in health issues, often making the difference in patient survival. Increasing demand of E-databases can be met with the formation of consortia only, as E-databases are the main feature of consortia these days. Important observation is that these databases have become addiction for the users.

Library Consortia

Information explosion, diversity of user need, financial crunch and impossibility of self-sufficiency has led to the formation of consortia at local, regional, national and international level. A library consortium is an association of a group of libraries to achieve mutually the common objective.

Working in an atmosphere, which is fully affected by *Information Communication Technology* (ICT), librarians are mastering the use of electronic resources to better understand and meet the information needs of the users and further train them in using new searching tools for better search.

Consortia provide the following common benefits to the libraries involved:

- Access to otherwise un-subscribed reading materials.
- Scope for electronic archives.
- Getting deep discounts through joint pricing negotiations.
- Developing common resources databases.
- Effective document delivery system.
- Enhanced search facilities
- Better scope for developing a union catalogue among participating libraries.
- By forming consortia, librarians are contributing to the economy of their country by saving Government revenue to a great extent. Following are some of the big and successful consortia's of India.

E-DATABASE

Understanding the user needs play an important role in growing the libraries and librarians; otherwise the library profession may grey in future. To meet the increasing and advanced demands of the user, consortia are playing an important role. Secondly to avail full fruit of consortia a very sincere suggestion to library professionals is to be in touch with whole of the new technology, bridging the libraries through I.T and ICT. One should know the inside out of all the E-databases and involved I.T application.An E-database is an organized collection of information, of a particular subject or multidisciplinary subject areas; Information within an Edatabase can be searched and retrieved electronically.

Edatabase can be full-text or bibliographic. Full-text databases contain the whole content of an article such as citation information, text, illustrations, diagrams and tables. Bibliographic databases contain only citation information of an article, such as author name, journal title and publication date and page numbers. There are many Edatabases and all these databases have various features of searching techniques and tools, which are being used by the librarians to help the users in finding best information in less time.

Some of the popular medical E-databases are mentioned below:

- Academic Search Premier:
  - BMJ
  - MEDLINE
  - OVID

- PROQUEST
- PUBMED
- SCOPUS
- WEB OF SCIENCE
- HINARI

Almost all the reputed publishers have come up with the Edatabases like Oxford University Press, American academy of Pediatrics, Cambridge University press and many more. All these e-databases can be considered as the latest technological innovation in the field of information.

DATA MINING TECHNIQUES ENHANCE LIBRARY SYSTEM

Suppose a library system has the following goals:

- Increase books borrowing rate.
- Attract more users to borrow books.
- Assist library professionals in making policy on the acquisition of duplicate copies and new publications.

The relationship between Data Mining and Library Management can be shown as in Figure.

Fig. The Cyclical Relationship between Data Mining and Library Management.

EXAMPLE

Consider a library whose books database includes the data of 2000 volumes of books, and the borrowing history of 5000 users who have borrowed books from library.From this database, we have developed a report system to represent the relationship between books and students. And then we use the data mining association rule to analyse the books of the same cluster borrowed by the students. A report chart of books will be produced, so that the library professionals will find references to the books for making a decision. Additionally, the library collection may be used more effectively.

The library database includes seven tables. The first of them is *BOOKS* which contains each of the books' basic information. The table *BOOKS* was improved from *MARCBOOKS* which comes from the previous library system. It kept most of the columns from MARCBOOKS.

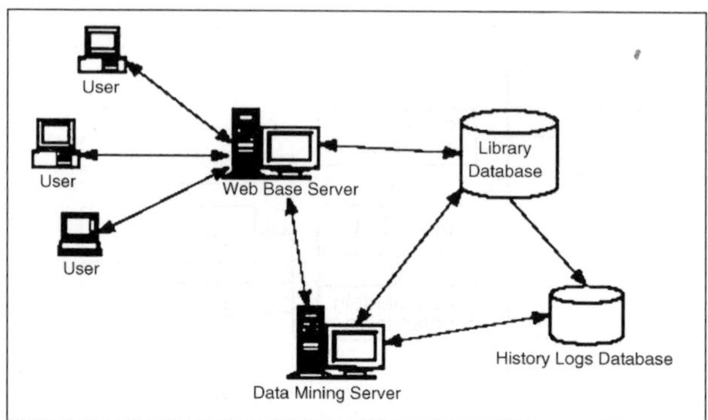

Fig. The Prototype of a Library Architecture.

Machine-readable Cataloguing (MARC) is a kind of metadata to describe a book. *USERS* has part of a student's basic information from the registration system and coordinates with the library system. *COPY* describes the actual volumes in the library. *LOCATION* reports the real location of each book. *CIRCUL* records each circulation of a book. *RESERVATION* has the information that is stored when a user holds a book. Figure shows the schema of these tables. Between each table, there is a key column that sometimes is a primary key in one of them. For instance, the relation key between *BOOKS* and *COPY* is ISBN.

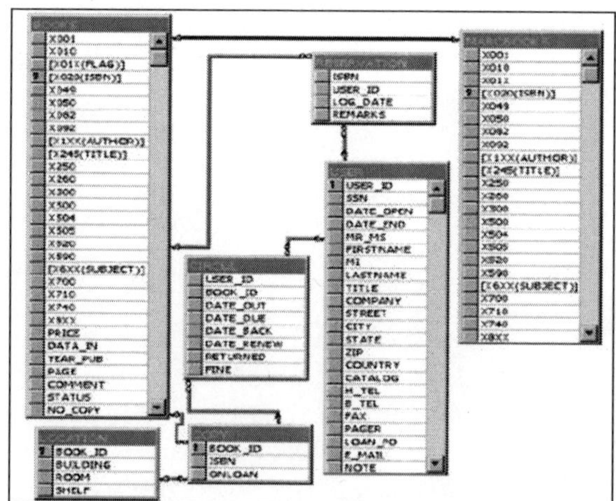

Fig. The Schema of the Library Database.

The data mining system is under statistics in a library system. It is an advantageous part of the library system. The process between the main page of data mining and its four functions is shown in Fig. On the main page of data mining, the administrator has four functions to execute. The first function is backup the *CIRCUL*. The second one is the list of top ten books. The third one is to execute rule. The final one is rule manager. The following paragraphs are describing them.

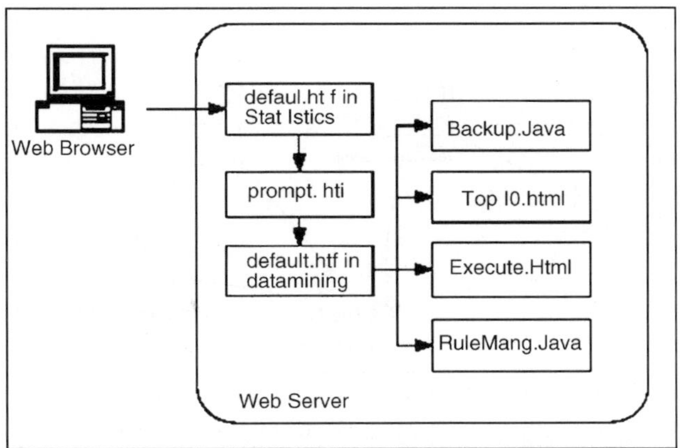

Fig. The Main Process of the Data Mining System.

LIBRARY INFORMATION SYSTEM AND INFORMATION TECHNOLOGY

In library information system, information technology has had a clear and persuasive impact in almost every area of the library. The most significant development in information technology over the last few years or so is digital technology.

Digital technology is revolutionizing the traditional concepts of preservation and access in library and archive communities. The applications of digital system and computing system in the libraries have been a subject of interest to present day professional librarians.

More recently the libraries have sought to implement increasingly complex solution that involved distributed networking and access to remote information resources. During the eighties, the whole focus of the librarians shifted towards library automation but in the nineties it has shifted towards digitization. The phrase library automation has been generally accepted within the profession to encompass early automation activities, yet it does not do justice to the current state of affaires as libraries have move well beyond the automation of internal procedures. In Manipur, however, applications of technologies in libraries are lagging far behind.

There are two university libraries, 74 affiliated colleges, nine public libraries, one state central library at Imphal and others at different districts of Manipur and many high and higher secondary schools libraries. But most of the libraries function in the traditional way with conventional printed shelf collection except some libraries like Manipur University library, Central Agricultural Library, RIMS Library, DOEACC Library etc. These libraries have initiated automation. Manipur University Library started automation since 1989 in the areas such as cataloguing, serial control, information retrieval and circulation recently.

This library provides internet facility, OPAC and has become one of the important nodes in the academic libraries system. As far as college libraries are concerned collections of information resources which support the faculty and students are not up to the mark because of lack planned systematic approach to the development of resources. Many of college libraries built up their collection of printed materials as activities and services are yet to be automated. Only one college library *i.e.* Modern College library has started Data entry using CDS/ISIS.

Books are still the only important channel for dissemi-nation of information. The librarian and other supporting professional staff are not well qualified and trained with the new modern technology. As far as infrastructures are concern a large majority of libraries have not yet automated their activities as they are handicapped to switch over to computeri-zation and modernization because of lack of infrastructural facilities like computer hardware, software, and human-ware. And most of the libraries are not provided internet facility.

Regarding school and higher secondary school libraries, majority of school libraries are not able to provide even the facilities of a traditional library. From the discussion it is evident that the libraries in Manipur, except some, automation of the operations and services progressing very slowly. Automation as well as conversion of digital library will not be possible within five year though plan for automation exist.

In Manipur it is not an easy task to develop digital library system as automation in the library is totally absent.Keeping in views of the reasons, authority should take initiative for promoting library automation by implementing new IT in the libraries of Manipur so that users from different communities can get the universe of knowledge available in the digital format.

PROBLEMS OF DIGITAL LIBRARIES SYSTEMS

Problems faced while entering into a digital libraries systems in Manipur can be summarized as:

- Libraries exist only in the traditional form and there is no electronic library/digital resource;
- Most of the libraries function with inadequate number professional staff required for smooth functioning and there is a general unwillingness to develop digital library system;
- Even if the librarian and some professionals are qualified they certainly lag behind because of lack of awareness about value of information, cooperation and coordination in the resource building and sharing of information and poor communication skill;

- Total absence of hardware, software and trained human power is another reason;
- A highly irregular and unpredictable power supply; and
- Libraries lack standardization of methods due to unwillingness to adapt to new requirements;
- Presently large majority of library have no computer and no internet facility and other infrastructural facilities required to exploit the opportunities provided by electronic media. Therefore, the best use of electronic publication on-line and network access are not possible;
- Lack of financial support due to the acute financial problem the state is facing.

In fact, the main problems faced seem to be lack of financial resources and lack of computer education without which automation in the libraries are not possible.

PROSPECT OF INFORMATION REVOLUTION

The dawn of information revolution is considered to be one of the marvelous achievements of the 20th century. The rapid growth and development of IT has resulted in the development of digital library, tools and skill relating to encoding information objects in digital format.

The application of digital technologies within the library comes along with the development of computer technology. Keeping the points in view it is necessary to consider some perspective of digital library. Digital library not only creates and develops modern libraries but also transforms many existing libraries.

Digital Library introduced the concept of hypertext, facilitates networking in order to communicate and exchange digital information from source location to destination. It also facilitates preservation, storage, and communication of diverse multimedia objects but also provides intensive access from multiple locations and enrich teaching and learning environment which is not possible with the traditional library.

Due to information explosion and existence of information society, everybody is aware of the newly developed technologies. This new developments are reflected in LIS education and in those libraries with existing infrastructure, services and network. In fact, there is a complete change in activities, role of library, librarians and other professionals (staff). Most of the librarians in Manipur have now entered in the technological era of communication dominated by film and electronic media.

The libraries are expected to be an automated information system having pervasive impact in almost every areas of library-be it the online catalogue, online database, online searching, document delivery, inter library loan, circulation etc. Clearly, the impact of automated system in libraries has been pervasive and significant.

INFORMATION EXPLOSION AND THE DIRECT RELATION OF INFORMATION TO DEVELOPMENTS

The present information explosion and the direct relation of information to developments in all walks of life emphasizes the need to give greater priority to the planning of systems which give library and information services to the people. Such systems can only be planned at national levels, if the total information resources of the nation is to be pooled together in a federal country like India, and shared between the cons-tituent states to make it available to all the users who require it in an equally and unbiased way at optimal cost.

Such library and information systems are to be founded upon sound legislation, if they are to attain their objectives the Society's information need has become so imperative that, many of the national and international library organizations has started to stress the urgent need for national library systems working together and sharing their services and materials at international level to provide better services to the people.

Better can be defined here in quantitative and qualitative terms. Such national level and international level networking and resource sharing between library systems make possible service at lower cost, convenience of access, access to more materials and more rapid availability of materials.

PREAMBLE OF STATE ACTS

The preamble of a Library Act should summarise and state the aims and objectives of that Library Act. Even though the preamble of KPLA went on to explain the existing situations and the intentions with which the Act was initiated in an elaborate and vague form, it has given what is to be in preamble just before the preamble in precise and clear words as a long title ofthe Act. This summary or long title of the Act which we have to consider as preamble contains the basic concept of modern public library service which the actual preamble failed to state and the KPLA in its totality failed to support.

Like the Model Act, this summary provides for the establishment and maintenance of a system of public libraries and for the comprehensive development and organisation of all kinds of library and information services required for the people. The long title that follows the title of the Act in KPLA states, it is: An Act to consolidate and unify the library laws in the State and to provide for the reorganisation of the entire library system in the State of Kerala with a view to the develop-ment and maintenance of a comprehensive rural and urban library service and for matters connected therewith or incidental thereto.

Ranganathan has laid clear emphasis on legislation for public library service and for the organisation of a comprehensive library system. But all other Acts except KPLA provides for establishment and maintenance of public libraries only. They all cling to the obsolete concept of treating public libraries as independent units in their collection and services. So in this statement of the purpose of the Act, KPLA has accepted the most modern concept of Public Library legislation and the statement is a distinct improvement over those in all other existing State Acts.

THE MODEL ACT OF S.R. RANGANATHAN

To attain these objectives Dr. S.R. Ranganathan had framed the first model public libraries Act in 1930 which he placed for discussion at the Educational Conference at Banaras. Before framing the Act, this internationally reputed library scientist had travelled through most countries of the world where library legislation existed and had evaluated them and in many countries his ideas helped them to improve the systems.

In his Library Development Plan which he submitted in 1947 to Government of India he had included a union library bill and a revised state library bill also which envisaged the national public library and information system according to the most modern principles. Another model library Act was drafted in 1963 by a committee under the chairmanship of D.M. Sen on behalf of the Ministry of Education, Government of India. In 1966 the Library Legislation Sub Committee of the Planning Commission also prepared a model bill.

The library Acts that came into existence in Madras, Hyderabad, Andhra, Karnataka and Maharastra totally or partially accept the ideas of Rang ana than as reflected in his Model Acts and bills. These States became the laboratories where the ideas evolved by Ranganathan were experimented and observed.In the light of these observations and suggestions contained in the other model bills and Acts, Ranganathan has improved his model Act by rectifying the clauses found to be defective in working and by adding new provisions that seemed essential.

This model libraries Act was published in 1972. This is the latest and most advanced Model Act. Ten States out of the 25 States and 7 union territories have enacted library legislation. They are Madras 1948, Andhra 1960, Karnataka 1965, Maharastra 1967, West Bengal 1979, Manipur 1985, Kerala 1989 and Haryana 1989.Others are Goa and Mizoram. But none of them are considered perfect or efficient.

So in this comparative analysis of the essential aspects of State Public Library Acts, the Model Public Library Act, 1972 of Dr. S.R. Ranganathan is taken as the measuring rod or ideal situation with which the State Act is compared.

Whenever some notable additional provisions or improvements are found in other existing Acts the same is discussed at the concerned contexts. The Kerala Act to which stress is given in this study and Ranganathan's Model Act of 1972 will be referred herein after as KPLA and Model Act respectively.

PURPOSE AND ADVISING OF STATE LIBRARY COMMITTEE

The Model Act provides for a *State Library Committee* (SLC) for the purpose of advising the SLA on all matters arising under the Act. All existing State Acts and Model Bills enacted or drafted in India provide for appointment of such a Committee or Council. KPLA names it as Kerala State Library Council. All Acts of the states except Kerala's have prescribed its membership on somewhat similar lines. All Acts provides that this body will be headed by Minister for Education. Despite differences in nomenclature and composition the function of this committee or council envisaged everywhere is basically the same *i.e.,* to advise the SLA or State Government in all matters arising out of the Act.

Kerala State Library Council (KSLC)

A careful analysis of the Kerala State Library Council (KSLC) in comparison with the SLC as provided in the Model Act or other State Acts will reveal that it is not a councilor committee of advisory nature as SLCs are. KSLC is an SLC and at the same time an SLA by itself. Naming it as a council is a difference in terminology only. Instead of appointing a Minister as SLA as in Mysore it appoints a body as SLA. But the Act fails to name it as SLA. The duties, powers and functions assigned to KSLC is inclusive of all those assigned to SLA and SLC in Model Act.Sub-section 1 of the Section 3 of KPLA dealing with the constitution and composition of KSLC states9; KSLC shall be a body corporate having perpetual succession and a common seal with power, to acquire hold and dispose of property, both movable and immovable and to enter into contracts and shall by its name sue and be sued. This is an adaptation of the class related to Karnataka State Library Authority of Karnataka Act. No other Act including Model Act has so clearly defined the nature of this body and assigned so much powers as this like the Acts of Kerala and Karnataka. The powers and functions assigned to KSLC includes both the advisory functions of the committees and councils provided by Model Act and other Acts and the duties assigned to SLA by Model Act and Karnataka Act.

Sub-sections of section 8 of KPLA provides that the KSLC may:

- Advise the government of all matters connected with the administration of that Act and . . . the overall library policy of the State.
- Co-ordinate the working of the District Library Councils and Taluk Library Unions and...supervise and direct all matters relating to library service in the state.
- Establish one or more State Libraries . . . at such place or places in the State as may be considered necessary.
- Appoint and control such officers and servants as may be necessary for the efficient performance of its duties and functions under this Act and the rules made there under.

- Give to the District Library Councils and Taluk Library unions directions in the performance of their functions under this Act and . . . they shall not in-the discharge of their functions under this Act depart from directions given by the KSLC.

While we consider these classes and compare them with the parellel sections of the Model Act or other Acts it becomes clear that the classes which assigns the duties, powers and functions of KSLC is a distinct improvement from all others. KPLA has identified most of the functions and duties expected from such a body and very clearly assigned them to it without giving space for doubt and vagueness.

Composition of KSLC

If KSLC is to become able to fulfil such duties and functions expected from it, the composition of the body should be done accordingly. Membership of such a body should include persons who have contributed to the growth of knowledge, who has evolved or developed methods and techniques for collecting, organising and disseminating information and who have wide experience in related fields of activity. It is not the method of representation but the quality of representation that will make possible the efficient functioning of the system.

The sections which prescribe the membership of SLA in Karnataka Act and SLC in Model Act and other State Acts prescribe their membership on somewhat similar lines. Prof. P.B. Mangla in his study of library legislation opines that it should be a body having representatives from various institutions, organisations, government etc. interested in and connected with the growth and development of library and information services in the State.

The Model Act, the opinion of experts and recommen-dations of committees set for studying library legislation agrees that such a body should include among its members; the Minister for Libraries if there is one, otherwise Minister for Education, then Minister in charge of Local-Self-Government, Director of Libraries, State Librarian, sufficient number of representatives from State Legislative Assembly by election from among themselves, Secretary to Government for Education, representatives elected from Local Library Authorities by rotation to limit size of the body, representatives of associations of library profession and experts with specialization in library and information services and represen-tatives of Universities of the State.

It would be essential that the Minister in charge of Libraries should act as *ex-officio* chairman and the Director of Public Libraries or State Librarian should act as ex-officio secretary of the committee.

The rationale behind such a composition of this body is that it is a body which is to advise the government and discuss continuously on a most important responsibility of the government, that is organisation and dissemination of information required by the society. But disregarding all these principles KPLA provides for constituting a body of members who were not suitable to undertake this work.

The section 3 sub-section (2) related to the composition of the KSLC in KPLA provides: The KSLC shall consist of one member each from Taluks, elected by the general body of the District Library councils, and five members of whom one shall be a librarian, another a person belonging to the scheduled caste or scheduled tribe and another a woman nominated by the government. Library and information service is an intellectual service. It goes without saying that this body as provided in KPLA will not be able to fulfil satisfactorily the purpose for which it is intended.

In these days of information explosion and flooding of vast and varied types of books and other printed materials that originates every minute without wide familiarity of all spheres of knowledge and expertise in handling their information in most effective way at minimum cost the body which heads such a system will be having a mere formal and useless existence. As we have seen in section 8 of KPLA the most important function of KSLC is to advise the government on all matters connected with the administration of this Act and overall library policy ofthe State.

It is not clear how this committee will be competent to render such expert technical advise when it has only persons as members, who has come through election without expertise or knowledge about information work and without even any educational qualifications. Library and information service to the people if provided efficiently will be the continuously active service of government and will require expert advise everyday on many matters.

The KSLC's inability to provide such expert advise will make government's efforts futile and to overcome this, govern-ment will be forced to create a continuous chain of Advisory Committees which is also not very practicable. While no hard and fast rule can be laid down about the size of this body it is generally felt that it should not have more than twenty members. The KSLC may remain a supreme body in name only for real powers of the council have been passed over to a smaller body which is the executive committee. But it also becomes an unwieldy body with membership of 25 persons.

Thus KSLC has acquired all the defects existing in SLAs and SLCs into one body. This Executive Committee is a new addition in our library Acts. But the findings of Ashok Mehta Committee and various committees appointed by many State Governments to study Panchayat Raj Institutions advise us against such an elected body like KSLC for organising important service as library and information service to the people. Instead of adopting the constitution and composition of SLA and SLC provided by the Model Act or followed by the other State Acts KPLA gave legal sanction to the organi-zational set up of an association that was already existing there, that is Kerala Granthasala Sangham.

The constitution and composition of KSLC and its Executive Committee is the same followed by Sangham for its general body and Bharanasamithi. In all other provisions KPLA follows the same pattern of Sangham with some minor alterations. For more than half a century Sangham was pressurizing the Government to give legal sanction to Sangham to be the SLA and to accept its system as it is,as State's Library System.

But experts have continuously pointed out during this period the futility of such a system for library and information service. But Sangham objected government's all other attempts to enact a modern library system legislation and at last come out successful in legalizing its own system. But this in fact totally prevents the State from having an advanced library legislation and developing its library and information services in conformity with the requirements of the time.

CONCEPTS OF THE STATE LIBRARY AUTHORITY

The concept of the *State Library Authority* (SLA) underwent an evolution from State Library Committee to Minister of Education or Libraries; everywhere in the world. The Model Act recommends that for the purpose of promoting and organising a library system in the State the Ministry for Education of the State shall be the SLA.

It shall be the duty of the SLA to provide; for an adequate library and information service in the State and, for the progressive development of the institutions devoted to the purpose and to secure the effective execution by *Local Library Authorities* (LLA) of the national policy for providing adequate library service to the people in every locality. In the existing' State Acts only Karnataka Public Library Act, 1965 provides and clearly names SLA.

The Act provides for the constitution and composition of the SLA.6 SLA shall be a body corporate having perpetual succession and a common seal with power, to acquire, hold and dispose of property and to contract and may by the same time sue and be sued. It consists of twenty members from the fields concerned with information creation, organisation and services, with Minister for Education who shall ex officio be the President and State Librarian who shall ex officio be the Secretary of SLA. But it is desirable to make only one person, instead of a corporate body to be the supreme authority for providing this very important service, for that gives a unified command from administrative points of view.

And this person should not be any person less than the Minister for Education, because he is directly responsible to the legislature and his term of office being limited to a period of five years he is ultimately responsible to the people. Hewit who made a study of the library legislation in India; it will be observed that two kinds of supreme authority are favoured in existing legislation and in the drafts of the model bills framed in India. One is a body of persons *i.e.,* State Library Councilor Committee and second is a Minister of State. He suggests the second as the better of the two, mainly because a Minister is responsible to his legislature, and through it, to the electors and many be called to account therein. A body of persons even though a Minister may be President or Chairman thereof is not so easily questioned.

In any case; so important an activity as the provision for public library and information service to the people fully justifies direct representation in State Legislature. So all the studies on library legislations and the evaluation of existing legislations throughout the world and especially in third world counties, like that of Gardners's study comes to the conclusion that providing up of a body or a person as SLA and clearly naming and defining its powers and functions is certainly essential for the successful working of library Acts. But KPLA is very vague in this aspect and it fails to name a person or body as SLA.

DEPARTMENT OF PUBLIC LIBRARIES AND OFFICIALS

It is generally emphasized that in order to develop a system of public libraries in a State or country on proper lines, it is essential that a separate department of public libraries be created at par with the department of education and that the former should not be a part of the later or any other' department. The Acts of Andhra, Maharashtra, West Bengal and Karnataka prescribe for the creation of separate department of Public Libraries.

Director of Public Libraries

Most of the recommendations related to public library system legislation emphasizes that the department of Public Libraries should be headed by a Director of Public Libraries (DPL), whose rank must be equivalent to that of Director of Education. He must be a person with qualification and experience in Library and Information Science.

Emphasis on his being a professional is laid because it is he to whom the whole public library system in the State would look for guidance and inspiration and his professional outlook would normally greatly help the development of the system on desired lines.

The first public library Act in this country; the Madras Public Library Act, 1948 provided for the appointment of DPL. Andhra, Maharastra and West Bengal also prescribes for the creation of DPL. In Madras and Andhra the Director of Public Instruction is made the ex-officio Director of Public Libraries also.

The disadvantages of such an administrative set-up are quite obvious. The Department of Public Libraries becomes an additional burden to the Director of Public Instruction. This new department will be looked upon as an uninvited guest. A. R. Hewit has rightly pointed out that many of the duties of Director of Public Libraries would require technical knowledge and skill in librarianship. So professional experts only can undertake this responsibility efficiently.

State Library

All the Acts except KPLA which is not providing for these offices, combines the responsibilities of developing and managing the State Central Library Superintending and directing all matters related to the State library system in a single person called State Librarian or DPL.

The Model Act also recommends this pattern. But the Sinha Committee report suggested the creation of two separate posts for this purpose when it said "The DPL may have the overall responsibility to organize develop and supervise the public library system as the Head of the Department of Public Libraries.

The State Librarian should have the responsibility to manage supervise and develop State Central Library and should be the Chief Technical Advisor of the DPL, with no responsibility for the administration of the service in the State. This responsibility should be entirely that of DPL. But in KPLA there is no provision for appointing a Director of Libraries or State Librarian. While the class by class discussion of the Bill was going on in Assembly Mr. V.M. Sudheeran; member presented an amendment to add a new clause in the Act providing for appointment of a Director of Libraries. But was not considered.

Administration

For the administration of public libraries all the State Acts have created a department or directorate of public libraries. It is put under the charge of Director of Libraries or State Librarian who is to be the *ex-officio* Secretary of SLA. The functions of these posts as prescribed by all Acts including the Model Act are: to supervise and direct all matters relating to public libraries, to direct and control the working of LLAs, submit reports to Government and deal with schemes and plans relating to libraries. Many of the highly technical and specialized works of State Central Library also is to be supervised by them.

So it is clear that these posts which are carrying heavy responsibility concerning various matters-financial, advisory, administrative, technical, supervisory and so on-under the Act would require technical knowledge and skill in library and information service. So the Secretary or High Officer of this body should be a whole time officer having the prescribed qualifications to practice the library profession. Disregarding all the facts KPLA assigns all these duties and powers 'to a Secretary elected by members of the Executive Committee ofKSLC.

Section 3 sub-section (5) of KPLA provides that the elected members of the Executive Committee shall elect a President, Vice-President, Secretary and Joint Secretary from among themselves to be the President, Vice-President, Secretary and Joint Secretary respectively of the State Library Council and of the Executive Committee. Their term of office will be for three years.KPLA assigns to the Secretary of KSLC the duties and powers which other State

Acts assign to State Librarian or Director of Libraries. Section 9 Sub-section (1) States: the Secretary of the State Library Council shall be Chief Executive Authority of KSLC.

The nature of the office of Secretary of KSLC requires professional knowledge and experience as well as continuity of office for the successful operation of the Act, so it is inevitable that this provision will prevent KPLA from fulfilling the objectives for which a modern library legislation should exist. This serious defect of the Act has been pointed out by many members during the discussion of the bill.

Dr. M.Kuttappan has brought to the notice of the Assembly that such an important system like that for library and information service requires qualified government officials as their secretaries at State, District and Taluk levels. The period of an elected non-official member may be over by three years and if he misappropriates government fund allotted for library development it will not be possible for the government to take action on him. Sri Ishac Kurikkal suggested an amend-ment to the Bill to provide that the Secretary of the SLC shall be appointed by the Government on the advice of the Kerala Public Service Commission.

Another member Sri Kodiyeri Balakrishnan opined that the Secretary of KSLC should be appointed by Government and the Act should specify the qualifications and method of appointment for this post. Sri Ramesh Chennitthala presented an amendment to add the following sub-clause in KPLA namely: The Secretary shall be a person not below the rank of a Joint Secretary to Government appointed by Government from among persons qualified and competent to hold such post. But all these suggestions were rejected and principles were disregarded to maintain a democratic system for constituting the SLA.

Library Co-operation

To make the best possible use of the document resources not only in the public library system but also in other types of libraries in the State such as universities, special libraries etc, a system of inter library co-operation needs to be developed in the state as a whole. It would also be useful and economical if centralization of different aspects such as acquisition programme, technical processing etc. of documents should be introduced at State level or at different levels of the system. The KPLA gives no such provision for co-operation or centralized processing and the institution which is to give leadership in such activities that is SCL is absent in KPLA.

State Central Library

The existing State legislations and the Model Act provide for a State Central Library (SCL) as an integral part of the Public Library Service. The SCL is normally the copy right collection. It should collect as far as its resources allow, expensive work and literature published abroad, material for which the local public library would have little need and could not afford. All the countries of the world possessing adequate library systems, have national library systems and all have national central library as distinct from the other libraries in the system, but is accessible to all through any library of the system.

The same role of National Central Library to the National system is done by SCL to the State system. Usually the library legislations designate the biggest collection available in the State as SCL and makes its resources and services available to the system. Even though various Acts and Model Act give different names to SCL like State Service Library, etc. in a public library system only one such library will be maintained and its resources will be shared by all participating units. Maintaining more than one SCL is unnecessary duplication of work and waste of resources.

Most of the State Acts and Model bills drafted, designate the biggest public library existing in the State as SCL and adopts it to the system and shares its resources among participating units. But instead of designating Trivandrum Public Library, the oldest and biggest collection in the State as SCL, the KPLA deems it to be one of the many State libraries it will establish.

The Act provides for no SCL in its system. Instead it provides that KSLC shall establish one or more state libraries at such place or places in the State as may be considered necessary. The relation of State libraries with other state libraries and different level service units and the purpose of more than one such institution is not defined in the Act.

State Library Service

State Library Service brings the manpower of the State in one pool and thus avoids the waste of time and money involved in filling up posts that would otherwise involve, if every Local Library Authority were to appoint the staff independently. A State Library Service further avoids the influence of members of the Local Library Authority in day-to-day management of libraries. Mysore Act has created a special state library service and it ensures proper administration and economy through State Library Service. But KPLA gives to KSLC and Local Library Authorities that is DLC and TLU the powers to appoint and control required officers and servants.

INTERNET SEARCHING IN LIBRARY

In 300 B.C., the Library of Alexandria held some half million scrolls and served as a cultural centre for the world, uniting the thoughts of Greek, Egyptian, Macedonian and Babylonian culture. The Letter of Aristeas, the library had "a large budget in order to collect, if possible, all the books in the world." Whole fields of study such as geometry and grammar grew from the scholars who had the fortune to travel to and study at Alexandria.In 2003 A.D., the Internet forms a distributed library of billions of pages, one that is accessible to anyone, anywhere in the world, at the click of a mouse.

Every day hundreds of millions of 'trips' to the library start with a query to an Internet search engine. If I want to research a topic such as 'Library of Alexandria,' I can type those words to a search engine and in less than a second have access to a list of 14,000 pages, sorted by their usefulness to the query. This unprecedented ease of access to information has revolutionised the way research is done by students, scientists, journalists, shoppers, and others. It opens up an online marketplace of products, services, and ideas that benefits both information providers and seekers; sellers and buyers; consumers and advertisers.

How is it that an Internet Search engine can find the answers to a query so quickly? It is a four-step process:

- Crawling the Web, following links to find pages;
- Indexing the pages to create an index from every word to every place it occurs;
- Ranking the pages so the best ones show up first; and
- Displaying the results in a way that is easy for the user to understand.

Crawling is conceptually quite simple: starting at some well-known sites on the web, recursively follow every hypertext link, recording the pages encountered along the way. In computer science this is called the transitive closure of the link relation. However, the conceptual simplicity hides a large number of practical complications: sites may be busy or down at one point, and come back to life later; pages may be duplicated at multiple sites and must be dealt with accordingly; many pages have text that does not conform to the standards for HTML, HTTP redirection, robot exclusion, or other protocols; some information is hard to access because it is hidden behind a form, Flash animation or Javascript programme.

Finally, the necessity of crawling 100 million pages a day means that building a crawler is an exercise in distributed computing, requiring many computers that must work together and schedule their actions so as to get to all the pages without overwhelming any one site with too many requests at once. A search engine's index is similar to the index in the back of a book: it is used to find the pages on which a word occurs.

There are two main differences: the search engine's index lists every occurrence of every word, not just the important concepts, and the number of pages is in the billions, not hundreds. Various techniques of compression and clever representation are used to keep the index 'small,' but it is still measured in terabytes, which again means that distributed computing is required. Most modern search engines index link data as well as word data.It is useful to know how many pages link to a given page, and what are the quality of those pages.

This kind of analysis is similar to citation analysis in bibliographic work, and helps establish which pages are authoritative. Algorithms such as PageRank and HITS are used to assign a numeric measure of authority to each page. For example, the PageRank algorithm says that the rank of a page is a function of the sum of the ranks of the pages that link to the page. If we let PR(*p*) be the PageRank of page *p*, Out(*p*) be the number of outgoing links from page *p*, Links(*p*) be the set of pages that link to page *p* and N be the total number of pages in the index, then we can define PageRank by

$$PR(p) = r / N + (1 -_r) \sum_i \subset Links(p)^{PR(i)/Out(i)}$$

where r is a parameter that indicates the probability that a user will choose not to follow a link, but will instead restart at some other page. The *r/N* term means that each of the *N* pages is equally likely to be the restart point, although it is also possible to use a smaller subset of well-known pages as the restart candidates. Note that the formula for PageRank is recursive– PR appears on both the right-and left-hand sides of the equation.

The equation can be solved by iterating several times, or by standard linear algebra techniques for computing the Eigen values of a matrix. The two steps are query independent–they do not depend on the user's query, and thus can be done before a query is issued with the cost shared among all users. This is why a search takes a second or less, rather than the days it would take if a search engine had to crawl the web anew for each query. We now consider what happens when a user types a query. Consider the query, where the square brackets denote the beginning and end of the query, and the quotation marks indicate that the enclosed words must be found as an exact phrase match.

The first step in responding to this query is to look in the index for the hit lists corresponding to each of the four words 'National,' 'Academies,' 'computer' and 'science.' These four lists are then intersected to yield the set of pages that mention all four words. Because 'National Academies' was entered as a phrase, only hits where these two words appear adjacent and in that order are counted. The result is a list of 19,000 or so pages. The next step is ranking these 19,000 pages to decide which ones are most relevant. In traditional information retrieval this is done by counting the number of occurrences of each word, weighing rare words more heavily than frequent words, and normalising for the length of the page.

A number of refinements on this scheme have been developed, so it is common to give more credit for pages where the words occur near each other, where the words are in bold or large font, or in a title, or where the words occur in the anchor text of a link that points to the page. In addition the query-independent authority of each page is factored in. The result is a numeric score for each page that can be used to sort them best-first. Traditionally this is done by listing a short description of each result in rank-sorted order. The description will include the title of the page and may include additional information such as a short abstract or excerpt from the page.Some search engines generate query-independent abstracts while others customise each excerpt to show at least some of the words from the query.

Displaying this kind of query-dependent excerpt means that the search engine must keep a copy of the full text of the pages at a cost of several more terabytes. Some search engines attempt to cluster the result pages into coherent categories or folders, although this technology is not yet mature. Studies have shown that the most popular uses of computers are e-mail, word processing and Internet searching. Of the three, Internet searching is by far the most sophisticated example of computer science technology. Building a high-quality search engine requires extensive knowledge and experience in information retrieval, data structure design, user interfaces, and distributed systems implementation.

Future advances in searching will increasingly depend on statistical natural language processing and machine learning techniques. With so much data–billions of pages, tens of billions of links, and hundreds of millions of queries per day–it makes sense to use data mining approaches to automatically improve the system. For example, several search engines now do spelling correction of user queries.It turns out that the vast amount of correctly and incorrectly spelled text available to a search engine makes it easier to create a good spelling corrector than traditional techniques based on dictionaries. It is likely that there will be other examples of text understanding that can be done better with a data-oriented approach; this is an area that search engines are just beginning to explore.

OPEN DATA, INTERNET RESOURCES WEB SITES AND LITERACY

The public, graphic Internet is a young technology. It is so young that it has only endured one significant change. It has morphed from being a passive information tool where large companies and organisations posted documents and has become, as well, a place where anyone can and does contribute opinions about events and thoughts or their personal lives. We are beginning to see a third major change in the web. This change is characterised by people being sent information that their profile suggests they might like to receive. Singles Around Me (SAM) is a dating app for smartphones. It links to social media profiles and lets users know when single people who match their interests are physically close, in any city. This is a huge shift from a web that provided passive web pages waiting to be viewed.

FOUR PRIORITIES FOR THE 21ST CENTURY PUBLIC LIBRARY SERVICE

- Place the library as the hub of a community.
- Make the most of digital technology and creative media.

- Ensure that libraries are resilient and sustainable.
- Deliver the right skills for those who work for libraries.

The key issues emerging in this research are similar to those we handle with the wider arts and cultural sector. It is because there is such a close fit with the Arts Council's five long term goals that we will be able to develop solutions to these challenges from which both libraries and arts organisations can benefit.

Place the Library as the Hub of a Community

We know that, in future, many people are likely to lead more isolated lives. More will work from home and more will live alone. Opportunities to meet in free public spaces for a wide variety of purposes will be increasingly important. Our findings show that libraries will continue to be valued as trusted, safe, democratic places that offer valuable resources and expertise to support the activities of the people who use them.

Libraries' physical space will be more flexible and integrated with a virtual presence that includes web-based reading groups, social networking and links to other online resources. People will engage in creative and cultural activities as well as reading and learning, exchanging ideas, conversation and knowledge.

Space shared with community based services (such as council, health, business support, and learning organisations) will be better for local people, and will bring benefits such as skills exchanges, reaching more people and cutting costs.

The challenge: the use of a library's space:

- Re-think the way library spaces are used to encourage shared and creative activity while continuing to welcome those who want to explore on their own.
- Integrate the library's physical and virtual spaces.
- Sustain enough spaces offered by libraries to meet the needs of their communities.

Make the most of Digital Technology and Creative Media

Digital technology is developing rapidly and will continue to have a major impact on the way we obtain and consume information, culture and the written word. Beyond the library building, people will expect a more interactive experience and to be able to gain access to library services all day, every day, particularly while on the move.

Libraries should be at the heart of digital innovation. They should develop their role in actively connecting communities and helping people to experience, experiment with and master new technologies. Digital technology will be the key to future library service delivery but our research points out that its true potential will not be achieved unless the principle of an open, enabling ICT infrastructure is agreed by local authorities and library services.This would allow libraries to innovate, and to share or jointly adopt services more efficiently.

By making it easier to develop national services and enable local innovation, people will get access to more resources, information and support. Many assume that digital information sources and online services are accessible to everyone.

But a digital divide still exists because a significant number of people lack the confidence, the necessary skills or the desire to make effective use of technology. Some who do, are held back by poor digital connections or can't afford them. Public libraries will ensure that no-one needs to be left behind or excluded.

The challenge: using technology:

- Improve the quality and consistency of the virtual library experience
- Develop an open ICT infrastructure that encourages innovation and better service
- Enable libraries to lend the full range of e-books, including remotely

Ensure that Libraries are Resilient and Sustainable

Our research, along with reductions in public expenditure, makes clear that libraries will need to reduce costs and find other sources of funding to supplement local authority support. Alongside this, communities are becoming more involved in the design and delivery of library services. To find the right solution, councillors in local authorities are considering whether they should change the way their library service is governed, or whether they can share aspects of their service with others.

Our research indicates that, as with many other public services, this trend will continue and grow, and the debate about community involvement in public libraries needs to be seen in this wider context. We do not suggest that any one approach is the right one in all circumstances but we have published guidance, based on experience to date, that we suggest should be taken into account.

Some library services are already doing this and we believe that they could be role models, not just among libraries, but for all public services. This kind of community involvement will become seen not as a cost-cutting tool but as a normal way of working, with staff and users developing ideas and creating services together.

The challenge: cutting costs, finding new sources of funds and new ways of working:

- Create a positive environment for communities and individuals to become actively involved in the design and delivery of their library services

- Encourage the development of new approaches to governing and managing libraries that make it more likely that they will survive and succeed.
- Equip libraries to be commissioned to deliver other public services, and to commission other organisations to deliver library services

Deliver the Right Skills for those Who Work for Libraries

Our research indicates that one of the major challenges facing public libraries in the future is ensuring that library staff have effective leadership and delivery skills for a rapidly evolving service. Librarians will need to be active in their communities, encouraging people to get involved with their library. That involvement will include local people identifying what their priorities are as well as volunteering and community managed services.

Supporting people in using digital resources competently and confidently will become increasingly important. Those who work in libraries will need to improve their skills in organising and helping users to find their way through complicated information sources.

They will become more pro-active in inspiring new services in partnership with others, and their leaders will need to be more entrepreneurial and adept in communicating and marketing their services.

Our research indicates that not enough people working in libraries are equipped to tackle these changes and take on these roles, and that current training is not always relevant for the current and future needs of those working in public libraries.

The challenge: developing the skills of those who work in libraries:

- Ensure those responsible for libraries have the right range of skills and experience to lead their services successfully
- Encourage those working in libraries to offer creative and innovative ways to use library spaces, books and other resources
- Ensure that library staff have the skills to develop and respond to digital developments and to support digital users.

INTERNET TRAINING FOR ACADEMIC LIBRARY STAFF

Educational institutions are being encouraged by the Government and other organisations to upgrade their resources for research and education. Consequently the academic libraries of the higher education institutions are also being upgraded. Internet has proved to be boon in this endeavor. Internet has helped these libraries to be interconnected and share their resources and also to access resources in remote locations.

Internet connections have been growing in the recent years with good connectivity and access. But are these libraries fully geared up especially in terms of their employees' skills to be able to fully utilise the Internet for the benefit of the academic community?

It has already been widely discussed that training is essential for the staffs to work in a network and automated environment. The Library Association Working Party on Training cites in its Policy Statement that training "is of fundamental importance to all levels of staffs working in all types of library", contributing to "greater efficiency and continuity, with real cost benefits". Since, technology keeps on changing it becomes even more necessary for the staff to be trained in Internet.

OBJECTIVES

The present study aims to understand the status of Internet training for the academic library staff within greater Guwahati. Since, the importance of Internet is growing in today's academic environment therefore the issue of training the academic library staff in handling Internet is becoming important.

So this study will investigate the various training methods used in the academic libraries, the content of such training, problems encountered and whether any evaluation is undertaken for such training. The investigation will also try to reveal the attitudes of the library managers with regard to training their staff on Internet.

SCOPE

The present study was based on a sample of academic libraries from greater Guwahati selected randomly. Since, there are many academic libraries within greater Guwahati only those were selected which had a functional Internet connection.

These include the following libraries:

- Hem Barua library (B.Borooah college).
- KKHandique Library (Gauhati University).
- Dr. BKB Library (Gauhati Commerce College).
- Central Library (IIT Guwahati).
- IASST Library (Institute of Advanced Studies in Science and technology).
- KC Das Commerce College Library.

METHODOLOGY

In order to understand the status of Internet training for the staffs of the academic libraries a sample of six academic libraries was taken. A questionnaire-based survey of the sample was conducted. The questionnaire contained both close-ended questions and open-ended questions. The questionnaire was prepared based on some existing studies already done on understanding the Internet training of academic library staff. Comprehending the importance of the study the author personally went to the respective libraries to collect the data.

INTERNET AND ITS USE IN ACADEMIC LIBRARIES

Many of us by now are familiar with Internet especially those working in the academic libraries. This is because the academic libraries have been the pioneer in the field of automation and Internet. Internet has become essential for today's education and research in the academic institutions. Library being a hub of research and academic activities are therefore being provided with Internet connections. The Internet is a unique information resource, bringing a wide range of material from around the world to a local machine. One of the earliest usages of the Internet was to access the OPAC, *i.e.*, the Online Public Access Catalogues of different libraries or within a campus.

The union catalogues which lists the holdings of several libraries was another important tool accessible through net. Another area of growing importance for academic libraries is that of electronic journals. Big publishing houses like Elsevier, Springer, ACM, etc., are providing packages of their journals to libraries in electronic form via Internet. So at nominal subscription the libraries can access to these costly journals, which are becoming increasingly popular with the users. Thus grew consortia based subscription in India.

INDEST, INFONET and CSIR Consortium are the examples of library consortia for sharing journals and bibliographic information. These consortia based journal subscription are available through the Internet. The Indian National Digital Library in Engineering Science and Technology, *i.e.*, INDEST was set up by the Ministry of Human resource Development (MHRD) for subscription to electronic resources for 38 institutions including IISc, IITs, NITs, IIMs, etc., Over 6000 e-journals are accessible through this consortium, which has its headquarters in IIT Delhi. Infonet Contortia is set up by UGC and operated through its INFLIBNET Centre, Ahmedabad. Over 100 Universities are its members.

It covers disciplines like Arts, Sciences, Mathematics and statistics, etc., About 4000 full text electronic journals from 25 publishers are currently accessible. CSIR e-journal Consortia provides access to 3300+ e-journals from 11 publishers to all CSIR SandT staff of different CSIR institutions located around India. These consortia not only provide full text access but they also give access to bibliographic databases like COMPENDEX, INSPEC SciFinder Scholar, and Web of Science, etc. Many open access materials important for education and research are available on the Internet. They are very useful in the context that they are not fee based and also don't have restricted access and are thus becoming very popular with students and researchers. Communicating with users is very important in academic libraries.

Widespread access to the Internet has also created new means of communicating with users. In some cases, Internet technologies are used to reproduce an existing service in another medium, such as online "suggestion boxes". However, there is "added value" to such a service as users can mail in their suggestions from terminals on or off campus at a time convenient to them. E-mail enquiry or reference services also represent an extension of mainstream library activity - although some academic librarians initially had concerns about being able to meet the demand of such a service. Reference and enquiry services in academic libraries in the main seek to teach their users how to search for information themselves, rather than answering the enquiries themselves, as is more likely to be the case in a special library.

A significant number of British academic libraries have adopted electronic mail enquiry or information services - at the University of Hull the "e-mail help line" is treated as an extension of the Enquiry Desk service. Anecdotal evidence suggests that electronic enquiry services are not overwhelmed, and most users do stay within the parameters of the service. The most successful e-mail enquiry services have developed their procedures and boundaries prior to the service going live. As many enquiries fall into the category of Frequently Asked Questions, these can thus be answered by existing position statements.

Electronic mail also has great potential to cut down on the mountain of paperwork involved in sending out recall notices, notifying readers that items can be collected, etc. Some library systems allow students to renew loans (provided no other reader is waiting for the book) directly via the OPAC or to request a renewal via e-mail. Similarly, weblogs or simply blogs are now becoming very popular on the Internet as a communication medium.

A library weblog can be used to:

- Providing news information for users.
- Providing links to recommend internet sources.
- Book reviews, information about new books.
- Providing entertainment or amusement for users.
- Providing news or information for librarians.
- Book discussions.
- Provide news or information for the trustees.
- Provide research tips.
- Communication among the librarians (in a library system).

The library can make good use of the electronic mail system of Internet, *i.e.*, E-mail to communicate reservation alert, current awareness services like SDI, new arrivals of books and journals, receiving interlibrary loan request and sending overdue notices to the users. In addition to these specialist services academic librarians also make use of the Internet information that is available to all users. Much bibliographical and price information can be found from online bookstores and Web sites for professional organisations and publishers. A wide range of factual information from government and NGO sources is available too. Although librarians have more skepticism about the well-publicised Web search tools than most users, such services can be valuable, particularly for easily defined topics (such as names or abbreviations) and the sheer range of material indexed, subjects covered and the speed with which they search can make them useful when a clear starting point is not obvious.

They may not always retrieve a full answer, but may give helpful clues. Internet resources are just another information medium academic librarians are extending their skills to encompass it. So they may offer a current awareness service to teaching and research staff to inform them of new Web sites and discussion lists; they will apply established criteria to assessing the content of information sources or the effectiveness of secondary services like search tools. The hypertext nature of the Web makes it easy to make additional explanation or instruction for a resource as an optional choice. This concept of instruction at the point and time of use is harder to achieve in the physical library.

WHY INTERNET TRAINING IS NECESSARY

In the Internet age there is acute need of Internet specialists. These specialists will be armed with the necessary skills and training to help the users to locate their information pin pointedly and efficiently on the net. Libraries specially the academic libraries would have a great demand for these specialists. Internet connectivity in the academic libraries is growing day by day. So, the present administration of the academic institutions should take necessary steps to equip the library staff with the required skills and training on Internet. Training can help to understand many essential aspects of the Internet such as follows:

- Are we using the right type of Internet connection for our needs? Are we getting a good deal?
- How quickly can we find what we looking for on the Internet? We should be able to find useful information about virtually any topic in less than a minute. If you're taking longer, you're doing something wrong.
- How do we know if we are safe? Most people who contract viruses or other nastiest thought they were protected.
- Are we using e-mail correctly? Or are we really annoying we our colleagues and they are too polite to tell us? We might be unpleasantly surprised to learn the truth.
- How do we avoid those terrible pop-up windows?
- How do we know if information is real or a hoax?
- How can we make surfing faster?
- How can we get the maximum satisfaction without spending more time on net?

As noted by Paula L. Matthews while employing Internet in academic libraries one of the important issues for the administrator is the implementation library staff training. "A lack of training can result in:

- Poor staff performance;
- Lack of motivation;

- High staff turnover;
- Resistance to change;
- Costly errors or accidents;
- Unfulfilled objectives;
- Undesirable low standards of service.

Academic librarians may well draw on training materials available on the Internet for the higher education community. Recently the issue of whether librarians should learn HTML (Hyper-Text Markup Language) was debated on a North American discussion list. The conclusion was that knowledge of basic HTML was necessary in order to prepare presentations and information guides, which are an integral part of the librarian's professional role. As an increasing number of academic libraries experience some measure of "convergence" with other academic support services, library staff has many opportunities to augment their IT skills and collaborate with colleagues in other services.

The combination of technical knowledge and the ability to evaluate information sources is a powerful argument for the continued need for LIS professionals in higher education. The users of the Academic libraries including some faculty member do not have net skills. In such cases the academic library staff has to come forward to help them. For readiness the staff should have some kind of net skills. The transition of traditional library resources to technology based library resources has put a lot of pressure on the academic library staff. Unless the staff is kept upto- date on Internet skills he will face more pressure to work in such conditions. So training of staff has become a necessity in today's context

SURVEY ANALYSIS AND DISCUSSION

Kirpatrik on his study on the training of academic library staff on IT found that a high 52.9 percent of the staff responded that they received individual training by coworker. This means that the most preferred method of training as founded on this study was internal training. Matthews has also found on his investigation that internal training was the most popular choice (100 per cent) of the 15 libraries that were included in his exploratory study. External training was least preferred. The high cost involved in external training was the cited as the chief cause for discouragement. Another factor was time.

The library mangers cited lack of manpower as the reason for not preferring sending staff to receive external training. Commonly used training methods include both formal and informal. Formal training or off – the – job training involves practical courses on specific topics in a developed programme for new conceptual, analytical and problem solving skills whereas, on – the – job training is a basic training method where a trainee is being shown the ways a job can be done through instruction and supervision.

The present study was however concentrated on the internal and external training methods. The internal training methods are basically on the job training. The internal training methods for Internet training includes lectures, presentations, demonstrations, workshops, tutorials, free search/browsing time and handouts. In the process of the above investigation as tabulate in Table it is found that 5 out of the 6 academic libraries, *i.e.*, 83 per cent of the respondents identified in Guwahati have undertaken internal Internet training.

Table. Internal vs External Training Preference for Internet Training of Staff.

Sl. No.	Name of the Institution	Internal Training	External Training
1.	Hem Barua Library	Yes	No
	(B. Borooah College)		
2.	KK Handique Library	Yes	No
	(Gauhati University)		
3.	Dr. BKB Library (Gauhati	Yes	No
	Commerce College)		
4.	Central Library (IITG)	Yes	No
5.	IASST Library	Yes	No
6.	KC Das Commerce College	Yes	No
	Percentage (percent)	**5/6 (83)**	**1/6 (17)**

Only 1 out of the 6 libraries has opted for external training citing it as more effective than internal training. Regarding the methods adopted or likely to be adopted in Internet training as tabulated in Table, majority 5/6 (83 per cent) has not preferred lecture as a good training.

A co-worker or the librarian himself gives lecture on specific topics. Demonstrations were another method found suitable for Internet training as it was opted by 5 (83 per cent) out of the total libraries surveyed. Other methods found popular among the libraries includes free searching or giving browsing time (67 per cent) to staffs.

This method although very effective is also difficult because the staff has to give sufficient time which may not be practical in difficult circumstances like busy schedule, budget constrains. It was surprising to find in the study that none of the libraries had opted handouts for internet training of staff (0 per cent). Because of the nature of Internet, which changes on a daily basis, guidance documentation is difficult to provide, as it can very soon be out of date. But as founded by Matthews *et al.* handouts are very popular and staff are often anxious to have a document they can refer to when they are no longer in a situation where help is at hand. Workshops were also sparsely selected as a training method as only 17 per cent opted for it. The common disadvantage cited included time and budget constraints. Only 1 out of the 6 libraries has opted for external training citing it as more effective than internal training. Majority of the libraries cited cost as the main. Since, such Internet training in specifically applicable in libraries are not conducted locally. Mangers are ill prepared to send some staff to take training outside. The contents of the Internet training did not very much among the six surveyed libraries as show in Table. The common contents included E-mail, WWW and browsers. Those libraries, *i.e.*, mainly the college libraries felt that training on accessing e- journals were unnecessary as none of them had e- journals in their library.

IIT- Guwahati, IASST and Gauhati University which has a sufficient collection of e- journals had answered that they had trained or likely to train their staff on e-journals. Many of the staffs that got Internet training had developed the skills to use Internet as a reference tool and as a communication tool such as Internet. Assisting users in Internet was another skill developed by such training. But none of the libraries reported on the development of publishing skills as an outcome of the training. The common reason cited was that it was felt too sophisticated in the present context. Information on Internet training was not available to the staff readily. Many of the respondents felt that remoteness of this part of the world as factor for this. Only two of the respondents, , *viz.,* IIT- Guwahati and K. C. Das Commerce College cited that such information are readily available to them. The most common problem cited by the respondents was that the staff was mostly technically unqualified for Internet.

This was especially in the case of the college libraries where mostly no technical persons worked in the library. However none of the libraries had done any evaluation on the training of the staff in Internet. Workload and time constraints were sited as the major reason for not undertaking such evaluations. On the future plans majority of the respondents showed willingness on their part to participate in Internet training. However their viewpoint was that some local leading institutions like Gauhati University, IIT Guwahati or the likes of National Informatics Centre (NIC) should organise such skill development Programmes where they are ready to participate.

FINDINGS

- Nearly all the libraries reported that they did not have a formal programme on Internet training as they felt such training was not needed in the present context.
- In majority of the libraries internal training was the most preferred.
- E-mail, WWW, browsers were the most common contents included in the training.
- Majority of the respondents said that information on Internet training were mostly unavailable to them.

- Majority felt that publishing skills on internet were not required for them
- Majority felt that basic skills developed by such training included ability to use Internet as a reference and communication tool and also ability to assist users.
- Majority cited that having non-technical staff in library as the main problem in Internet training.
- Constant electric failure was another problem cited by the respondents in conducting Internet training.
- No formal evaluation was done in any of the surveyed libraries.
- On future plans majority of the respondents had shown the willingness for Internet training provided that some reputed institutions of this reason comes forward in giving guidance for such training.

SUGGESTIONS

- Internet training of the staff should be given due importance.
- Individual libraries should develop a formal Programme for giving Internet training to their taff.
- Librarians should explore all the options including external training courses on the Internet.
- There is strong need for some leading Institutions of the region to take initiative where the staffs of academic libraries can be sent at periodic intervals to update their skills on Internet.
- Such Programmes are taking place outside Assam as in DRTC, INFLIBNET centres, etc., but institutions are not willing to sent staff for such training due to financial and other constraints.

IMPACT OF INTERNET ON LIBRARY AND INFORMATION SERVICES

Perhaps no other recent innovation has impacted the library profession to such a great extent as Internet. Not only is our world becoming an interconnected global community, but this early use of the Internet has changed the fundamental roles, paradigms, and organisational culture of libraries and librarians as well, which created profound impact on LandIS by offering new modes of information delivery and a vast information source.

There is a continuing evolution of the roles and functions of libraries and librarians, which appears to parallel the growth of acceptance and use of the Internet by library professionals. The innovative use of Internet technologies enable us to reach both local and distant users much more easily and effectively than hither to possible. Technologies such as e-mail and Web provides tremendous opportunities for library and Inf. Scientists to deliver the information to the desktops of our users. Web offers significant advantage by integrating different library and information services with a common user interface offered by Web browsers. Realising the potentials, many libraries are rushing to getting the connectivity. The following listing will give an idea of which various functions of libraries may take advantage from Internet and Web technologies.

Acquisition:

- Correspondance with Book seller and Publisher.
- Reminders, Price verification
- Biblographic details and downloading of bib. records etc
- Ordering, billing
- Bookshops are on-line, *e.g.,* amazon.com

Classification:

- Network resources
  - Available on the net
  - Subscribed or free or trial basis
- Dewey Online
- Maths. Classification System
- Engineering Electronics Lib. Classification
- Search engines – such as yahoo use DDC.

Collection Development:

- Ownership vs Access
- Subscribe in print or e-form
- Subscribe in print as well as in e-form
- Pay-per-use
- Consortial approach

Cataloguing:

- Cataloguing of network resources
- Online Catalogues
- WorldCat (OCLC)
- WebOPAC – web sites
- MARC adds 856 field
- OCLC Scorpian project- MARC and AACR2
- Metadata standards - Dublin core

Circulation:

- Remote login
- Status check
- OPAC access
- Reminder to users
- User requests
- Direct borrowing
- ILL

Resource Sharing:

- Union Catalogue
  - Access, adding, downloading

- Access to databases over networks
  - Ohionet, ILLINET, WLN, OCLC, BID (UK)
  - Full text journals access, etc.

Services:

- ILL
- Document Delivery Service, *e.g.,* Ariel
- Reference/ Inf. Services
- CAS
  - Recent additions,
  - Contents pages
- SDI
  - From library collection
  - Databases
  - Internet Sources
- OPAC
- Database access
  - Bibliographical
  - Full text
  - Many vendors and organisations are moving to Internet (web) access

Subject Lists/ Gateways:

- Internet Public Library
- *EEVL* – Engineering
- *SOSIG* – Social Science
- *OMNI*- Medical
- *ADAM* – Arts, Design, etc.

User Education:

- Through E-mail
- Through Web
- Setting Intranet.

Preservation and Storage:

- The Internet is also a medium for the preservation and storage of information. In past, libraries were seen as the main storage facility of information. As society becomes increasingly more digital and more information resides on the Internet, the focus on storage and preservation is shifting. For example, some academic libraries are now faced with the problem of whether or not to purchase serials that can be just as easily accessed on-line. Preservation of these same media also becomes an issue of economics, not the 'just in case' preservation ideology of the past paradigm. Co joined to the function preservation is the destruction of information. Because the Internet can be seen as a medium for preserving information, the process of destruction of information also is affected. As more and more information is created and stored on the Internet, the capacity to store this information is also decreasing.

RETRIEVAL OF INFORMATION

Directories, Search Engines, Meta Search Engines and Information Gateways/Virtual Libraries etc are widely used to retrieve relevant information from Internet.

Search Engines:

- They are also called Meta crawlers or multi search engines
- Do not crawl the web compiling their own searchable databases
- Search the databases of multiple sets of individual search engines simultaneously from a single site and using the same interface.
- They function as intermediary
- Present the results of their searches in two ways
  - Single lists
  - Multiple Lists.
- There are three types of meta search engines,
  - Listing
  - Options
  - Automatic
- While you query, options less
- Cover all major search engines
- Do not return all results retrieved, they take only top ones from the list.
- They are very fast.
- Use them when you are in a hurry
- Helpful when you want to have quick overview on a subject and/or unique term.
- Use them when you are,
  - Conducting a relatively simple search
  - Not having any luck pulling up documents in your search.

RESOURCES AVAILABLE ON THE INTERNET

The advent of IT and other communication technologies changed all means of information services and sources. The Internet has given the world numerous easy-to-use and inexpensive research tools. Internet is changing the way we view information sources. Information bundled in World Wide Web in the form of structured and Non-structured sources create huge problem for professionals who are dealing with information. The shift in publication process takes place as individuals, institutions, publishers, professional associations, business houses and many others are publishing information on Internet.

Electronic publishing is considered as the speedy, accurate and effective way of communication among academia and research community, and becoming a favorite idea among information professionals to experiment with. The library and information professionals have a vital role to play in organising the information and bridging the *information gap*. Internet has become a part of library environment today. Internet for reference work in the library is gaining popularity. It can be successfully utilised for providing short-range and long-range reference service because various primary and secondary sources of information are available online from many sites. As information professionals, we can arrange the sources on net as we come across, in a structured manner.

These can be;

- E-journals
- E-books
- Standards
- E-TDs
- Preprints
- Library catalogue
- Bibliographical Tools
- Share wares
- Old books
- News papers
- Dictionaries
- Magazines
- Encyclopaedias
- Databases
- Directories
- Films
- Maps
- Technical reports
- Audio/Video
- Proceedings
- Patents
- Web sites of Companies, Institutions, Organisations, Associations, etc.

Evaluation of Information Sources

When we access or retrieve something on the Web, we need to decide whether the information is useful, reliable, and appropriate for our purposes. The resources identified can also occasionally contain inaccurate and misleading information.

The nature of the Internet and WWW makes it easy for almost anyone to create and disperse information. People also have considerable freedom and variety in the formats with which they publish information on the Web. We have to double -check the facts before giving it to users. Here we need to use some general guidelines or criteria when evaluating information sources. We should ask the following questions about whatever information we found:

- Who is the author or Institution?
- How current is the information?
- Who is the audience?
- Is the content accurate and objective?
- What is the purpose of the information?
- How easy to use it?

More than that, we can consider coverage, presentation and arrangement of information in the sources to find out its value. The tremendous increase in online information sources made the searching difficult, where organising skill is required for library and information professionals.

Libraries role is also enhanced where they will have to adapt to changing environment. The scope is only limited to the imagination of information professionals, where they have to acquire thorough understanding of changes in their profession.

Willingness to take up the challenges in information resource management is the need of the hour for us.

WEB SITE FOR A LIBRARY

The roles of libraries and the Internet in providing information in the 21st century are firmly intertwined. It behooves any librarian working today to understand not only how to find things on the World Wide Web, but to have a basic understanding of how it works. Librarians will be called on to become information architects, to be able to create Web sites with clearly stated goals, that are aesthetically pleasing and filled with relevent content and functionality.

As more and more libraries set up comprehensive Web sites, there becomes an increasing demand for librarians who have an understanding of HTML, as well as other types of Internet programming skills such as javascript, SQL, CGI, ASP, and Cold Fusion. Librarians should know the principles of setting up an efficient information resource. As the Internet becomes more interactive, there is a push Towards making databases accessible online; the best example of this is the library card catalog. Other interactive options include e-mail and bulletin board service, and moving from CD-ROMs to online subscriptions.

A library Web site is not merely establishing a presence on the Internet. It can be a virtual addition to the existing library structure, reaching out to patrons around the clock and providing valuable information resources.

Additionally, a library's Web site is an important source of information about the library.

The library's Internet policies, special programming, and new materials can all be made viewable at any time from the Web site. Libraries, too, should be designing their own Web sites that serve as portals to interesting sites that have been reviewed and annotated by professional librarians. Librarians will continue to play an important role as information professionals in the Information Age, well into the 21st century.

MARKETING OF LIBRARY SERVICES

In recent years, libraries of all types from all countries have found it necessary to compete for both money and clients as major changes have occurred.

The Internet brings a whole new dimension of competition that public, academic, and special libraries are facing daily. Whereas budget problems have been around for some time, the recent competition from the Internet can translate into fewer users, despite the fact that the Internet is also a crucial tool used by librarians for research and marketing.

Because of all of these existing challenges and intensifying changes at least a handful of libraries have turned to 'tried and true' business models for improved planning and development, and that they are employing marketing plans as one method for moving forward.

As time goes on, libraries must think about marketing of their services and resources to achieve goals. It is important to clarify what marketing means in a library environment.

Marketing is not so much about 'selling' information products to researchers, as it is more about spreading the word about potentially useful new tools. It is also about keeping users informed about library activities and involving them in collection development. It is more about integrating new research tools into existing, effective research processes, and in some way enhancing researchers' work, rather than selling the tool to users as an end in itself.

As librarians market new tools, they should know how the tools may offer clarity, and not simply contribute to noise for the users. Effective marketing can only occur when librarians understand, at least in a broad sense, what the scientists, professors, and graduate students are already doing to keep informed, and what their research projects are about.

LIBRARY TECHNOLOGY: PLANNING FOR THE FUTURE

Whether public, private, or corporate, libraries are experiencing rapid changes as technology increasingly permeates their methodology and functionality. These technological changes affect all levels of librarianship, and management of new library resources and new expectations of staff must adapt accordingly. As suggested, discuss management of resources and staff in today's fluctuating technological environment. In the first part, as suggested, use a systems development model to organize the discussion of resource management. In the second part, as suggested, turn our attention to issues that arise in the intersection between staff and technology by focusing on barriers to learning, online learning alternatives, and changes in staff development practices.

6

Development of Public Libraries

INTRODUCTION

Public libraries arose worldwide along with growth in education, literacy, and publications. Every country has its own public library history with influential leaders. Monarchs, wealthy people, and philanthropists have all made a contribution to society in the form of public library development. India is no exception. Libraries were established in ancient India mainly by the patronage extended by emperors, major capitalists, and scholars. Indian emperors and kings were supported scholars and scholarship. There is evidence of well-developed libraries even in the sixth century A.D. The famous Nalanda University in Bihar had its own magnificent library with a massive collection of manuscripts covering the universe of knowledge. Admission to library was restricted to scholars.

Other ancient universities, such as Taxila and Vikramashila, also had valuable libraries. Muslim influence in India during the 13th century A.D. marked the dawn of another era of learning and scholarship. The Mughal period gave a further stimulus to the growth of libraries. Mughal rulers attached considerable importance to libraries and appointed scholars as librarians. The Mughal emperors were patrons of art and literature. In the period of Emperor Babur, Humayun, and Akbar many new libraries were established and existing ones further developed. Mughal libraries featured magnificent buildings, rare manuscripts, and scholar librarians. The names of Maharaja Sawai Man Singh of Jaipur and Maharaja Ranjit Singh of Punjab will be remembered with appreciation in the history of library services in India. The Maharaja of Tanjuar started the famous Saraswati Mahal Library in 17th century A.D. It remains a unique institution in its nature of collection and services Libraries established by the kings and capitalists functioned like private institutions and the admission was limited. Service to the general public had to wait for the British. Unfortunately, the arrival of the British and resulting political disorder also brought chaos to the Indian way of life. This was a severe blow to the cultural heritage of India, which had arisen from the Indus valley civilization. When libraries began developing in India during the early nineteenth century, they were a western product. In 1808, the Government of Bombay proposed to register libraries, which were to be given copies of books published from the "funds for the encouragement of literature". According to the "Sinha Committee", this was the beginning of the first phase of public library development in India. During the first half of the 19th century, the three presidency towns of Bombay, Calcutta, and Madras had public libraries. These libraries were mostly financed by Europeans residing in these towns.

Of these, the establishment of the public library at Calcutta in 1835 was the most significant. This was the library which later developed into the National Library of India. Almost simultaneous, subscription libraries were started in many Indian cities. These were, of course, not public libraries in the true sense of the term, and did not provide free books for all. Founded in imitation of their western counterparts, the use of these libraries was confined to small, affluent portion of society. The first three decades of the 20th century can be looked on as the golden age of the Indian library system. On January 31, 1902, the Imperial Library Act was passed and Lord Curzon transformed the Calcutta Public Library into the Imperial Library in 1906. Developments in Baroda were also notable. Espranza sums them up:

- The development of public libraries in Baroda was unique. Baroda developed a network of public libraries to serve the entire Princely State. Maharaja Sayaji Rao Gaekwad III of Baroda who traveled all over the world was deeply impressed by the role played by public libraries in the promotion of education in the United States and thought of extending such benefits to his own subjects. In 1910 he invited an American expert, William Alson Borden to organize the public library system for his state. The public library movement that flourished in Baroda was a glorious one. But that was not a general trend of that period because in no other part of India, a parallel development occurred.

Yet another development during the period was the organisation of a host of conferences such as:

- The first conference of library workers and persons interested in the library movement was held at Beswada, Andhra in 1914.
- The first All India Library Conference of Librarians was held in 1918 at Lahore.
- The first All India Library Conference was held at Calcutta in 1933.
- The first All India Public Library Conference was held at Madras in 1934.

With the existence of democratic governments in several provinces beginning in 1937, another phase of the library movement began. Between 1937 and 1942, a number of village libraries and travelling libraries sprang up in Assam, Bihar, Punjab, and Travancore. It was estimated that there were about 13,000 village libraries in India in 1942. Another remarkable development was the appointment of the 'Library Development Committee' by the Government of Bombay, with A.A.A. Fyzee as its chairman. The Committee ambitiously recommended a comprehensive library system to be implemented in three successive stages. Because of financial constraints, the government could only implement part of the recommendations.

AFTER INDEPENDENCE

After independence, the growth of libraries in general has been remarkable, although not as remarkable as that of academic and special libraries. At the time of independence, India was facing a host of challenges. Those in the rural population, 88 percent of the total, were nearly all illiterate. Transportation was poor and mass media merely nominal. Nevertheless, the public library scene in India improved considerably during the post independence period, though it is still lacking on several fronts. Verma and Agrawal argue that to compare our public libraries with those of the developed nations on equal footing, we have to go a long way. The 1951 census, the first conducted after independence, found 2,843 local governments in the urban and rural areas in India, of which 320 were rural district boards.

Only about one third of local governments maintained public libraries, about 950. In addition, there were about 1,500 subscription libraries. So-called public libraries were primarily reading rooms with a few hundred books for reading on the premises. The Delhi public library deserves special mention. It was founded in 1951 as the first UNESCO Public Library Pilot Project under the joint auspices of UNESCO and Government of India. The purpose of the library was to adapt "modern techniques to Indian conditions" and to serve as a model public library for Asia. The establishment of Delhi Public Library, the involvement of union government in the public library movement, and the enactment of public library legislation in some states are the main factors which contributed to the improvement of public libraries after independence. Although the government of India allotted funds for public library development in its five-year plans, this funding was not connected to effective planning.

ADVISORY COMMITTEE FOR LIBRARIES

The Government of India appointed a committee in 1957 to report on the status of public library development in the country. It is also called the Sinha Committee, after its chair, the late Dr. A.P. Sinha, who was at that time Director of Public Instruction in Bihar. The Sinha Committee's charge included:

- Determining present reading needs, how they are met, and what part existing library systems play in meeting the needs;
- Determining reading tastes, what agencies provide suitable literature, and how reading taste can be improved;

- Recommending future library structure in India;
- Recommending areas of cooperation between libraries and education systems;
- Considering the training of librarians and the conditions of their service;
- Recommending the administrative and financial measures necessary to support public libraries in India.

The committee submitted its report to Dr. K.L. Shrimali, who was Minister for Education, on the 12th of November, 1958. The Committee described the situation as dismal and called libraries in most cases, "a stagnant pool of books," because new books were not added regularly. The committee at the same time observed that wherever large collections did exist, they were not fully used because of rigid rules. Library users were not trusted and were required to deposit large sums of money as a kind of insurance, which lower income people could not afford. As of March 1954 there were 32,000 libraries in India, with a little more than 7,100,000 books and a total circulation of about 37,700,000. The report observed that genuine public library service was rarity, and that public library service throughout the country was unsatisfactory. The committee recommended creating state library networks based on uniform library legislation. The chief recommendations of the report were:

- Library service should be made free to every citizen of India;
- The hierarchy of public library service in the country should begin with National Library, and proceed to State Central Library, District Library, Block Library, and Panchayat Library;
- An independent Director of Social Education and Libraries should be set up in every state, with a fulltime senior class-1 officer of the rank of Deputy Director of Education to plan, organize, and administer library services;
- An All India Library Advisory Council should be constituted as a central agency to review and assess the work done at the state level;
- Library Associations should actively assist the development of libraries in the country;
- University libraries should cooperate with public library systems by allowing selected public readers to use their collection;
- State governments should accept responsibility for public library services in their states;
- Librarians and social education workers should cooperate to promote literacy;
- A library cess of six paisa for each rupee of property tax should be levied with the permission of local bodies.
- The Government of India should match the amount collected in the states. State governments should also give matching grants to local

bodies over the succeeding 25 years, their contribution should be raised to three times the cess collected.

- State and national governments should enact comprehensive state library laws incorporating the right of every citizen to have free access to libraries. The Government of India should provide necessary financial assistance to the state governments for this purpose.

RAJA RAM MOHAN ROY LIBRARY FOUNDATION

Another positive step taken by the Central Government was the establishment of the *Raja Ram Mohan Roy Library Foundation* (RRRLF) at Calcutta on May 22, 1972, as a part of the bicentenary celebrations of the birth of Raja Ram Mohan Roy, a social reformer of the early 19th century. Its objectives are library development in general and rural library development in particular. It provides financial assistance to public libraries in the form of matching grants. It assists State Central Libraries and District Central Libraries, which has helped many states and Union Territories develop rural public library services.

MAIN OBJECTIVES OF RRRLF

The main objectives of RRRLF are:

- Promotion of the library movement in India;
- The adoption of a national library policy by the central and state governments;
- Development of a National Library System by integrating the services of National Libraries, State Central Libraries, District Libraries, and other types of libraries through an interlibrary lending system;
- Propagation and adoption of library legislation in the country;
- Provision of financial and technical assistance to libraries;
- Provision of financial assistance to voluntary organizations and library associations for the promotion of library development;
- Periodic publication of reports on library development;
- To act as a clearing house for ideas and information on library development in India and abroad;
- To advise the Government of India library development;
- Promotion of research in problems of library development

The primary objective of RRRLF is the promotion of the library movement. The rest are subsidiary objectives. RRRLF is the first government-sponsored body specifically created for this purpose. The foundation also has a programme of assistance to libraries for workshops, conferences, and exhibits. The foundation has taken the major initiative for the formulation of a national policy on library and information systems by the Government of India. The current programmes of assistance are:

- Collection building;
- Rural libraries and mobile library service for rural areas;
- Seminars, workshops, conferences, training courses, and exhibits;
- Facilities and equipment for storage and display of materials;
- Public library buildings;
- Television and VCR equipment for educational purposes;
- Assistance to voluntary organisations providing public library services;
- Assistance to children's libraries or children's sections of general public libraries

During the last three decades, the foundation has assisted more than 500 libraries, including many in rural areas

NATIONAL POLICY ON LIBRARY AND INFORMATION SYSTEM (NAPLIS)

In 1985, a committee was set up under the chairmanship of Prof. D.P. Chattopadhyay to formulate a *National Policy on Library and Information System* (NAPLIS). The Committee submitted its report in May 1986. Following that, another committee looked at implications of the report and created an action plan for its implementation.The Empowerment Committee submitted its report in April 1988 and an Implementation Cell was formed to implement its recommendations within a period of six months. Yet another Working Group, under the Joint Secretary to the Government of India in the Department of Culture, was constituted to examine its recommendations for implementation. The Working Group submitted its report in July 1993 and suggested implementing only 29 of 60 recommendations made by the NAPLIS. The following are some of the recommendations of NAPLIS related to public libraries:

- Proposals for maintenance and development of public libraries should preferably come from State Legislative Enactment. The Central Government may revise the Model Public Library Bill. Funds for library development should come from each state, either from general revenue or from local taxation. Central Government agencies may provide funds under Plan Expenditure.
- Efforts should emphasize rural public libraries. A village or a cluster of villages with an adequate population should have a community library/rural community centre, which will also serve as an information centre. Resources from various agencies engaged in the public health, adult education, State and central government, etc., should be used to build up and maintain this centre.
- The central government increase its assistance to state governments in the development of public libraries. The RRRLF, as the national agency for coordinating and assisting the development of public libraries, should be suitably strengthened in order to do this.

- Standards and guidelines for library service should be created.
- There should be a system of national libraries consisting of National Library, Calcutta as the National Library of India, National Depository libraries in Delhi, Bombay, Madras, National Subject Libraries, and others. These national libraries should form part of one integrated system.
- A National Commission on Libraries and Information System or National Commission on Informatics and Documentation may be constituted by an Act of Parliament to serve under the Ministry of Human Resource Development. The Commission will have representation from appropriate central and state agencies and could provide guidance and coordinate library development programmes in all sectors. This body will have the primary responsibility for the implementation of NAPLIS programmes.
- National Depository libraries; Connemara Public library, Chennai; Central Library, Bombay; and Delhi Public Library, Delhi should concentrate on development of collections and preservation of Indian culture produced in the languages of their regions, supplementing and complementing the efforts of the Indian National Library.
- The Indian National Bibliography should have a comprehensive coverage of the national output of documents and should be updated regularly. This responsibility should be vested in the National Library.
- Government should create a national awareness of the need to preserve the nation's cultural heritage. National libraries should be responsible, with preservation facilities created there. Links between libraries, archives, and museums should be established for the purpose of national preservation.
- The Ministry of Rural Development has a plan for one community centre in every Panchayat Centre. The Department of Culture and the Ministry of Rural Development have agreed to provide library services at each of these Rural Community Centres.
- An important link should be established between community centre library and primary schools. If the schools do not have libraries of their own, the community centre library should provide children with adequate services.
- A community centre library should have an important role in adult education programmes.
- A district library should provide facilities and recreation for the disabled and low-income people, *e.g.*, literature in Braille.
- Libraries should be built in areas of tribal concentration and in minority communities to help in developing and sustaining their distinctive cultures.

- Libraries should be equipped with relevant resources, such as publications covering Open University and vocational educational courses, for their role in support of distance education.
- All public libraries within a state should form a part of a network extending from village library through community centre library, district library, and state network, and should be linked to the national information grid.

1951-1956

- The first five-year plan for educational development included a proposal for "Improvement of Library Service." This proposal envisioned a network of libraries throughout the country, coordinated by National Central Library at New Delhi
- During the first five-year plan, nine state governments, *i.e.*, Assam, Madhya Pradesh, West Bengal, Punjab, PEPSU, Rajasthan, Savarashtra, Bhopal, and Vindhya Pradesh, decided to set up State Central Libraries.

1956-1961

- At this time, the government allocated funds to set up a national network of libraries in its 320 districts. As a result, most states established State Central Libraries and District Libraries as the main distributing centres

1961-1966

During this period, the system of central government assistance to the states was changed, and funding for libraries was kept to a minimum. It was up to the individual states to take initiative and develop their public libraries. The programme to assist state governments in establishing state central libraries, district central libraries, and block development libraries was abandoned.The decision was a major setback to the development of public libraries. During this period four national libraries were established at Delhi, Calcutta, Bombay, and Madras. A Working Group on libraries was appointed by the Planning Commission in 1964 to take a stock of library development. The working group submitted its report on 7th September 1965 with following recommendations:

- The central and state governments should share responsibility for providing adequate public library service. New government agencies in the central government under the Minister of Education, a directorate of libraries and a state library advisory council in each state should be set up to execute the programmes effectively.
- State central libraries should be established in four states: Madhya Pradesh, Mysore, Nagaland, and Orissa.

- States which do not possess adequate functional buildings for their state central libraries should be provided with library buildings.
- The state central library must have a children's section.
- There should be 335 District Libraries for the 327 districts in the country, *i.e.*, in large and populous districts, two district libraries may be provided.
- New buildings should be constructed for the existing 100 district libraries.
- Block libraries are the chief feeding centre for the rural reading public, and therefore, 2,500 new block libraries, covering 75 per cent of blocks in the country should be constructed.
- A sum of 10 million rupees shall be provided for distribution of grant in aid to such libraries of urban and rural areas which depend on subscription and donations.
- Three public libraries on model of Delhi Public Library should be set up
- The Institute of Library Science established by the Ministry of Education at Delhi University in 1958-59, and then closed in 1962, should be reopened. Such institutes should be established at the state levels also to train graduate and undergraduate librarians to meet future requirements.
- A sum of `.10,000 shall be allocated as financial assistance to all national level and state level library associations to create library consciousness in the country by organizing seminars, conducting surveys, and producing library literature.
- A programme of book production should be undertaken.
- A draft of the Library Act should be produced

1969-1974

This plan proposed a substantial sum for the social education programme. A much lower sum was allocated. Of this, only a very small amount was available for the development of libraries in the country.

1974-1979

This plan included measures to strengthen the buildings, collections, and staff of the central and state libraries, as well as strengthening the district, block, and village libraries. During this period, attempts were made to develop a district-level library system, so that district library could act as a leader for the smaller libraries in the district. The adult education programme was the hallmark of this plan. The programme was to be supported by a network of libraries at the village and block levels and various community centres. Thus steps were taken to strengthen not only the village and block libraries, but also the central, state libraries and the district libraries.

1980-85

This plan emphasized establishing a network of rural public libraries to sustain literacy and disseminate information to rural areas. It discussed the necessity of integrating school and college libraries with the system of public libraries. During this period, 26 states or union territories out of 31 had established state central libraries and 291 district libraries.

1985-90

During this period, the Commission's objective was to address the needs of 90 million people in the Adult Education Programme. The network of libraries was to play a role in the development of literature for neo-literates. Library systems were to be strengthened, with specific attention given to improvement of facilities at national level institutions. An important development was the 1986 adoption of National Literacy Mission, which emphasised the education of women and the establishment of rural libraries. In addition, the RRRLF set up an Integrated Research Cell-cum-Computer Unit for promoting research in librarianship and database of public libraries in the country There were two annual plans for the years 1990-91 and 1991-92.

1992-97

During this period it was proposed to reorganize the Central Reference Library into the National Bibliographical and Documentation Centre, which would also have a computer centre. The Delhi Public Library set up two new libraries in its service area. RRRLF created programmes to help state central libraries purchase reprographic equipment, to help libraries process rare books, and to give special assistance to networks of public libraries that were at least 100 years old.

1997-2002

During the 9th five year plan, the National Library, Kolkatta, undertook several major initiatives to upgrade and modernize its collection building programme, reader services, and conservation of library material. The major activities completed during the period were automation of the circulation system in the lending section, setting up of a local area network, improved reader services, and more efficient collection management. The conservation activities in the library got a major advance with the purchase of modern equipment to preserve rare books and other materials. The Central Reference Library, Kolkatta computerised various functions during the Ninth Plan. As a result, the publication of the *Indian National Bibliography* is now up to date, with records available online.

Funds were provided to the Delhi Public Library and Central Secretariat Library, Delhi, for acquisition of new material in different languages and media as well as for modernizing their infrastructure. The benefits of these efforts can be seen in improved reader services, networking, and resource sharing. The Central Secretariat Library organized a number of computer training programmes for resource sharing, standardization of cataloguing formats, and co-operative acquisition. Funds for modernizing and computerization were also provided from central grants to the Connemara Library, Chennai, Thanjavur Maharaja Serovji Sarasvati Mahal Library, Thanjavur and the State Central Library, Mumbai. Besides these, the RRRLF provided assistance to public libraries across the country for collections and storage, construction, and seminars and workshops.

Tenth Five-Year Plan (Action Plan)

The Planning Commission proposed further modernization of central and public libraries during the Tenth Plan. A national bibliographic database would be developed to encourage resource sharing, networking, and to improve reader services. The Commission resolved to strengthen public library infrastructure through the RRRLF. The Tenth Plan focused on upgrading existing libraries, including private collections, and widening the programme for bibliographic control and documentation. To make readers services more comprehensive and effective, the National Library is expected to act as the ultimate referral centre for various subjects. To keep pace with the latest developments in information technology in public libraries, the upgrading and networking of central and state libraries was also planned.

PUBLIC LIBRARY

A public library is a library that is accessible by the public and is generally funded from public sources and operated by civil servants. There are five fundamental characteristics shared by public libraries. The first is that they are supported by taxes; they are governed by a board to serve the public interest; they are open to all and every community member can access the collection; they are entirely voluntary in that no one is ever forced to use the services provided; and public libraries provide basic services without charge.

Public libraries exist in many countries across the world and are often considered an essential part of having an educated and literate population. Public libraries are distinct from research libraries, school libraries, and other special libraries in that their mandate is to serve the general public's information needs. Public Libraries also provide free services such as preschool story times to encourage early literacy, quiet study and work areas for students and professionals, or book clubs to encourage appreciation of literature in adults. Public libraries typically allow users to take books and other materials off the premises temporarily; they also have non-circulating reference collections and provide computer and Internet access to patrons.

SERVICES OFFERED

In addition to print books and periodicals, most public libraries today have a wide array of other media including audiobooks, e-books, CDs, cassettes, videotapes, DVDs, and video games, as well as facilities to access the Internet and inter-library loans. Readers' advisory is a fundamental public library service that involves suggesting fiction and non-fiction titles. Public libraries may also provide other services, such as community meeting rooms, storytelling sessions for infants, toddlers, preschool children, or after-school programmes, all with an intention of developing early literacy skills and a love of books. In person and on-line programmes for reader development, language learning, homework help, free lectures and cultural performances, and other community service programmes are common offerings. One of the most popular programmes offered in public libraries are summer reading programmes for children, families, and adults.

In rural areas, the local public library may have, in addition to its main branch, a mobile library service, consisting of one or more buses furnished as a small public library, serving the countryside according to a regular schedule. Public libraries also provide materials for children, often housed in a special section. Child oriented web sites with on-line educational games and programmes specifically designed for younger library users are becoming increasingly popular. Services may be provided for other groups, such as large print or Braille materials, Books on tape, young adult literature and other materials for teenagers, or materials in other than the national language.

California and Nevada now offer a new service called Link. This new programme links county libraries across the two states, allowing patrons access to books their library may not have in their collection. Librarians at most public libraries provide reference and research help to the general public, usually at a reference desk but can often be done by telephone interview. As online discussion and social networking allow for remote access, reference is becoming available virtually through the use of the Internet and e-mail. Depending on the size of the library, there may be more than one desk; at some smaller libraries all transactions may occur at one desk, while large urban public libraries may employ subject-specialist librarians with the ability to staff multiple reference or information desks to answer queries about particular topics at any time during regular operating hours. Often the children's section in a public library has its own reference desk. Public libraries are also increasingly making use of web 2.0 services, including the use of online social networks by libraries. Public libraries in some countries pay authors when their books are borrowed from libraries. These are known as Public Lending Right programme.

COMMERCIAL AND GOVERNMENTAL SERVICES

As more commercial and governmental services are being provided online, public libraries increasingly provide Internet access for users who otherwise would not be able to connect to these services. Part of the public library mission has become attempting to help bridge the digital divide. A study conducted in 2006 found that "72.5 percent of library branches report that they are the only provider of free public computer and Internet access in their communities". A 2008 study found that "100 percent of rural, high poverty outlets provide public Internet access, a significant increase from 85.7 percent last year". The *American Library Association* (ALA), addresses this role of libraries as part of "access to information" and "equity of access"; part of the profession's ethical commitment that "no one should be denied information because he or she cannot afford the cost of a book or periodical, have access to the internet or information in any of its various formats." In addition to access, many public libraries offer training and support to computer users.

Once access has been achieved, there still remains a large gap in people's online abilities and skills. For many communities, the public library is the only agency offering free computer classes and information technology learning. As of 2008, 73.4 percent of public libraries offered information technology training of some form, including information literacy skills and homework assignment help.

A significant service provided by public libraries is assisting people with e-government access and use of federal, state and local government information, forms and services. Internationally, public libraries offer *information and communication technology* (ICT) services, giving "access to information and knowledge" the "highest priority." While different countries and areas of the world have their own requirements, general services offered include free connection to the Internet, training in using the Internet, and relevant content in appropriate languages. In addition to typical public library financing, *non-governmental organizations* (NGOs) and business fund services that assist public libraries in combating the digital divide.

ORIGINS AS A SOCIAL INSTITUTION

The culmination of centuries of advances in the printing press, moveable type, paper, ink, publishing, and distribution, combined with an ever growing middle class, increased commercial activity and consumption, new radical ideas, massive population growth and higher literacy rates forged the public library into the form that it is today. Public libraries are not a new idea; Romans made scrolls in dry rooms available to patrons of the baths, and tried with some success to establish libraries within the empire.

Naturally, only those few that could afford an education would be able to use the library, where those less than rich or without control of money; women, children and slaves could not. In the middle of the 19th century, the push for truly public libraries, paid for by taxes and run by the state gained force after numerous depressions, droughts, wars and revolutions in Europe, felt mostly by the working class. Matthew Battles states that:

- "It was in these years of class conflict and economic terror that the public library movement swept through Britain, as the nation's progressive elite recognized that the light of cultural and intellectual energy was lacking in the lives of commoners".

Libraries had often been started with a donation, an endowment or were bequeathed to various, parishes, churches, schools or towns, and these social and institutional libraries formed the base of many academic and public library collections of today. Andrew Carnegie had the biggest influence in financing libraries in the United States of America, from the east to west coast. From just 1900 to 1917, almost 1,700 libraries were constructed by Carnegie's foundation, insisting that local communities first guarantee tax support of each library built.The establishment of circulating libraries by booksellers and publishers provided a means of gaining profit and creating social centers within the community. The circulating libraries not only provided a place to sell books, but also a place to lend books for a price. These circulating libraries provided a variety of materials including the increasingly popular novels. Although the circulating libraries filled an important role in society, members of the middle and upper classes often looked down upon these libraries that regularly sold material from their collections and provided materials that were less sophisticated. Circulating libraries also charged a subscription fee, however the fees were set to entice their patrons, providing subscriptions on a yearly, quarterly or monthly basis, without expecting the subscribers to purchase a share in the circulating library.

Circulating libraries were not exclusively lending institutions and often provided a place for other forms of commercial activity, which may or may not be related to print. This was necessary because the circulating libraries did not generate enough funds through subscription fees collected from its borrowers. As a commerce venture, it was important to consider the contributing factors such as other goods or services available to the subscribers. Many claims have been made for the title of "first public library" for various libraries in various countries, with at least some of the confusion arising from differing interpretations of what should be considered a true "public library".

Difficulties in establishing what policies were in effect at different times in the history of particular libraries also add to the confusion. The first libraries open to the public were the collections of Greek and Latin scrolls which were available in the dry sections of the many buildings that made up the huge Roman baths of the Roman empire. However, they were not lending libraries. The "halls of science" run by different Islamic sects in many cities of North Africa and the Middle East in the 9th century were open to the public. Some of them had written lending policies, but they were very restrictive. Most patrons were expected to consult the books on site. The later European university libraries were not open to the general public, but accessible by scholars.

HISTORY

A public library is a library funded by public money, such as taxpayer money. The purpose of a public library is to provide books, Internet access and many other resources to the public for free. Even DVDs and movies are available for free rentals. Public libraries are not new, in fact the first organization that was considered to be a public library was created in the late 1500s.

- The first public library was created in England. At that time, the only people who were able to use libraries were individuals who joined a cathedral or were enrolled in college. This public library was called Francis Trigge Chained Library. This public library actually still exists and is famous for its long standing history of giving the people free access to all library resources. Although this library was the first, it stood nearly alone in its existence until the mid 1800s. That was the time period in which public libraries began to become popular.
- In England, Parliament decided to make a committee dedicated to considering the creation of multiple public libraries. The committee was supposed to decide if a public library was something that would benefit the public. The committee reported back that public libraries would be beneficial, since so many people were poor. The recommendation was to open multiple public libraries throughout the country. This decision led to the Public Libraries Act of 1850. The act allowed all cities to collect taxes for public library support, providing that the population of the city had at least 10,000 people.
- This was quickly followed by the Public School Law, created in 1870. The point of this law was to raise the literacy rate of the public, since it was very low at the time. The only people who really knew how to read were rich people and scholars. Obviously, this literacy need increased the need for public libraries. By the 1870s, over 50 cities had created public libraries of their own. Only 30 years later, the number of public libraries hit 300. This was the time when public libraries began opening everywhere, and the United States began funding them as well. A public library was funded by public money, but it was also common for the people to help out these public libraries grow and flourish. Womens' clubs and the wealthy donated books to these public libraries to improve their selections.

Today, there are hundreds of thousands of public libraries in the world. The larger the city, the more public libraries will be found there. Unfortunately, despite the great need and desire for public libraries, funding for them are cut consistently by the state legislature. Large amounts of money to fund public libraries are made by private donors who have the wealth and desire to see a public library being used.

17TH CENTURY

In the early years of the 17th century, many famous collegiate and town libraries were founded throughout the country. Francis Trigge Chained Library of St. Wulfram's Church, Grantham, Lincolnshire was founded in 1598 by the rector of nearby Welbourne. Norwich City library was established in 1608, and Chetham's Library in Manchester, which claims to be the oldest public library in the English-speaking world, opened in 1653.

Other early town libraries of the UK include those of:

- Ipswich (1612),
- Bristol (founded in 1613 and opened in 1615), and
- Leicester (1632).

Shrewsbury School also opened its library to townsfolk. In Bristol, an early library that allowed access to the public was that of the Kalendars or Kalendaries, a brotherhood of clergy and laity who were attached to the Church of All-Hallowen or All Saints. Records show that in 1464, provision was made for a library to be erected in the house of the Kalendars, and reference is made to a deed of that date by which it was "appointed that all who wish to enter for the sake of instruction shall have 'free access and recess' at certain times".

EARLY 18TH CENTURY

At the turn of the 18th century, libraries were becoming increasingly public and were more frequently lending libraries. The 18th century saw the switch from closed parochial libraries to lending libraries. Before this time, public libraries were parochial in nature and libraries frequently chained their books to desks. Libraries also were not uniformly open to the public. In 1790, The Public Library Act would not be passed for another sixty-seven years. Even though the British Museum existed at this time and contained over 50,000 books, the national library was not open to the public, or even to a majority of the population. Access to the Museum depended on passes, of which there was sometimes a waiting period of three to four weeks.

Moreover, the library was not open to browsing. Once a pass to the library had been issued, the reader was taken on a tour of the library. Many readers complained that the tour was much too short. At the turn of the century, there were virtually no public libraries in the sense in which we now understand the term, *i.e.*, libraries provided from public funds and freely accessible to all. Only one important library in Great Britain, namely Chetham's Library in Manchester, was fully and freely accessible to the public.

However, there had come into being a whole network of library provision on a private or institutional basis. Subscription libraries, both private and commercial, provided the middle and middle to upper class with a variety of books for moderate fees.

The increase in secular literature at this time encouraged the spread of lending libraries, especially the commercial subscription libraries. Commercial subscription libraries began when booksellers began renting out extra copies of books in the mid-18th century. Steven Fischer estimates that in 1790, there were 'about six hundred rental and lending libraries, with a clientele of some fifty thousand. The mid to late 18th century saw a virtual epidemic of feminine reading as novels became more and more popular. Novels, while frowned upon in society, were extremely popular. In England there were many who lamented at the 'villanous profane and obscene books' and the opposition to the circulating library, on moral grounds, persisted well into the 19th century. Still, many establishments must have circulated many times the number of novels as of any other genre. In 1797, Thomas Wilson wrote in *The Use of Circulating Libraries*: "Consider, that for a successful circulating library, the collection must contain 70 per cent fiction". However, the overall percentage of novels mainly depended on the proprietor of the circulating library. While some circulating libraries were almost completely novels, others had less than 10 per cent of their overall collection in the form of novels. The national average at the turn of the century hovered around novels comprising about 20 per cent of the total collection. Novels varied from other types of books in many ways.

They were read primarily for enjoyment instead of for study. They did not provide academic knowledge or spiritual guidance; thus they were read quickly and far fewer times than other books. These were the perfect books for commercial subscription libraries to lend. Since books were read for pure enjoyment rather than for scholarly work, books needed to become both cheaper and smaller. Small duodecimo editions of books were preferred to the large folio editions. Folio editions were read at a desk, while the small duodecimo editions could be easily read like the paperbacks of today. Much like paperbacks of today, many of the novels in circulating libraries were unbound.

At this period of time, many people chose to bind their books in leather. Many circulating libraries skipped this process. Circulating libraries were not in the business of preserving books; their owners wanted to lend books as many times as they possibly could. Circulating libraries had ushered in a completely new way of reading. Reading was no longer simply an academic pursuit or an attempt to gain spiritual guidance. Reading became a social activity. Many circulating libraries were attached to the shops of milliners or drapers. They served as much for social gossip and the meeting of friends as coffee shops do today. Another factor in the growth of subscription libraries was the increasing cost of books. In the last two decades of the century, especially, prices were practically doubled, so that a quarto work cost a guinea, an octavo 10 shillings or 12 shillings, and a duodecimo cost 4 shillings per volume.

Price apart, moreover, books were difficult to procure outside London, since local booksellers could not afford to carry large stocks. Commercial libraries, since they were usually associated with booksellers, and also since they had a greater number of patrons, were able to accumulate greater numbers of books. The United Public Library was said to have a collection of some 52,000 volumes-–twice as many as any private subscription library in the country at that period. These libraries, since they functioned as a business, also lent books to non-subscribers on a per-book system.

PRIVATE SUBSCRIPTION LIBRARIES

Private subscription libraries functioned in much the same manner as commercial subscription libraries, though they varied in many important ways. One of the most popular versions of the private subscription library was a gentleman's only library. The gentlemen's subscription libraries, sometimes known as proprietary libraries, were nearly all organized on a common pattern. Membership was restricted to the proprietors or shareholders, and ranged from a dozen or two to between four and five hundred. The entrance fee, *i.e.*, the purchase price of a share, was in early days usually a guinea, but rose sharply as the century advanced, often reaching four or five guineas during the French wars; the annual subscription, during the same period, rose from about six shillings to ten shillings or more.

The book-stock was, by modern standards, small and was accommodated, at the outset, in makeshift premises--very often over a bookshop, with the bookseller acting as librarian and receiving an honourarium for his pains. The Liverpool Subscription library was a gentlemen only library. In 1798, it was renamed the Athenaeum when it was rebuilt with a newsroom and coffeehouse. It had an entrance fee of one guinea and annual subscription of five shillings. While no records survive of the commercial library lendings, we have the Bristol Library's continuous record of borrowings from 1773 to 1857. An analysis of the registers for the first twelve years provides some fascinating glimpses of middle-class reading habits in a mercantile community at this period. The largest and most popular sections of the library were History, Antiquities, and Geography, with 283 titles and 6,121 borrowings, and Belles Lettres, with 238 titles and 3,313 borrowings. Far below came Theology and Ecclesiastical History, Natural History and Chemistry, Philosophy, Jurisprudence, Miscellanies, Mathematics, etc., and Medicine and Anatomy, all with fewer than 100 titles. The most popular single work was John Hawkesworth's *Account of Voyages... in the Southern Hemisphere* which was borrowed on 201 occasions.

The records also show that in 1796, membership had risen by 1/3 to 198 subscribers and the titles increased five-fold to 4,987. This mirrors the increase in reading interests. A patron list from the Bath Municipal Library shows that from 1793 to 1799, the library held a stable 30 per cent of their patrons as female. It was also uncommon for these libraries to have buildings designated solely as the library building during the 1790s, though in the 19th century, many libraries would begin building elaborate permanent residences. Bristol, Birmingham, and Liverpool were the few libraries with their own building. The accommodations varied from the shelf for a few dozen volumes in the country stationer's or draper's shop, to the expansion to a back room, to the spacious elegant areas of Hookham's or those at the resorts like Scarborough, and four in a row at Margate. Private subscription libraries held a greater amount of control over both membership and the types of books in the library. There was almost a complete elimination of cheap fiction in the private societies. Subscription libraries prided themselves on respectability. The highest percentage of subscribers were often landed proprietors, gentry, and old professions. Towards the end of the 18th century and in the first decades of the nineteenth the need for books and general education made itself felt among social classes created by the beginnings of the Industrial Revolution.

The late 18th century saw a rise in subscription libraries intended for the use of tradesmen. In 1797, there was established at Kendal what was known as the Economical Library, "designed principally for the use and instruction of the working classes." There was also the Artizans' library established at Birmingham in 1799. The entrance fee was 3 shillings. The subscription was 1 shilling 6 pence per quarter. This was a library of general literature. Novels, at first excluded, were afterwards admitted on condition that they did not account for more than one-tenth of the annual income.

RATE-SUPPORTED LIBRARIES

Although by the mid-19th century, England could claim 274 subscription libraries and Scotland, 266, the foundation of the modern public library system in the UK is the Public Libraries Act 1850. Prior to this, the municipalities of Warrington and Salford established libraries in their museums, under the terms of the Museums Act of 1845.Warrington Municipal Library opened in 1848. Salford Museum and Art Gallery first opened in November 1850 as "The Royal Museum and Public Library", as the first unconditionally free public library in England. The library in Campfield, Manchester was the first library to operate a *free* lending library without subscription in 1852. Norwich lays claims to being the first municipality to adopt the Public Libraries Act 1850 but theirs was the eleventh library to open, in 1857, being the eleventh in the country after:

- Winchester,
- Manchester,
- Liverpool,
- Bolton,
- Kidderminster,
- Cambridge,

- Birkenhead and
- Sheffield.

The Scottish-American philanthropist and businessman, Andrew Carnegie, helped to increase the number of public libraries from the late 19th century. County libraries are a later development which were made possible by the establishment of County Councils in 1888. They normally have a large central library in a major town with smaller branch libraries in other towns and a mobile library service covering rural areas.

NORTH AMERICA

Canada

In 1779 Frederick Haldimand, the Governor of Québec City, founded the first subscription library in Canada. Until then, Canada's libraries were mostly religious institutions, and the general public was not admitted. However, even though "Haldimand's library, like other subscription libraries, appealed primarily to an urban elite", it was the nation's first step towards the public library as it is known today. Haldimand's library later merged with the Literary and Historical Society of Quebec, which displays the original Québec Library collection within its library. This and similar association/social libraries were examples of early prototypes of public libraries.

They were public in that membership was allowed regardless of class or religion, and many in Canada eventually evolved into free public libraries. "Subsequently legislative collections were established in 1791 in Upper and in 1792 in Lower Canada; and in 1796 the first public library was founded in Montreal. In 1800, libraries were established in King's College, Nova Scotia, and at Niagara, where the first public library in Upper Canada operated for twenty years, in spite of losses during the War of 1812.". In Saint John, New Brunswick in 1883, following the efforts of Colonel James Domville in procuring a collection of materials to replace the many private collections lost in the Great Fire of Saint John, New Brunswick the first free, tax-supported public library was established. Guelph, Ontario and Toronto, Ontario opened public libraries that same year as well. Due to Canada's size and diversity, the development of the modern Canadian public library was more of a slow evolution than a quick transition as each of the provinces' specific conditions had first to be addressed.

The public library therefore took on many forms in Canada's earlier years; the three most prevalent of these forms were school-district libraries, Mechanics Institutes, and association/social libraries. In 1850, school-district libraries were initiated in Canada. Public servant Joseph Howe started one in Nova Scotia, and politician Egerton Ryerson started one in Ontario. New Brunswick and Prince Edward Island followed suit in 1858 and 1877, respectively. The hope was that both children and adults could benefit from the local school authorities, where financial assistance was provided from colonial legislatures, but the departments of education proved to be too centralizing for locals and this practiced was phased out. Mechanics Institutes also contained libraries that the working class could access inexpensively.

The first Canadian library of its kind was established in 1828 in Montréal, Québec. Other communities took up this idea as well – notably those in Halifax, Nova Scotia, Hamilton, Ontario, Toronto, Ontario and Victoria, British Columbia. Like the school-district libraries, these institutes eventually ceased or were replaced by public libraries. The public library that opened in Toronto, Ontario, was mostly due to a campaign by city alderman John Hallam. James Bain became the first chief librarian, and built a comprehensive collection of Canadian literature and history.

The Toronto Public Library was one of the first libraries to choose free status, and it was the largest of them all. Its development flourished after 1900 when Carnegie grants began to aid in building construction and the expansion of collections and services. During this time, open access and children's departments were introduced, and standard cataloguing and classification systems were adopted. Many of the original branches, funded by a Carnegie grant, still stand and continue to be operated by the Toronto Public Library. Other provinces were affected by Carnegie as well and followed Ontario's lead in legislating tax support for library services. British Columbia acted in 1891, Manitoba in 1899, Saskatchewan in 1906, and in Alberta, the first legislation officially passed by the legislative assembly was the Library Act.

The act was passed March 15, 1907. The next provinces to follow were New Brunswick in 1929, Newfoundland in 1935, Prince Edward Island in 1936, Nova Scotia in 1937, Québec in1959, and then the Northwest Territories in 1966. As they stand today, public libraries in Canada are "governed by provincial statues and are primarily financed by municipal tax revenues and other local income, with provincial grants supplementing local funding. [They are also] the responsibility of a local or regional library board with authority to appoint or dismiss employees, control library property, establish policies, and budget for library operations." Though the services offered vary from local branch to local branch, public libraries in Canada are not only places to read and borrow books; they are also hubs of community services, such as early reading programmes, computer access, and tutoring and literacy help for children and adults.

Throughout the years, Canadian libraries have been subject to the political and economic influence of the nation. During World War II, public libraries experienced development setbacks, but expansion resumed in 1945. Then, in the 1960s, Canadian public libraries felt the benefits of the era's emphasis on education – service expanded, buildings were remodeled or constructed from scratch, and Centennial Grants were provided in order to improve the system. This period of growth ended in due to the inflationary period in the 1970s and the two recessions during the 1980s. However, in the late 1990s this trend reversed and the National Core Library Statistics Programme reported in 1999 that public libraries served 28.5 million municipal residents – a total of 93 per cent of the Canadian population. Nevertheless, in 2011 the tides turned for public libraries in Canada once again, specifically in Toronto. The city is now undergoing a heated debate regarding Mayor Rob Ford's proposed budget cuts for the Toronto Public Library, which is currently one of the most efficient public library systems in all of North America.

Mexico

In 1646, Don Juan de Palafox y Mendoza, bishop of Puebla and Viceroy of New Spain, expelled the Jesuits from New Spain, and with the confiscated books founded the Biblioteca Palafoxiana–the first public library in New Spain. It was in Puebla and open to all readers. The Biblioteca Palafoxiana exists today and is listed on the UNESCO Memory of the World Programme.

United States

As the United States developed from the 18th century to today, growing more populous and wealthier, factors such as a push for education and desire to share knowledge led to broad public support for free libraries. In addition, money donations by private philanthropists provided the seed capital to get many libraries started. In some instances, collectors donated vast book collections. William James Sidis in *The Tribes and the States* claimed the public library, as such, was an American invention. But exactly what constitutes a "free public library" is subject to dispute, and the term "invention" doesn't seem applicable to the many facets of an institution such as a library. Throughout history, knowledge in different forms has been shared in different ways.

Writing was recorded on papyrus and stored in scrolls and kept in vast libraries such as the Library of Alexandria in Egypt. In ancient Greece, knowledge was passed by one person reading aloud to a group of scribes from a text; this resulted in sometimes different and error-prone versions of the same text. Monks in the Middle Ages copied manuscripts by hand. After the invention of the printing press by Johann Gutenberg, books became prevalent, and different institutions such as universities and governments and churches found ways to keep and share them. There are disputes about which was the *first* public library in the nation. Early American cities such as Boston and Philadelphia and New York had the first organized collections of books, but which library was truly "public" is subject to dispute. Sidis claims the first public library was Boston's in 1636, although the official Boston Public Library was organized later in 1852. In 1698, Charleston's St. Philip's Church Parsonage had a parish library. In 1731, Benjamin Franklin and his friends, sometimes called "the Junto", operated the Library Company of Philadelphia partly as a means to settle arguments and partly as a means to advance themselves through sharing information. Franklin's *subscription library* allowed members to buy "shares" and combined funds were used to buy more books; in return, members could borrow books and use the library.

Today, the Library Company continues to exist as a non-profit, independent research library. A town in Massachusetts wanted to name itself Franklin in honour of the famous Pennsylvanian, and in return, Benjamin Franklin donated books for use by local residents; while Franklin had been asked to donate a church bell instead, he declined on the basis that "sense" was preferable to "sound". One source considers the Franklin library in Massachusetts to be the first public library in the United States. Another source claims the library in Darby, Pennsylvania which opened in 1743 is the "oldest continuously operating free public library" in the United States. But other libraries claim to be the first public library, including the Scoville library in Salisbury, Connecticut, which was established in 1803. The library in the New Hampshire town of Peterborough claims to be the first *publicly-funded* library; it opened in 1833. And a library in Massachusetts in the town of Arlington claims to have had the first free *children's library*; it opened in 1835.

Finances

In the trend from private to public libraries, big city libraries had the largest book collections and the most funding. The forerunner of the New York Public Library in Manhattan was a library established by the Earl of Ballamont around 1700. A newspaper described the call for the "first public librarian" demanding that "he must not be too young, for this would render him liable to be despised by the youth" and "he must be of an even temper" with "great diligence" and "sufficient learning" and "have a genius peculiarly adapted to the calling." In 1849, the library was officially established, and consolidated in 1901. Today, it is considered to be one of the most important public libraries in the nation.

New York governor and book lover Samuel J. Tilden bequeathed millions to build the New York Public Library. He believed Americans should have access to books and a free education if desired. In 2005, the library offered the "NYPL Digital Gallery" which made a collection of 275,000 images viewable over the web; while most of the contents are in the public domain, some images are still subject to copyright rules. In 1902, one account suggested "the village library is growing more and more an indispensable adjunct to American village life." Around the turn from the 19th to the 20th century, Scottish-American businessman Andrew Carnegie donated over $60 million, which was a vast fortune in 20th century dollars, to build over 2,811 free public library buildings in the United States. They were often known as *Carnegie libraries*.

Carnegie envisioned that libraries would "bring books and information to all people." Libraries have been started with wills from other benefactors; for example, the Bacon Free Library in South Natick, Massachusetts was founded in 1881 after a benefactor left $15,000 in a will; it has operated as a public library since then. Once the idea of the public library as an agency worthy of taxation was broadly established during the nineteenth and early twentieth centuries, librarians through actions of the American Library Association and its division devoted to public libraries, the Public Library Association, sought ways to identify standards and guidelines to ensure quality service. In 2009, with the economic downturn, many public libraries have budget shortfalls. The library in Darby, Pennsylvania found expenses were greater than revenues from local property taxes, state funds, and investment income; it was on the risk of closing, according to a newspaper report. Many public libraries face budgetary problems; the report noted that "tax dollars that support them are dwindling as property tax revenue declines along with home values and sales taxes fall as consumers spend less. As local funding drops, libraries are turning to their endowments and draining the investments." Many libraries have foundations behind them to support them financially, and rely on the help of well-heeled donors as well as local corporations for funds.

Services

Most public libraries today are supported by tax monies from local and state governments, and some have foundations to support them with additional capital. Libraries lend books and materials freely, but charge fines if materials are returned late or damaged. Libraries often keep many historical documents relevant to their particular town, and serve as a resource for historians in some instances; for example, the Queens Public Library kept letters written by unrecognized Tiffany lamp designer Clara Driscoll, and the letters remained in the library until a curator discovered them. In 2009, big city libraries have multiple branches and offer numerous services. For example, the Boston Public Library has 26 neighbourhood branches and offers free Internet service; it has two restaurants and an online store which features reproductions of photographs and artwork; and it promotes itself with a web site. It answers more than one million reference questions annually.

The library uses wireless technology software networks to offer more services and keep costs under control. The Boston library offers digitized content, video, a wider range of formats and, as a result, "research documents now have broader accessibility within the community and around the world," and help communities by offering public access computers, mobile Wi-fi access, and free job search tools. Libraries promote cultural awareness; in Newark, New Jersey, the public library celebrated black history with exhibits and programmes. Libraries also partner with schools and community organizations to promote literacy and learning. One account suggested libraries were essential to "economic competitiveness" as well as "neighbourhood vitality" and help some people find jobs. Some library buildings are notable for their particular architectural styles; in the town of Beaver Dam, Wisconsin, architects designed the Williams Free Library in the style of Richardsonian Romanesque.

EUROPE

France

The National Library of France is one of the oldest libraries in the world still in service today as it traces its origin to the royal library founded at the Louvre by King Charles V in 1368, but at the time it was conceived as the private library of the French kings and it opened to the public only in 1692, during the reign of Louis XIV. Claude Sallier, the philologist and churchman, had an idea that was advanced for its era–to make culture accessible to all. From 1737 to 1750 he made books available to the town of Saulieu, forming France's first public library. The pioneer of modern public libraries in France was Eugène Morel, a writer and one of the librarians at the Bibliothèque nationale. He put forward his ideas in the 1910 book *La Librairie publique*.

Italy

The Malatestiana Library also known as the Malatesta Novello Library, is a public library dating from 1452 in Cesena, Emilia-Romagna. It was the first European civic library, *i.e.*, belonging to the Commune and open to everybody. It was commissioned by the Lord of Cesena, Malatesta Novello. The works were directed by Matteo Nuti of Fano and lasted from 1447 to 1452.

Poland

The Za^{3}uski Library was built in Warsaw 1747–1795 by Józef Andrzej Za^{3}uski and his brother, Andrzej Stanis^{3}aw Za^{3}uski, both Roman Catholic bishops. The library was open to the public and indeed was the first Polish public library, the biggest in Poland and one of the earliest public libraries in Europe. In 1794, the library was looted on orders from Catherine II of Russia. Much of the material was returned in the period of 1842-1920, but once again the library was decimated during World War II during the period following the Warsaw Uprising. The Za^{3}uski Library was succeeded by the creation of the National Library of Poland in 1928.

Australia

Library services in Australia developed along different paths in the different States. In 1809 the Reverend Samuel Marsden advertised in England for donations to help found a 'Lending Library for the general benefit of the inhabitants of New South Wales'. The library would cover 'Divinity and Morals, History, Voyages and Travels, Agriculture in all its branches, Mineralogy and

Practical Mechanics'. No Public Library came to fruition from this although some of the books brought to the colony after this call survive in the library of Moore Theological College. The place of Public Libraries was filled by Mechanics' Institutes, schools of arts, athenaeums and literary institutes. Some of these provided free library services to visitors.

However lending rights were available only to members who were required to pay a subscription. In 1856, the Victorian colonial government opened the Melbourne Public Library. This was however purely a reference library. In September 1869, the *New South Wales* (NSW) government opened as the Free Public Library, Sydney by purchasing a bankrupt subscription library. In 1896, the Brisbane Public Library was established. The Library's collection, purchased by the Queensland Government from the private collection of Mr. Justice Harding.

In 1932, the Carnegie Corporation of New York, funded a survey into Australian libraries. It found 'wretched little institutes' which were 'cemeteries of old and forgotten books'. There was also criticism of the limited public access, poor staff training, unsatisfactory collections, lack of non-fiction, absence of catalogues and poor levels of service for children. Lending libraries in Sydney and Prahran were praised as examples of services which were doing well, but these were seen as exceptions. In NSW, The Free Library Movement was established in response to the Munn-Pitt Report. This collection of concerned citizens, progress associations, returned servicemen and trade unions advocated a system of public libraries to serve the needs of all people. The birth of the movement took place at a public meeting in the Chatswood-Willoughby School of Arts, Sydney, in 1935. George Brain, President of the Middle Harbour Progress Association, ran the meeting. George Brain initiated the resolution which brought the Free Library Movement into existence in NSW as well as the election of provisional office bearers, including himself as Honourary Secretary.

This movement was stalled by the onset of World War II in 1939. In 1943, the Queensland Parliament passed the Libraries Act, establishing the Library Board of Queensland to manage the operations of the Public Library of Queensland, and coordinate and improve library facilities throughout the State of Queensland. In November 1943, at the official opening of the new Public Library of New South Wales building, William McKell, the New South Wales Premier, announced that the Library Act would be fully proclaimed from 1 January 1944. After the war, and with George Brain now in NSW parliament as a principle advocate for the Free Library Movement, the passing of Library Acts in NSW and the other states at the end of the war marked the beginning of modern public libraries in Australia. Even after the war, the development of free lending libraries in Australia had been agonizingly slow: it was not until the 1960s that local governments began to establish public libraries in suburban areas.

Currently there are 1402 Australian public libraries plus 78 mobile libraries. Australians generate more than 110 million library visits per year. There are more than 9.9 million library members more than 41.5 million items to use and borrow, plus more than 11,600 computers for public use. It costs $882.3 million to run Australian public libraries. They return at least $2.6 billion-worth of community benefits. All this costs Australians $830 million - just over 10c a day each with a benchmark for best practice funding being 20c per day. The 2007 *Americans for Libraries Council* (ALC) report on library valuation stated, 'A benefit-to-cost ratio of 3:1 or better is common among the library valuation studies ALC reviewed. Because this type of economic analysis is commonly used across industries and businesses, it puts libraries into an evaluative framework that permits comparisons with other types of organizations. When this occurs, public libraries consistently outpace other sectors, such as transportation, health, and education, on the efficient use of tax dollars.'

ROLE OF PUBLIC LIBRARIES IN EGOVERNMENT

The E-Government Act of 2002 states the goal of E-Government as enhancing "governmental functions and service," achieving "more efficient performance," and increasing "access to Government information, and...citizen participation in Government". Since the passage of the E-Government Act, E-Government has quickly become an increasingly popular element of service delivery at the federal, state and local levels. If E-Government services are planned and executed well, they allow government agencies to increase effectiveness and efficiency, and can increase citizen trust in government. The challenges that libraries encounter in providing E-Government vary geographically, as planning and execution of E-Government service varies between states, municipalities, and counties.

Even different agencies within county governments approach E-Government in a number of different ways, and with varying levels of success. In addition to increasing effectiveness and efficiency of services, governments have increased their use of E-Government in an effort to cut operating costs. The Florida *Department of Children and Families'* (DCF) eliminated almost ten thousand staff positions between 1999 and 2007 with the introduction of its ACCESS Florida E-Government programme, three thousand of which are attributable directly to the ACCESS Florida initiative. The DCF ACESS programme is a "modernized public assistance service delivery system... based on streamlined workflows, policy simplification, technology innovations and partnership with local community organizations".

This programme largely eliminates DCF offices, instead, funneling applicants and programme participants to a network of Community Partners for assistance with applications and administration of accounts. DCF now counts public libraries among its Community Partners – agencies and organizations willing to provide Internet access and service assistance applicants. A close examination of the DCF Community partners list reveals that, in most counties, libraries are the only partners charged with providing free Internet access to any citizen who enters requesting service.

Other partners are limited to specific constituencies. Since 1994, the Information Use Management and Policy Institute at Florida State University has conducted a national survey of public library internet connectivity. Between 1994 and 2007, Internet availability in libraries grew from approximately 21 per cent to over 99 per cent. Bertot, Jaeger, Langa and McClure write, "...by meeting user information needs through public access computing and Internet services, public libraries were able to serve a larger community need for access to e–government services and resources". The 2008 national survey found that approximately 95 per cent of public libraries provide asneeded assistance to patrons with understanding and using E-Government resources, while 69 per cent help with E-Government applications and services. Sixty three percent of respondents indicated that the public library was the only free public internet access point in the surrounding community.

Thus, public libraries provide substantial E-Government service and resource support. One can view Government to Citizen EGovernment as a three-part system comprised of the public, the government agency involved and the networks and points of access that allow citizens to participate in EGovernment with that agency. By seeking EGovernment information at the library and requesting assistance from librarians, citizens have added a fourth component to the system: the local librarian as a surrogate agency service provider. In this capacity, the librarian facilitates what ideally develops into discourse around the design of the E-Government implementation in question.

As Bertot, Jaeger and McClure write, "to develop citizen-oriented EGovernment services that achieve cost savings implies that governments...actively seek to discover what citizens want from E-Government" Dittrich, Ekelin, Elovaara, Eriksen and Hansson's 2003 article also provides a useful framework for understanding the implications of this "fourth party" service provider.

The article outlines a four-part chain of interaction in E-Government development that includes developers (agencies), local designers (developers), service providers (libraries) and citizens. According to the framework proposed by the Dittrich *et al.*, it is in the best interest of all parties to collaboratively develop effective ways to collect and channel patron feedback for successful, iterative development of the E-Government system. Citizens in need of government services do not bear sole responsibility for involving librarians in EGovernment service. Some agencies refer citizens to public libraries to access web-based forms or applications that are not available in their offices.The DCF ACCESS web site encourages applicants to "apply for public assistance (food stamps, temporary cash assistance, and Medicaid) using the internet wherever it is available including home, a library, or a school".

Because they are, in many cases, the only organizations offering free Internet access in their communities, the public library plays an instrumental role in leveling out differences in citizen access to personal computers and the Internet, moving the E-Government system away from exclusion of segments of the population, and towards "design for all". In this role, many libraries have begun to evolve into "one-stop shops" that now include assistance with government service programmes, access, and delivery. This is a substantive departure from a longstanding role of public libraries that serve as access points to government information and forms (*i.e.*, tax forms during tax season). For example, though librarians provided tax forms in the past, they did not serve as tax accountants who assisted patrons complete and file their taxes. Now, citizens come to the library seeking government programme and services assistance, not simply access to information. This shift seems to occur in direct relation to government agencies cutting back in their provision of programme support services due to the adoption of E-Government technologies.

PURPOSE AND OBJECTIVES

The purpose of this exploratory study was to identify the E-Government related needs of citizens who access government related information at the library, and to identify current library E-Government practices in order to provide practical guidance to public libraries in meeting the needs of local community members they serve. Specifically, the study addresses the following questions:

- What E-Government services and resources do public libraries typically provide?
- What types of E-Government assistance and/or resources do members of libraries' community members request?
- Why do citizens seek E-Government services and resources at the public library?
- What barriers and issues do librarians face in providing E-Government services and resources?

Answers to these questions can help ascertain EGovernment needs from a user perspective, but also foster understanding the impacts of E-Government on community-based support organizations such as public libraries.

The study was exploratory and used an iterative multi-method approach. Limited to public libraries in the state of Florida, the study used:

- Interviews with public librarians. The interviews explored and identified the E-Government services public librarians provided, and the issues encountered by public librarians in providing EGovernment services and resources.

- E-Government workshops. The study team conducted five E-Government workshops in key geographic regions to explore EGovernment service provision by libraries in the regions.
- Survey of workshop attendees. The survey asked librarians to identify the most frequently provided E-Government services, and to identify issues encountered by patrons seeking E-Government assistance in local libraries.
- Librarian-maintained reference log files. The log files captured specific E-Government service and resource transactions provided to users in libraries.
- User survey. The survey explored the reasons why users came to the public library for EGovernment services and resources, library services requested and used to engage in EGovernment services, and issues encountered while engaging in E-Government services. The survey was available in English, Spanish, and French Creole. The survey was primarily in print format, though a web-based Survey Monkey version of the survey was available in English.

The interviews and workshops informed the development of the log file and user surveys. User surveys and log files were pre-tested to ensure their usability and ability to capture valid and reliable data.

Sampling Strategy and Data Quality

The study team employed a combination of purposeful and cluster sampling for the study's data collection efforts. The study team identified and selected public librarians who provided E-Government services in their libraries, both face-to-face and through developed web sites that contained a range of information regarding federal, state, and local government services.

The study team also conducted workshops in four key geographic regions throughout the state of Florida to explore library E-Government involvement and services. Given the diversity of the state of Florida and its various communities, the regional workshops provided the study team with variations in E-Government services due to user needs in each of the regions.

The individual interviews provided more in-depth information regarding librarian efforts to develop and offer E-Government services and resources in their libraries.

For the librarian logs and user surveys, the study team developed a cluster sampling approach to select libraries for participation based on:

- Library diversity – *e.g.*, urban, rural, and suburban; and geographic spread throughout the state of Florida;
- Community diversity – *e.g.*, poverty, immigrant, language, and a range of other library community factors; and
- Willingness to participate.

In all, 74 libraries agreed to participate in the study by maintaining library logs and distributing user surveys. The study team provided surveys in multiple languages based on librarian indications of the communities that the libraries served. The user surveys and log files were maintained and available for two weeks in March 2008. Overall, the study team interviewed nine public librarians individually, conducted workshops with 145 public librarians throughout the state, and received 415 librarian logs, and 210 usable user surveys. A total of 46 usable librarian surveys were collected during workshops. The data are limited due to the exploratory nature of the study and the purposeful and cluster sampling approaches. The five methodologies, however, provided detailed and overlapping findings regarding issues associated with providing E-Government services and resources in public libraries. By using an iterative and multi-method approach, the study team identified and triangulated perspectives on E Government in public libraries from both the public library and user populations.

KEY ISSUES

The study found a number of issues raised due to local, state and federal E-Government implementations, as described in the ensuing sections.

Access and the digital divide

The transfer of some services from face-to-face to Internet-only highlights the gap between those who have and do not have access to the Internet. The digital divide continues to exist, to the detriment of citizens without access. In many communities, public libraries provide the only free access to the Internet, and thus the only link to E-Government. In some cases, E-Government is a matter of convenience. Some patrons seek web sites and forms that make application for a service simpler than walking into an agency office or calling a phone number. In other cases, E-Government is the only option. The Florida Department of Children and Families, which deals primarily with a low-income constituency, has moved its services and applications to an Internet-based application system.

Since DCF closed many of its offices, applicants have begun seeking help at public libraries. In many locations in South Florida, the only way to make an appointment at the United States Citizenship and Immigration Service office, which processes immigrant visas, permanent residence and citizenship applications, is to use the web-based appointment system. ECitizenship and E-Participation rely on access to the Internet, making access an issue of democratic participation. But access is only part of the divide, and a basic one. Users require computer and Internet use training, information resource selection, web site navigation, and a range of other types of assistance to engage in successful E-Government efforts. It is not the case that the library simply opens its doors and provides access to a computer and the Internet. Rather, that technology access leads to a number of other types of assistance requests and needs from government service applicants and beneficiaries that agencies are unable or unwilling to provide.

Resolving Life Events: The Evolving Role of the Librarian as Case Worker

The increased emphasis on E-Government in public libraries threatens to alter the role of the librarian from neutrally situated information provider to that of social worker. Instead of being asked to provide information, reference staff report being asked to help patrons resolve problems, advise patrons on which forms they need to use, and at times, assist patrons in completing applications. Patron requests ranged from help with enrolling children in childcare, to finding family members, to setting up businesses, to help going through the trademark process. Increasingly, librarians are taking on the role of the social worker, referring patrons to one agency or another, and becoming more involved in patrons' personal lives.

In addition, the needs of citizens change over the course of the year. Librarian surveys, conducted in late 2007, suggested that the greatest volume of EGovernment services were provided on behalf of the Department of Children and Families. In contrast, librarian log data collected in early 2008 suggested that most E-Government services were provided on behalf of the IRS. Together, the data demonstrate that E-Government related information needs change fluidly with external life events, such as tax season, and DCF application deadlines. This evolution of librarian as information provider to case worker has multiple and profound implications. Not only is this a substantial shift in librarian duties, but it also requires librarians to become facile with multiple agency programmes. And, given that user life events can cut across multiple agencies, programmes, and eligible benefits, the knowledge and skills librarians need are numerous. A number of librarians commented that they had no training in being a social case worker and felt uncomfortable serving in that role.

Skills and Training

Librarians expressed concern and anxiety that they are unprepared to provide the services requested by users. While some agencies have made significant efforts to reach out to libraries and community centers that serve their target populations, many have not made any efforts to provide training to non-agency staff. As a result, libraries that embrace the role of E-Government service provider must pour significant resources into training staff, most often without assistance from local agencies. In short, librarians that engage in the provision of EGovernment services and resources are self-taught and can often lack an essential programmatic perspective. There is a need for increased communication and cooperation between libraries and the government agencies on state and local levels.

Local agency offices are often unaware of the level of service libraries are able to offer, and direct patrons to the library for services they may not provide. They also argued that state agencies often shut down local offices without consideration for the restrictions of the local library's funding, resources, or space. To some degree, librarians do not have a choice whether to assist or not assist someone needing help in using E-Government resources or services. If the person is present and needs assistance then the librarian will likely try to assist them as best they can – regardless of the level of training the librarian has received regarding E-Government. Thus, an area for additional research is the quality of the EGovernment services that librarians can provide – especially in the current Florida context of severe budget cutbacks, reduced library hours of operations and increasing overall library use.

Liability

As library staff members are asked to assist patrons with forms and applications, and to handle more sensitive personal information, librarians and administrators grow more concerned over possible liability issues. This anxiety includes civil and criminal concerns. Fear over possible lawsuits against library staff, administrators, and city/county councils, and criminal consequences associated with entering false information on behalf of library patrons lead some libraries to avoid EGovernment altogether. A few local library administrators restrict librarians from providing assistance with E-Government forms.

In some cases, library staff members are instructed to limit EGovernment help to locating forms as requested, and to provide no help in interpreting or completing applications. But overall, there are no clear guidelines as to "how much assistance" in filling out forms requiring a range of personal information and explanation is too much assistance on the part of the librarian.

Forcing Technology Management Changes

Library public access computer and Internet resources are not limitless. Libraries only have a certain number of public access computers available for use. Indeed, 82.5 per cent of libraries report that they have insufficient public access computers some or all of the time and 93.4 per cent have time limits on workstation use.

Given this, libraries have had to purchase, install, and maintain public access management software that manages user workstation registration process, enforces time limits, and resets the computers after each session.Time limits, imposed to alleviate public access computer and Internet access demands on limited library resources, are often in direct conflict with E-Government services requirements, which can often take considerable time and effort.

Librarians either have to try and remove the time limit features, set up E-Government workstations, or risk the loss of E-Government application and other information by users. Thus, EGovernment service provision can impose a substantial management and infrastructure burden on libraries.

An Unfunded Mandate: Resources and Burden Shifting

When state and federal agencies send citizens to county-funded public libraries to access EGovernment forms, schedule appointments and seek information instead of providing that information in the traditional office setting, they add to an overall increase in the number of patrons requesting EGovernment services. Library services are provided by local tax revenue and libraries' budgets are significantly stressed. The increase in EGovernment users taxes the human and financial resources of already strained local libraries, increasing costs associated with staff time, computer equipment, and Internet bandwidth. Although Florida's budget reductions represent an extreme case, reduced library funding is a national issue, made worse by downturns in the economy Agencies that choose to exchange face-to-face services for Internet based services are, in many cases, actually shifting personnel and operating costs to locally funded organizations that provide "free" public Internet access and assistance. Local agency offices are often unaware of what level of service libraries are prepared to offer, and direct patrons to the library for services they may not be in a position to provide. State agencies often shut down local offices without consideration for the restrictions of the local library's funding, resources, or space.

While some local libraries are able to absorb the costs associated with a spike in use, others cannot, and risk closure when local agency offices close their doors. This burden shift amounts to an unfunded mandate from state agencies to local, city and county governments that fund local library systems. Libraries are put in the position of providing services that they may not have the staff, expertise, equipment, or funding to deliver, or risk the ire of a patron base that provides the library's funding. Because public libraries are not legally mandated, community support is sometimes the only protection a library has at its disposal to maintain its operations. The extent to which reductions in state staffing at DCF, for example, have resulted in increased costs for public libraries in Florida, reductions in other library services, and staff time to meet E-Government service demands is an area for future investigation.

STATE LIBRARY AGENCIES

Continuing education for professional and support staff in all the professions has been receiving increasing emphasis in recent years. The need to update current practice through new knowledge and insight of societal conditions and client needs has had its impact in the library and information science fields. The advances in automation and technology, the proliferation of knowledge, and the growing recognition of the need to provide access to the rapid delivery of information in many formats have given priority emphasis to continuing library education as a means of responding to the changes taking place in our society. State library agencies have a continuing responsibility for a planned approach to the development of library and information services in each state. This planned approach includes the need for the continuing education of library personnel to meet changing service demands.

This article reviews the background for the continuing education role of the state library agency, the development of continuing education for libraries, the implications of these developments, current programmes in progress, and trends which may indicate future change. Historically, state library agencies have had the responsibility for statewide library development, particularly public library development. The provision of advice, assistance and consultant services has been one of the primary means employed. Included in the advisory activities were the conducting of workshops and other educational and staff development programmes. State library agencies having responsibility for school library development as units of state departments of education carried on similar programmes and activities to improve school libraries. Following the enactment of the federal *Library Services Act* (LSA), state library agencies moved into a new era of growth and influence. The requirement to develop state plans and the attendant emphasis on establishing libraries, creating library systems and extending library services created the need for staff development and continuing education activities as a major component in the achievement of desired objectives. A U.S. Office of Education study of state library extension resources and services compares the data from 1955-56 prior to LSA with the re- sources and services of state library agencies in 1960-61. For the purposes of this article, the report of consultant activity and training programmes during this period is of interest. Forty-eight states reported 16,466 field visits compared to 6544 in 1955-56; 44 states held or sponsored some 1600 training programmes for over 56,000 persons from 1956 to 1961.

These pro- grams served professional (36 percent) and non-professional (22 per-cent) personnel and public library trustees (26 percent). The responsibility of state library agencies for the planning and ad- ministration of federal funds under the Library Services Act of 1956 and the *Library Services and Construction Act* (LSCA) of 1964 gave added impetus to national documents and conferences concerned with improving the capabilities of state library agencies. These reports emphasize a stronger focus on goals, purposes and long-range plans with the attendant need for highly skilled consultants and related staff development activities in the field in order to implement the statewide programme. All state library agencies view continuing education and consultant services as a major responsibility of the agency. In a recent survey, about one-half of the state library agencies considered the continuing education responsibility to be a shared responsibility and not solely the responsibility or of the state library agency. In recent years national activities of major importance have contributed to an increased awareness of continuing education responsibility and to an increase in planned activities of state library agencies. In the regional hearing conducted in 1972 by the National Commission on *Libraries and Information Science* (NCLIS),one of the identified priorities was the availability of continuing education for the development and maintenance of competencies which are needed to deliver the library and information services required by the nation. Subsequently, NCLIS funded a study in 1973 to recommend a nationwide programme of continuing education which culminated in *Continuing Library and Information Science Education.*

This report made recommendations which eventually led to the formation of the *Continuing Library Education Network Exchange* (CLENE). The NCLIS report outlines the development of library continuing education and comments on the necessity for continuing life- long learning.' Based on responses from the field, an operational definition of continuing education was developed which includes the following:

- The implication that lifelong learning is necessary to keep the individual up to date,
- Assurance that the individual carries the basic responsibility for his/her own development,
- Diversification to new areas of interest, and
- Involvement in educational activities beyond those considered necessary for entrance into the field.

In comparison with other professions, the librarians felt that continuing education should be pro- vided for all levels of personnel, not solely professional, and that it not be limited to improved competence for the job held now or aspired to in the future. In its plan for continuing education, the report suggests roles and responsibilities of the individual agencies and organizations in order to coordinate efforts, including those of the individual employee, the employing library, the state library agency, the library schools, and state, regional and national associations. Major responsibilities outlined for the state library agencies include coordination of continuing education programmes on a statewide basis, identification of continuing education needs of the state, provision of a link between librarians in the state and national and regional plans, and the appointment of a continuing education coordinator on the state library agency staff. The other major responsibility is three- fold: the planning, implementation and evaluation of statewide continuing education programmes based on identified needs.

These initial efforts to provide a suggested outline of responsibilities continued to receive attention through CLENE as a newly formed national organization. State library agencies which joined CLENE as sustaining members, as well as the state library agency directors and continuing education staff members, influenced some of the priorities of CLENE. In 1976 CLENE received a USOE, Title II-B grant to provide an "Extended Institute to Train State Library Agency.Personnel to Implement and/or Strengthen Statewide Systems of Continuing Education for Library/Information/Media Personnel." The workshop phase of the institute was held November 7-13, 1976, at the Illinois State Library.

Continuing education personnel from twenty-five state library agencies met to develop planning and implementation skills in continuing education. For participating states the institute spurred development of statewide coordinated planning among providers of continuing education in the state. During this period several regional consortia of states were formed with a primary concern for continuing education. CELS grew out of a survey of members of six state library associations where the need for Continuing education was strongly expressed. State library agencies are major financial contributors to this programme.

The *Western Interstate Commission on Higher Education* (WICHE) had a major continuing education component funded in large part by five state library agencies. The Western Council of State Libraries has succeeded WICHE in this regional effort. In preparation for this article, state library agencies were asked to report on activities in needs assessment, programmes in continuing education, the extent of cooperation of other agencies in planning and implementing continuing education programmes, recent changes and improvements in state library agency continuing education programmes, and trends and new developments in continuing education. Forty responses to the questionnaire were received. State library replies indicate that all state library agencies have a responsibility for continuing education. Several have stated that the agency statutes define this responsibility but most suggest that agency planning documents cover these functions.

Cooperation with other continuing education agencies is extensive; 63 percent of the respondents work closely with state library associations, and 34 percent with library schools. State universities, higher education commissions, state departments of education, and other agencies were also listed. State staff are active participants on the continuing education committees of other agencies, and either library associations or the state library agency has formed a continuing education committee for coordinated planning and programmes. The formation of continuing education planning committees representing all types of libraries is a recent development in many states. These committees are in various stages of the development of guidelines, policy statements or state plans for coordinated continuing education programmes. Examples of plans underway can be found in Illinois, Michigan, Ohio and Louisiana. Oklahoma reported the formation of a state committee in 1978, Maryland in 1977.

Pennsylvania is planning a special project in 1978 with a director and task force to develop continuing education coordination. States participating in the

Western Council of State Libraries and CELS are the primary planners for the continuing *ed*ucation programme of the regional consortia. Coordinated planning appears to be one of the more significant activities now underway. Continuing education needs were identified by the majority through surveys and questionnaires at state, regional or local levels;consultations with local staffs and "perceived changes in the library climate," evaluation of current programmes and of new national library trends and programmes were also cited. The responses did not indicate the types of libraries involved in the needs assessment process. The influence of continuing education committees and recently formed task forces has not yet been felt to any great degree in the development of continuing education programmes as reported. The continuing education programmes sponsored by state library agencies are directed primarily to public library staffs, although programme offerings to reach a broader group were listed. All respondents listed public library directors and public library professional staff as participants; twenty-six listed non-professional public library staffs. However, twenty- one listed academic librarians;twelve, school librarians;twelve, multi-type participants; and two listed institutional and special library staffs.

Principal topics in continuing education programmes covered a wide range including copyright, networking, automation, planning, management, public relations and audiovisual materials. However, over one-third of the respondents offered basic or refresher courses to public library staffs in such areas as reference, children's services, storytelling, and young adult services. A few states mentioned law materials, oral history, censorship, and government documents. Workshops on community needs and development of special services to disadvantaged, senior citizens and other groups reflect the outreach programme priorities of some states. Wisconsin reported a continuing education programme for public library and staff through the University of Wisconsin using the *Education Telephone Network* (ETN). Once a month for about two hours, several topics are discussed by a group or panel. Local libraries may purchase sets of materials related to the programme. Topics covered in the last two years include:

- Networks,
- Censorship,
- School-public library cooperation,
- The independent adult learner,
- Deaf awareness, and
- Service to special groups.

Alaska and Hawaii reported the use of video cassettes to bring continuing education programmes to remote areas, and West Virginia reported that the capability now exists there to provide this form of continuing education programming. Frequently, continuing education programmes sponsored by the state library agency are executed by contract with a university or other educational organization. Some states do this extensively; others use this method for institutes in such areas as management. Recent changes and improvements in the continuing education activities of state library agencies reflected the increased emphasis and direction given a planned and coordinated programme. The establishment of a new position of continuing education coordinator was listed by five states; assignment of this responsibility to an established position was listed by many states.

Several states were engaged in "train the trainer" programmes with the shift to local library systems of responsibility for staff development and training in their own institutions, particularly for non-professional staff. State programmes will provide for more advanced and intensive training and attempt to ensure continuity in programme offerings. At least two states -North Carolina and Maryland -provide reimbursement to public library staffs for attending out-of-state institutes. The responsibility of the continuing education coordinator for developing and disseminating information on continuing education offerings in-state and nationally; for maintaining a master calendar; for providing continuing liaison with library schools, library associations and other educational agencies; and for assuring a programme of needs identification and developing plans to meet needs were mentioned.

These activities reflect to a marked degree the influence of the CLENE report and subsequent programmes and activities of CLENE. It should be noted that state library agency personnel active in CLENE are frequently those most active in continuing education development in their respective states. Several states commented that NCLIS and CLENE had provided the impetus for renewed continuing education activity at the state level; one saw CLENE as the key to noteworthy, effective state library agency work in continuing education. The continuing education programmes of CLENE itself provide state library agency personnel the opportunity to gain knowledge, exchange information, and encourage the further coordinated development of continuing education activities of state library agencies. Changes and trends seen as important and needed for further development of continuing education include the development of more non- traditional methods for the delivery of continuing education programmes, as well as education techniques more suitable to adult learners.

States ex- pressed the need for improved needs assessment and evaluation skills and techniques. At least one-half the states were interested in a recognition system for continuing education. This seemed to be the national trend of greatest interest. Some states are currently using the *continuing education unit* (CEU) in institutions of higher education for library programmes. CEUs are directly related to certification in several states. South Dakota State Library provides voluntary certification for public libraries based on CEUs. Michigan and North Carolina have proposals for recertification of public librarians through approved programmes in continuing education and the CEU.

The "college without walls" programme in New Hampshire and Vermont has prompted library staff to indicate that continuing education programmes should provide some academic credit. A nationally recognized CEU programme for librarians was specifically cited by several respondents. The study recently completed by CLENE, Model Continuing Education Recognition System in Library and Information Science, was first discussed in January at a CLENE meeting and is to be further examined and discussed at a national convention sponsored by NCLIS in June 1978. State library agencies will need to give the proposal and comments from the field serious study, since it has implications for an increased state library agency role.

This article has attempted to provide a summary of the development of continuing education responsibilities in state library agencies as viewed in the literature and reported from the agencies themselves. A few other points and issues need to be raised. State library agencies have a continuing responsibility for the improvement of the quality of library services in the state. In that respect they are in a unique position to assess the impact of continuing education programmes on library services in the state, and have a responsibility to do so.

There is no documentation to determine whether this is being done, but the need to develop the evaluation and performance criteria for this purpose is evident. In the author's opinion this would lead to fewer programmes of longer duration, involving participants in more appropriate learning situations and plans for implementation in their libraries.

Another issue is the responsibility of the individual for his own continuing education and for the pursuit of programmes that satisfy individual needs and interests. State library agency programmes are geared primarily to the perceived needs of the institution and to the priorities of the state library plans and objectives.

To the extent that these coincide with individual needs and interests and that participation is voluntary and encouraged, the interests of both can be served. By publicizing continuing education programmes at state, regional or national levels, state library agencies are helping individuals to become aware of other opportunities.

Each state library agency needs to define its own role in continuing library education in relation to those of library schools, library associations and other providers of continuing education programmes.

State library agencies should continue efforts to make possible situations in which innovators and practitioners can reach each other, invent ways to be mutually instructive and supportive, define steps by which to strengthen the drive towards improved continuing education programmes, and undertake cooperative endeavors that ultimately may matter greatly in the capacity of library personnel to deliver the library and information services needed in today's society.

USE OF PUBLIC LIBRARY SERVICES

Expert assessment of the nation's health care system suggests that it is slow in translating knowledge into practice and that patient care is not keeping abreast of advances in basic research. The American Medical Informatics Association recently proposed a plan for improving health care delivery. The plan focusses on clinical decision support, which "encompasses a variety of approaches for providing clinicians, staff, patients or other individuals with timely, relevant information that can improve decision making, prevent errors, and enhance health and health care."

The National Library of Medicine (NLM) can make a substantial contribution to improving national health by making a wide range of biomedical resources readily accessible to advanced information technology. There is a large, and growing, amount of online health-related information. Some resources are in the form of text readily accessible only to humans; examples include MEDLINE/PubMed and ClinicalTrials.gov. Other information is structured and includes biomedical vocabularies, clinical and molecular biology knowledge bases, and model organism annotation databases. Within NLM, examples include the Unified Medical Language System and Entrez Gene.

There are also several specialised biomedical databases, for example the BIND database and PharmGKB, as well as commercially curated drug databases, such as Micromedex DRUGDEX and DrugDigest. The growth of online information resources for biomedicine is outstripping access applications that could allow users to maximally exploit those resources. In order to take full advantage of available resources, the Library needs to provide services beyond traditional information retrieval. Emerging research provides the underpinnings for developing applications that accommodate the growth in online information. Advanced applications manipulate information, not just text, and provide visualisation of results and interconnections among multiple sources. Some research concentrates on extracting information from text. Other emerging systems focus on using the information extracted; examples include automatic summarisation, question answering, and knowledge discovery.

METHODS AND PROCEDURES

We discuss issues involved in constructing a Biomedical Knowledge Repository and illustrate an emerging Web application that exploits a preliminary version. The SemRep and Sem Gen natural language processing systems will be used to extract information in the form of semantic predications consisting of arguments and a predicate that represent relations between concepts asserted in text. Information in biomedical structured resources will be converted into a common format and all information will be integrated into the repository. Finally, a significant aspect of this project is the development of applications that exploit the Biomedical Knowledge Repository.

Extracting Predications from Text

Two programmes developed at LHNCBC will initially be used to extract semantic predications from ClinicalTrials.gov narrative and MEDLINE/PubMed citations for the repository. SemRep was devised to apply to the clinically oriented research literature, while SemGen addresses the genetic etiology of disease.

SemRep

SemRep is a rule-based symbolic natural language processing system developed for the biomedical research literature. As the first step in identifying semantic predications, SemRep produces an underspecified syntactic analysis based on the SPECIALIST Lexicon and the MedPost part-of-speech tagger. The most important aspect of this processing is the identification of simple noun phrases. In the next step, these are mapped to concepts in the Metathesaurus using MetaMap. Syntactic analysis in table, for example, contains Metathesaurus concepts and semantic types for the sentence in table.

Table. SemRep Analysis.

Sentence	Phenytoin induced gingival hyperplasia	(1)
Syntactic analysis	[[head(noun(phenytoin)), metaconc('Phenytoin' :[orch,phsu]))], [verb(induced)], head(noun(['gingival hyperplasia')), metaconc(' Gingival Hyperplasia':[dsyn]))]]	(2)
Semantic Network	'Pharmacological Substance' CAUSES 'Disease or Syndrome'	(3)
Semantic Predication	Phenytoin CAUSES Gingival Hyperplasia	(4)

SemRep relies on structures to translate syntactic structures into semantic predications. One aspect of this processing is 'indicator' rules which map syntactic elements to predicates in the Semantic Network.

Argument identification rules then find syntactically allowable noun phrases to serve as arguments for indicators. If an indicator and the noun phrases serving as its syntactic arguments can be interpreted as a semantic predication, the following condition must be met: The semantic types of the Metathe-saurus concepts for the noun phrases must match the semantic types serving as arguments of the indicated predicate in the Semantic Network. For example, in the structure given in table, the indicator *induced* maps to the Semantic Network relation in table. The concepts corresponding to the noun phrases *phenytoin* and *gingival hyperplasia* can serve as arguments because their semantic types match those in the Semantic Network relation. In the semantic predication produced as output, the Metathesaurus concepts from the noun phrases are substituted for the semantic types in the Semantic Network relation.

SemGen

SemGen was adapted from SemRep in order to identify semantic predications on the genetic etiology of disease. The main consideration in creating SemGen was the identification of gene and protein names as well as related genomic phenomena. For this SemGen relies on ABGene, in addition to MetaMap and the Metathesaurus. Since, the UMLS Semantic Network does not cover molecular genetics, ontological semantic relations for this domain were created for Sem Gen. The allowable relations were defined in two classes: gene-disease interactions and gene-gene interactions.

Other Systems

The information submitted to the repository by SemRep and SemGen could be supplemented with output from other natural language processing technologies that produce relationships. Phenotypic information from clinical narrative could be made accessible with the NLP system described by Friedman *et al.*. For molecular biology phenomena, several systems use syntactic templates and shallow parsing to produce a variety of relations, including gene and protein functions, protein interactions, and protein modifications such as phosphorylation. Friedman *et al.* use extensive linguistic processing for relations on molecular pathways, while Lussier *et al.* use a similar approach to identify phenotypic context for genetic phenomena.

Converting Structured Data into a Common Format

Since, relations in structured resources are already represented in some kind of formalism, their conversion to a common format is somewhat easier than extraction from text. However, the challenges in normalising such knowledge are not unlike those encountered with textual data. In both cases, knowledge extraction involves syntactic issues and semantic issues. Various formalisms are used to represent structured data, including relational databases, tables, graphs, etc. Currently, no universal conversion mechanism is available. Moreover, the semantics of the data is often implicit or limited, for example, to short column names in a database schema. The objective of the conversion is the creation of 'normalised knowledge'. This effort, in the context of knowledge management, is somewhat equivalent to term normalisation. Knowledge normalisation ensures that the same entity referred to in different resources is ultimately identified in such a way that it is recognised as a unique thing. Knowledge normalisation forms the basis for information and data integration.

Description of Resources

Over the past twenty years, NLM has developed many knowledge resources, from various perspectives. Terminological resources such as the *Unified Medical Language System* (UMLS) result from the integration of many existing terminologies and ontologies, represented in a common formalism–UMLS' Rich Release Format–and partially normalised. While synonymous terms are grouped together as names for a given concept, synonymous relationships are typically not identified as such.

Nevertheless, with some 8 million relations, the UMLS Metathesaurus constitutes an important resource, providing mostly hierarchical relations and co-occurrence relations. Another source of structured knowledge is represented by the many databases available under the umbrella of the NCBI's Entrez system. While some databases such as MEDLINE/PubMed and *Online Mendelian Inheritance in Man* (OMIM) are mostly textual resources, many other NCBI databases contain predominantly structured information.

Entrez Gene, for example, is a gene-centric resource in which a record provides gene properties such as names, associated diseases, function, sequence, etc. While numerous links have been created across the resources in the Entrez system for navigation purposes, such links typically require human interpretation and therefore cannot be used for knowledge discovery purposes in high-throughput systems. Finally, structured databases and knowledge bases are also available outside NLM. One example of large, publicly available genomic resource is represented by the genome annotations for the major model organisms. Here, the existence of a controlled vocabulary–the Gene Ontology–has contributed to developing unified functional annotations, integrated in systems such as the Mouse Genome Database and the Saccharomyces Genome Database. In the clinical domain, the various knowledge bases of drug information constitute important resources about drug-drug interactions, drug kinetics and metabolism, and indications and contraindications. DRUGDEX, produced by Micromedex, is an example of such a resource.

Representing Normalised Knowledge

One of the strengths of the World Wide Web is that it relies on textual information, easily created and interpreted by humans. This is also one of its principal limitations. The absence of explicit semantics prevents agents from being able to make sense of the information on the Web. This is the motivation of the Semantic Web, which aims at creating a vast collections of integrated and interoperable resources.

There is an obvious parallel between the Semantic Web and the Biomedical Knowledge Repository we propose to create. The technologies developed for the Semantic Web offer possible solutions to some of the challenges we face, including selecting a formalism for normalised biomedical knowledge and identification issues for biomedical entities.

It is worth noting that some of these issues are still actively being debated in the Semantic Web community, especially in the Semantic Web Health Care and Life Sciences Interest Group.

Formalism

Many of the resources produced by NLM and other organisations are available in XML, the eXtensible Markup Language. However, the semantics of XML is limited. In addition to XML, the World Wide Web Consortium (W3C) has produced the specifications of other formalisms for representing resources.

Collectively know as Semantic Web technologies, these specifications define the building blocks of the Semantic Web. Of particular interest to us is the Resource Description Framework. RDF extends the capabilities of the extensible markup language XML as it enables many-to-many relationships between resources and data. The resulting structure is a graph in which the nodes are resources or data and the edges are relationships.

The basic unit in RDF is therefore the equivalent of a triple, similar to a relation in the UMLS Metathesaurus or a predication extracted by SemRep. RDF integrates limited inference rules, enabling, for example, the definition of subclasses and subproperties. Some extensive resources such as UniProt have already been converted to RDF. The BioRDF task force of the W3C Semantic Web Health Care and Life Sciences Interest Group currently investigates methods whereby existing biomedical resources can be converted to RDF.

Such methods include XSLT, GRDDL and DB2RDF, among others. The *eXtensible Stylesheet Language Transformation* (XSLT) uses a stylesheet approach to converting XML to RDF. GRDDL specifies associations between markup languages–including XLM–and RDF. Finally, DB2RDF is used to convert databases to RDF.

Identification Issues

In order for RDF triples to form a graph–and for integrated knowledge to be interoperable-entities and relationships must be identified consistently and unambiguously. For example, if the disease *Neurofibromatosis 2* is identified by the code *SNOMEDCT:92503002* in one resource and by the code *MESH:D016518* in another, the RDF triples involving *SNOMEDCT:92503002* and *MESH:D016518* will not come together as expected unless both resource are converted to the other annotation system or mappings are created between the two systems. For example, the UMLS Metathesaurus could be used to convert or bridge between MeSH and SNOMED CT, in this case through the concept *C0027832*. The predications extracted from the literature by SemRep already use UMLS codes to identify biomedical entities. From a technical perspective, several technologies have been developed by various communities to implement identification mechanisms for RDF.

There are three major identification mechanisms:

- LSID (Life Science Identifier), promoted by the Life Sciences community. Examples of applications using LSID include Taverna and resources created by the BioPathways Consortium;

- Solutions based on the HTTP protocol, promoted by the W3C; and
- ARK (Archive Resource Key), promoted by the Digital Library community.

There are important differences among three mechanisms regarding location independence, backward compatibility, resolution mechanism and versioning. It is unclear at this time what mechanism would suit our needs best.

Pilot Project: Converting Entrez Gene to RDF

As a proof of concept, we converted the Entrez Gene database into RDF. The entire Gene database in its native ASN.1 format was downloaded by FTP from the NCBI web site and later converted to XML using the programme gene2xml provided by NCBI. Using the *eXtensible Stylesheet Language Transformation* (XSLT) approach, we mapped the element tags of the XML representation to more intuitive relationship names manually, and used them during the automatic conversion to RDF.

Finally, we stored this RDF version of Entrez Gene in the Oracle 10g relational database management system, which provides support for storing and querying native RDF data. The conversion process is illustrated in figure.

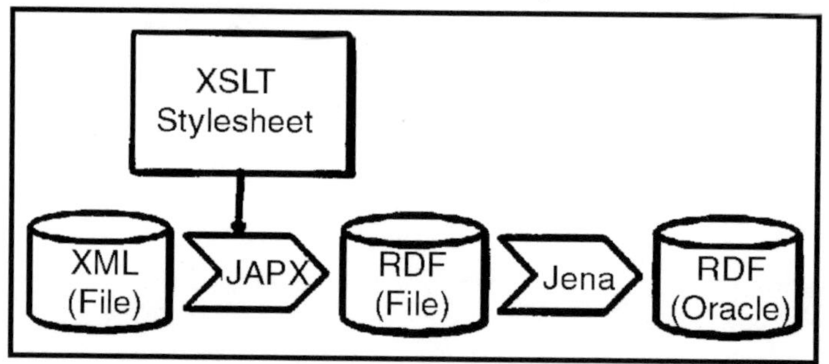

Fig. Overview of the Conversion of Enrez Gene from XML to RDF

Mapping XML Element Tags to RDF Properties

While XML data can be mechanically converted to RDF, the resulting RDF graph would be of limited interest because the semantics of the properties is most often implicit in XML and needs to be made explicit. Starting from one typical Entrez Gene record, we identified all its XML element tags, corresponding to the properties of the gene, as described in the Gene record. Examples of such properties include *<Genetrack_geneid>* and *<Genetrack_update-date>*, indicating the identifier and the update date of the gene record, respectively. A total of 124 unique elements tags were identified.

Because XML element tags represent gene properties, they were transformed into predicates in RDF. For example, *<Genetrack_geneid>* becomes *has_unique_geneid* and relates the gene record to its unique identifier in the Gene database. Note that the RDF property now conveys the notion–implicit in the XML representation–that the identifier is a unique identifier, corresponding to a primary key in a relational database.

Converting XML elements to RDF properties requires familiarity with the structure and content of the original record structure and is a key component to the mapping process. After eliminating redundant and superfluous XML element tags, 106 unique RDF properties were created. The mapping of Entrez gene XML element tags to RDF properties is specified formally using the XPath language and constitutes a stylesheet. This stylesheet is specific to the conversion of the Entrez Gene database.

Converting XML to RDF through XSLT

Once the stylesheet is created, it can serve as an auxiliary file for existing programmes realising the XML to RDF conversion. In other words, the major interest of this approach is that no specific code is required for the conversion, because the transformation logic resides entirely in the stylesheet.

We used JAXP, the Java *Application Programming Interface* (API) to XML, to implement the conversion. The resulting 411 million RDF triples were then loaded in a store using Oracle 10g using the Jena API.

Lessons Learned, Issues and Challenges

This experiment confirmed the feasibility of converting a large resource from XML to RDF. It also showed that the issues are not technical, but rather lie in the necessity of making explicit the relationships represented implicitly by element tags in XML.

This step requires the manual intervention of a domain expert. In our experience, it took less than a week for one person familiar with both bioinformatics and stylesheets to formalise the mapping between XML element tags and RDF properties. Although the stylesheet created is specific to the Entrez Gene database, it is expected that part of the expertise acquired during this transformation can be applied to transforming other NCBI resources.

The major unresolved issue concerns entity identification. If the RDF graph resulting from the conversion of Entrez Gene is to be integrated with clinical or bibliographic information, the diseases associated with genes must be represented not as literals as they currently are, but by their identifiers in the corresponding clinical and bibliographic controlled vocabularies, or with the *concept unique identifier* (CUI) in the UMLS Metathesaurus.

Only after such mapping will the RDF graph integrating Entrez Gene and, say, the Metathesaurus, support queries such as *Find all genes associated with neurodegenerative diseases*. The knowledge required in this cases comes in part from Entrez gene and from UMLS.

Integrating Predications: Biomedical Knowledge Repository

The Biomedical Knowledge Repository can be understood as a specialised version of the Semantic Web. It consists of an extensive collection of predications, represented in a common format, processable by computers. Biomedical terminologies and ontologies provide the concepts involved in the facts. Logical reasoners extend the capabilities of the repository by inferring new knowledge. Each fact in the repository is annotated with metainformation regarding its origin, making it possible for applications exploiting the repository to select facts of interest in a given context and for a particular task. Once it is fully populated, the Biomedical Knowledge Repository is expected to comprise several hundred million facts, collected from hundreds of sources.

Origin of the Predications

The Biomedical Knowledge Repository (BKR) comprises predications form three major sources: extracted from the biomedical literature by NLP programmes such as SemRep, converted from existing structured knowledge bases, and contributed by users. In our vision of the BKR, NLM not only contributes to populating the BKR, but also makes it available to the community as a framework for researchers to deposit their predications.Predications resulting from experiments, from alternative processing of the literature, and inferred from other predictions, for example, can be contributed by members of the community and made available to others. One measure of success of the BKR would be for it to become a standard repository for the knowledge created through biomedical research experiments. In order to maintain the consistency and integrity of the BKR, its developers would have to follow guidelines regarding formalism of the predications and identification mechanism for biomedical entities.

Metainformation Associated with the Predications

Just as few users need all the vocabularies in the UMLS Metathesaurus for a given purpose, it is unlikely that all predications will be equally useful for a given task, such as question answering. Instead, a mechanism supporting the selection of relevant sets of predications is needed. The metainformation associated with each predication enables this selection and may include the source of the predication, the method of extraction, the date of extraction, in addition to the usual metadata associated with MEDLINE/PubMed citations for predications extracted from the literature.

Researchers contributing predications to the BKR will be requested to annotate them with similar metainformation. Another form of contribution to the repository is to provide not predications, but annotations to existing predications. Such a contribution represents a form of collaborative curation of the repository by the community, similar to the framework developed by the SWAN project for the Alzheimer research community.

Storing the Predications

Several technological solutions, called RDF stores, have been developed for storing information in RDF format, generally implemented on top of some storage system. One such open source RDF database is Sesame. More recently, traditional database management systems have started offering direct support for native RDF triples. For example, version 10g of the Oracle system supports RDF in addition to the relational model. Since, we need to store large amounts of both RDF and traditional information, we started experimenting with Oracle 10g while converting Entrez Gene to RDF last summer. Preliminary results are encouraging although we might face optimisation issues.

Querying the Predications

Analogous to SQL for relational databases, SPARQL is the language for querying RDF. Like SQL, SPAQRL queries have a SELECT and a WHERE clause. However, in a SPARQL query, the WHERE clause follows the pattern of a RDF triple in which at least one element of the triple is replaced by a variable. In the BKR, the predications to be queried would first be selected based on their annotations. For example, a typical query supporting multidocument summarisation would be as follows. Select all predications from MEDLINE/PubMed returned by a PubMed query on *metabolic syndrome*, restricted to citations from *JAMA*, *Am J Cardiol.* and *J Hypertens.*, published between 2004 and 2005. Additionally, select those predications from the UMLS Metathesaurus and Entrez Gene having at least one node in common with those from the literature.

Integrating Predications

The query example presented above illustrates the interest of integrating knowledge under a unique framework. First, there is a unique namespace for all knowledge in the BKR. As suggested, largely rely on the UMLS for identifying biomedical entities. Second, once integrated into a graph, the predications can serve as a basis for inferencing, creating additional knowledge along the way. This represents an advantage over traditional database and information retrieval approaches. Finally, complex rules can be written to implement additional reasoning. For example, it is possible to restrict queries to those redundant predications asserted in more than 2 sources and for which the frequency of occurrence is above a certain threshold.

Estimated Size of the Repository

Once fully instantiated, the Biomedical Knowledge Repository is expected to comprise several hundred million predications extracted from the literature, terminological resources and structured knowledge bases. Assuming an average of ten predications is extracted from the title and abstract of each MEDLINE/

PubMed citation, we can expect about 150 million predications from MEDLINE/PubMed. The UMLS Metathesaurus records about 9 million relations, either symbolic or statistical. Some seven million functional annotations for the major model organism databases are recorded in the Gene Ontology database. Finally, our conversion experiment with Entrez Gene yielded over 400 million RDF triples. In this experiment, the objective was to systematically represent in RDF all the information present in the original XML file. In fact, part of this information would become metainformation in the context of the BKR, resulting in a significantly smaller number of triples to be actually contributed to the repository.

Exploiting the Repository: Semantic Medline Web Portal

As a pilot project to exploit a preliminary version of the Biomedical Knowledge Repository, we are developing a Web portal, called Semantic Medline, for managing the results of PubMed searches. The portal is designed as a Java-based Web application that seamlessly integrates PubMed, SemRep processing of the results of the search, automatic summarisation, and, finally, visualisation of the results, with links to the underlying citations and relevant additional knowledge in the UMLS Metathesaurus, the Genetics Home Reference, and Entrez Gene. Realtime access is achieved by pre-processing text from MEDLINE/PubMed abstracts and other sources with SemRep/SemGen and storing the results in a database.

Background

Several recent systems visualise the results of information identified in text as a way of providing users with enhanced access to the information retrieved. Results are often represented as a graph of interrelated relationships. The Telemakus project is based on relationships identified by hand and is meant to enable knowledge discovery through interactive visual maps of linked concepts among documents. Jensen *et al.* constructed literature networks of genes found relevant in gene expression data analysis.

Analysis is based on co-occurrence of genes in MEDLINE/PubMed abstracts. Van der Eijk *et al.* use various relations for literature-based discovery. The relationships represent co-occurrence of MeSH headings associated with MEDLINE/PubMed citations by a mapping programme. Feldman represent several gene-related relations in a graph. The relations were extracted with a type of underspecified natural language processing. Finally, Tao *et al.* visualise genomic information across both structured and textual databases.

Implementation

Semantic Medline is implemented as a three-tier, Java EE-based Web application. The three-tier architecture allows for the separation of user interface, application logic and data storage, providing improved performance, easier maintenance and scalability. We leverage mature open-source technologies in the development to the extent possible. The prototype runs in a Tomcat servlet container on an Apache Web server. It has been developed using the Apache Struts Web application framework. This framework encourages the use of *Model-View- Controller* (MVC) paradigm to provide a clean separation of application model, navigational code, and page design code through the use of Java Servlet API.

The controller is a Java servlet that mediates the application flow; the model comprises Java classes that represent the functionality of the semantic tools and the view is JSP pages that contain dynamic content. A MySQL database is used to store Semantic Medline data, which includes semantic predications extracted from MEDLINE/PubMed abstracts and ClinicalTrials.gov clinical study texts as well as a subset of UMLS Metathesaurus data. The database tables are prepopulated from plain text files that contain SemRep/SemGen output and Metathesaurus data using Perl scripts. Hibernate *object/relational mapping* (ORM) tool is used to programmatically access the database. We use such Hibernate features as database connection pooling and query caching for increased performance.

Using Semantic Medline

MEDLINE/PubMed contains more than 16 million citations drawn from nearly 4,600 journals with biomedical relevance. Searches often retrieve large numbers of items. For example, the query 'diabetes' returns 207,997 citations. Although users can restrict searches by language, date and publication type, results can still be large. For example, a query for treatment for diabetes, limited to articles published in 2003 and having an abstract in English finds 3,621 items; limiting this further to articles describing clinical trials still returns 390 citations. It is difficult for a user to effectively exploit the information in this many citations. Semantic Medline addresses this difficulty by allowing users to summarise the results of searches focused on one of several points of view, including diagnosis and treatment of disorders, drug interactions and adverse events, genetic basis of disease, and pharmacogenomics.

A clinical scenario based on a summary focused on drug interactions illustrates the potential use of Semantic Medline for taking advantage of the research literature in clinical practice. In a hypothetical situation, a patient presents with peptic ulcer and tests positive for *Helicobacter pylori*. The clinician has tried several standard regimens including two different triple regimens: and; however, the patient still tests positive for *H. pylori*.

In order to gain insight from recent research, the physician uses Semantic Medline to issue a PubMed search for lansoprazole. SemRep extracts 5,971 predications from 564 citations returned by this search, and automatic summarisation for drug interactions involving lansoprazole condenses the final list of predications to 182, which are visualised by the system as the interactive graph in figure. Figure provides an informative overview of recent research on lansoprazole represented as predications asserting INTERACTS_WITH. Each predication is linked to the MEDLINE/PubMed citation that generated it.

Of interest for this case are two predications in the graph: 'Lansoprazole INTERACTS_WITH Famotidine' and 'Famotidine INTERACTS_WITH CYPC19 Enzyme.' SemRep extracted the first predication from a citation with title seen in the first line of table and the second from a citation with in the second line.

Table. MEDLINE/PubMed Citations.

PMID	Title
15963082	Effect of concomitant dosing of famotidine with lansoprazole on gastric acid secretion in relation to CYP2C19 genotype status
15710002	Concomitant dosing of famotidine with a triple therapy increases the cure rates of Helicobacter pylori Infections in patients with the homozygous extensive metaboliser genotype of CYP2C19

Both citations discuss the salutary effect of combining famotidine with lansoprazole. In the second citation, which reports on a randomised controlled trial, the authors realised between 63 per cent to 100 per cent eradication of *H. pylori* with the addition of famotidine to a standard triple therapy and conclude that this is a promising option for patients who phenotypically are extensive metabolisers.

If the patient in this hypothetical scenario falls under this category, it would be a potentially valuable regimen to pursue.

EVALUATION PLAN

We intend to follow a multifaceted evaluation plan, focusing evaluation activities on specific aspects of the project.

Evaluating Extraction

For this project, effectiveness of information extracted from text crucially depends on the accuracy of SemRep and SemGen. We have performed linguistic evaluation across a wide variety of predicates that includes the clinical as well as the genetic domain.

Among the predicates evaluated were Treats, Prevents, Location_of, Causes, Isa, Interacts_ With, Affects, Disrupts, Process_of, Part_of, Manifestation_ of, Associated_With, Inhibits, Stimulates and PREDISPOSES. Recall on the extraction of semantic propositions with these predicates has ranged from 41 per cent to 74 per cent and precision from 68 per cent to 84 per cent. Previous evaluations have been reported in and as suggested, continue this evaluation paradigm. The framework for evaluating knowledge extraction from terminological and structured knowledge bases is not as well established as the evaluation of relation extraction from text. However, several aspects are particularly important. The rules used for the conversion need to be reviewed independently by several experts for a given knowledge base and integrated across databases in order to ensure consistency of the extraction of the relationships.

Key to the consistency of the graph is also the mapping of literals to concepts–the nodes in the RDF graph and their consistent representation by identifiers from authoritative sources.

Evaluating Integration

Ideally, the graph resulting from integrating knowledge from several sources is consistent both structurally and semantically. Therefore structural techniques based on graph theory and semantic approaches similar to reasoning services created for description logics are expected to play a central role in evaluating the quality of knowledge integration in the repository.

However, the UMLS Metathesaurus, while resulting from the integration of a much smaller body of terminological knowledge, is already not always structurally or semantically consistent.

Like the Metathesaurus, the Biomedical Knowledge Repository will allow contradictory predications to be represented as long as they occur in the original information sources. However, consistency is expected to be found at both structural and semantic levels on limited subsets of the repository.

Evaluating Applications

When evaluating applications such as automatic summarisation, it is useful to compare results against curated resources. Standard measures of performance can be calculated with respect to the reference standard chosen.

For treatment of disease, the British Medical Journal clinical evidence concise is one alternative. For drug interactions and adverse events, Micromedex DRUGDEX, DrugDigest, and the First DataBank's National Drug Data File can be used. A more ambitious method, requiring human experts, is task-based evaluation. Ultimately, user-centred evaluations such as the one described by McKeown must be considered.

PROJECT SCHEDULE

- *Year 1:* Pilot study, processing all of MEDLINE/PubMed, integrating Entrez Gene
- *Year 2:* Integrating UMLS and other NCBI resources
- *Year 3:* Annotating predications, opening the BKR to collaborative development and use.
- *Year 4:* Fully integrated ALS system available

PROJECT RESOURCES

This project relies on a range of existing competencies and resources and has the potential to federate research energies throughout the Lister Hill Center. In addition to the efforts of the two core component projects, Semantic Knowledge Representation and Medical Ontology Research, the success of this project relies on collaboration with the Indexing Initiative, the Lexical Systems Project, and ClinicalTrials.gov. The effectiveness of applications drawing on the repository could be strengthened by providing links to Visible Human images where appropriate. In order to accomplish the goals of this project additional staff and equipment are required: staff for creating and populating the repository and servers for providing effective access to the repository. Initially, PubMed and ClinicalTrials.gov will be processed by SemRep and SemGen and the predications extracted will be stored in the repository. Dedicated servers are required to process PubMed for this project.

7

Language used in Collective Catalogues of University Libraries

INTRODUCTION

It is a fact that the interactivity between thematic representation, indexing language and information retrieval is conducive to continuous evaluations of language perfor-mance during search strategies, guiding their refinement and use in the indexing of documents. The studies of Henzler, Betts and Marrable, Fidel and Gil Urdiciain demonstrated this relevance when they evaluated the performance of indexing language and of natural language in automated systems such as online catalogues and specialised databases.

The results obtained revealed that the combination in the use of terms of indexing language and natural language proves to be ideal when devising strategies, affording quality in the retrieval by subject carried out and expected by the user. In addition, Gil Urdiciain observes an increase in relevance in information retrieval with the use of indexing language, inserted in a context of high subject specialisation, placing the precision of database systems before recall.

The indexing languages, characterised as knowledge organisation systems that correspond to the lists of subject headings and thesauruses, are controlled languages built from the principles and meanings stemming from terms that are part of specialised language and natural language, representing the set of terms to recover the indexing information. They should be structured in a multidimensional plan, crossing cultural and geographical boundaries of access and representation, without disregarding the main functions which include eliminating ambiguity, controlling synonyms and establishing semantic relationships.

The primary function of indexing languages is to represent the content of documents in an information retrieval system, according to content, and its second function is to mediate information retrieval by representing the users questions, according to use, hence, playing a key role in the indexing and information retrieval processes and enabling the represen-tation of documented contents, thus facilitating user-search by topic whenever information needs to be accessed quickly and accurately. The considerations of Zeng and Boccato lay out the need for constantly updating the indexing languages used by online catalogues of university libraries, in line with the innate characteristic of scientific progress and the plethora of dynamic and progressive knowledge generated by universities.

The views and comments of librarians and users are collaborative to consolidate these processes, in light of the fact that they should be seen as individuals who interact, understand and interpret their environment and at the same time, share their knowledge with a community of interpreters. On this matter, Hjørland reports that the socio-cognitive views are interested in individual cognition, however, approaching it from a social context. Accordingly, the process of individual knowledge is associated with the historical, social and cultural context of units and information systems responsible for organising and retrieving information. Thus, the objective of this study is to evaluate the use of alphabetical indexing language of online collective catalogues, focusing on technologies of representation and information retrieval from the standpoint of university libraries and within the socio-cognitive context of librarians and users.

SUBJECT AND GENRE VOCABULARIES FOR THE SEMANTIC WEB

There are a vast number of controlled vocabularies for various forms of subject access to library materials. Some of these vocabularies are classification schemes, such as *Dewey Decimal Classification* (DDC) and *Library of Congress Classification* (LCC).

Others are controlled lists of subject headings or terms, which adhere to national and international guidelines for thesaurus construction, like the Library of Congress Subject Headings (LCSH), the two Thesauri for Graphic Materials: Subject Terms (TGM I) and Genre and Physical Characteristic Terms (TGM II), Guidelines on Subject Access to Individual Works of Fiction, Drama, Etc. (GSAFD), and the Ethnographic Thesaurus. Some of the subject thesauri published by The Getty, such as The Getty Thesaurus of Geographic Names (TGN) and The Art and Architecture Thesaurus (AAT) are truly hierarchical thesauri. Many of these controlled vocabularies are registered as DCMI Encoding Schemes in the DCMI Terms namespace.

Registered Encoding Schemes qualifying the DC Subject element include:

- Dewey Decimal Classification (DDC),
- Library of Congress Classification (LCC),
- Library of Congress Subject Headings (LCSH),
- Medical Subject Headings (MeSH),

- National Library of Medicine Classification (NLM),
- The Getty Thesaurus of Geographic Names (TGN),
- Universal Decimal Classification (UDC).

However, when these vocabularies are used as values of DC Subject in metadata records outside of the library context, the syndetic structure of the source vocabulary is all but lost. There is no way for search tools or other applications to make use of information about related terms and variant forms as part of the entry vocabulary. In some cases, item metadata for Dublin Core records is included within a larger system that relies heavily on MARC data, such as OCLC WorldCat. When this is true, many of the Library of Congress controlled vocabularies are indirectly linked to these Dublin Core records by virtue of the availability of MARC authority records for the controlled vocabularies in those systems.

Systems outside of these application environments need to be able to retrieve and translate or otherwise make use of MARC authority record data to make effective use of the hierarchies, equivalency relationships, and structures in the content of controlled vocabularies. These vocabularies present tremendous potential for improving access to web resources and Semantic Web data, as well as enhancing networked applications.

Search engine results could be dramatically improved, both in terms of precision and recall. Different subject vocabularies covering the same concept space could be merged together or associated, providing an environment where differences in terminology between different communities would provide less of a barrier to effective browsing of resources. Front-end interfaces could be built for a variety of online reference tools that take advantage of the rich structure of relationships between topics that is provided by controlled vocabularies. In some regards, libraries are only now realising the full potential of catalogue records to provide innovative and new browsing interfaces.

An example can be seen in North Carolina State Library's new, Endeca powered, catalogue interface, which is presently built entirely on the structure of bibliographic records. This new catalogue interface allows users to refine a search by navigating through record clusters that share a particular property. Drawing on the idea of faceted classification, clusters can be grouped by subtopic, genre, language, time-period, geographic region, and in a variety of other ways. These facets are derived from information in various access points, subject headings and subdivisions in a particular bibliographic result set.

It is easy to envision a similar technique being used to broaden searches and even to present initial browse interfaces to specific collections of information resources. When interfaces start to leverage the power of authority control in new and interesting ways, the benefit to users will be immense. Another example of initiatives to leverage authority control is OCLC Research's Terminology Services project to 'offer accessible, modular, Web-based terminology services'.

The Terminologies Pilot Project in October 2005 explored techniques for encoding sample vocabularies, means of mapping between them to help users identify relationships, and methods for incorporating the resulting services into other applications and tools. These services are the beginning of a rich tapestry of semantics that can be delivered within a user's current context, whatever that context is. In some cases, the services may be entirely carried out by server-side applications.Almost any application that serves content dynamically could include a navigation system that draws on the hierarchies and relationships between terms in LCSH, and could provide search interfaces that draw on term equi-valencies to retrieve a broader set of resources when doing keyword searches. Additionally, there could be services that exist within client side applications, pulling vocabulary structures from the network and integrating them into authoring tools.

One such service component prototyped for the OCLC pilot uses the Microsoft Office 2003 Research Services Pane to access genre terms. "... if a college student wishes to categorise a reading list of fiction titles based on genre, he could copy the titles into a Microsoft Excel 2003 workbook, open the Research services pane, send a search to the OCLC Research GSAFD vocabulary service, and then place the results into his document". This provides the user with the ability to browse and search genre categorisations without having to leave the application in which the search results will be used.

Additionally, the more sources of data are made available in this way, the more automated the process can be. If the Research Services Pane had access to bibliographic records, genre or subject categorisation could be fully automated and available at the touch of a button. A cataloguer could use a similar tool to suggest appropriate terms from a controlled vocabulary, which will lead to lots of cost saving opportunities. Similar applications could be developed as browser plug-ins or extensions.

A sidebar application could be built for FireFox that could harness the power of controlled vocabularies when browsing Web resource that provide some degree of keyword tagging or folksonomy support. Imagine browsing a resource like Flickr and being able to query LCSH for relationships that may be defined between subject terms through the tags labelling the subject of a particular photographic image and tags for various related concepts.

The sidebar could include hyper-linked broader, narrower, equivalent, and associative terms that would pull together additional photographs tagged with those related terms. In a different context, such an application could attempt to scan html source code for word frequency and try to guess the primary topics, returning related terms from a controlled vocabulary, and perhaps linking to search engine results for the concepts represented. Additionally, a similar service could be provided using a word highlighted by the user. The possibilities are endless.

NAME AUTHORITY FOR THE SEMANTIC WEB

The benefits of authority control–search precision, more powerful navigation, collocation, and linking between various tools and resources–apply to metadata about the creators of resources as well as to subject access. The library community is well positioned to play a significant role in these developments. Libraries have been dealing with identification, disambiguation, and collocation of names of content creators since, the beginning of cataloguing. The different forms of name used by the same creator in various print publications and other types of resources have always led to some degree of difficulty in grouping works together.

The syndetic structure of name authority files has proven itself a very useful tool to help collocate works by an author regardless of the form of name on a particular item. The proliferation of resources on the Web extends the scope of the collocation problem. Initiatives are appearing in the Web community to help provide better mechanisms for identifying persons, families, and corporate entities that have a role with respect to information resources.

InterParty is a European Commission funded project exploring the interoperation of 'party identifiers,' which would provide standard identification numbers to serve the same purpose that authorised forms of names serve in library applications: to help collocate and disambiguate individual content creators. More recently, some of the InterParty members and others submitted a similar proposal for International Standard Party Identifiers (ISPI) as an ISO standard.

More directly related to Semantic Web Development is the Friend Of A Friend (FOAF) project. FOAF is about "creating a Web of machine-readable homepages describing people, the links between them and the things they create and do". Finding ways to integrate these initiatives with existing mechanisms for name authority control in libraries can help to bring library catalogues into the mix of tools available on the Web.

Additionally, the availability of library authority data in a more Web-friendly format has the potential to positively influence the organisation of the broad spectrum of Web content already available. The development of a Virtual International Authority File (VIAF) has been a key idea moving forward this initiative.

Virtual International Authority File (VIAF)

Presently, authority files are maintained and developed by a large range of national bibliographic agencies. To make the most of this potential, it is useful to first integrate the somewhat disparate sources of authority data that exist even within the library community. These agencies develop files that are generally focused on the creators of content relevant to a particular national and cultural identity. As geographic boundaries become more and more porous, and culture becomes much more international, there is increasingly overlap between the authority files maintained by these agencies.

The concept of a Virtual International Authority File (VIAF) has been discussed since, the 1970's within the International Federation of Library Associations and Institutions (IFLA). Initially, IFLA envisioned a single shared file; more recently the concept has evolved into one of linking existing national and regional authority files. The primary objective of this vision is to facilitate sharing the workload and reducing cataloguing costs within the library community. The community is expanding, especially in Europe, where libraries are viewed as one of many 'memory institutions', along with archives, museums, and rights management agencies.

Ideally, authority files can be freely shared among all of these communities. A shared file would reduce the cost of doing authority work by avoiding repetition of effort while combining various forms of names that are particular to resource published within the context of a particular region, culture, or nation. Combining or clustering the forms of name will result in a much richer set of authority information, enabling users to access information in the language, scripts, and form they prefer.

Additionally, a single international authority file system will be far morc useful when integrated into various Web retrieval tools and Web content descriptions. Such a tool could be used by a wide range of Web systems to improve the precision of user's searches and to provide the user's preferred display of the language and script of names. Authority records are used to collocate resources that utilise varying forms of name, but collocation does not need to dictate the script or language used by the end user display.

Figure shows how a single entity–whether it is a concept, person, place, or thing–has a variety of labels that identify it in different languages and scripts. Traditionally, library systems have relied on a preferred label for all entities, although the preference would vary depending on the geographic context of the system.

Merging or linking records that utilise different languages and scripts allows the end-user to select the language and script used to display information about entities irrespective of system's default preference. This is appropriate in a truly global Web, where geographic and national boundaries are considerably less significant.

A variety of projects have sought to address this language challenge in recent years, exploring mechanisms to combine individual authority files. One such project, the European Commission funded Author project converted a sample of authority records from five European bibliographic agencies in France, England, Belgium, Spain, and Portugal into the UNIMARC format and made them available as a searchable file. "The challenge was that each library has its own language, cataloguing rules, bibliographic record format and local system for its online authority file". Combining these records into a single UNIMARC file required a large amount of record normalisation. No attempt was made to link the records for the same entity.

More recently, OCLC Online Computer Library Center Inc., the Library of Congress, and Die Deutsche Biblioteck (DDB) began a joint project to test the idea of a VIAF. OCLC used matching algorithms to link name authority records of these two national bibliographic agencies and built a server to store the combined records. Additional phases of the project will involve ongoing maintenance to update the central file when either source is updated and possibly the development of a multilingual end user interface. Following the evaluation of the project, the addition of new partners will be explored, particularly those potential partners with non-roman authority records.

LEVERAGING A VIAF ON THE SEMANTIC WEB

When combined with developments in the broader metadata, Web-design, and Semantic Web communities, the power and utility of VIAF outside of libraries becomes clear. Authority record data can be associated more easily with a variety of Web resources, allowing users and potentially machines to immediately start to evaluate the information they are looking at. A quick search of bibliographic data related to a given resource author allows the retrieval of her dissertation, which could be mined for data about the degree granting institution.

Other bibliographic records could be retrieved to help evaluate the original Web resource and related works could offer pathways to additional relevant resources. As other resources start including metadata that uses identifiers or headings to link to a VIAF, the opportunity to connect more interesting bits of information can add significant value to any Web-based information resource. Wikipedia entries, journal articles, Who's Who biographical info, an individual's blog, their homepage, or the homepage of their place of work can all be interconnected, as well as linked to journal articles, bibliographic records in catalogues and in e-commerce sites, and a variety of other scholarly resources. These interconnections have extensive implications for research.

Once there is a corpus of biographical information combined into a data store that is connected to authority data, the information can be used to make inferences about any document, article, Web page, or blog entry that turns up when searching for information. For example, imagine a blog post that includes information about its author's identity. This information could be referenced against available biographical data and used to make inferences about the veracity and objectivity of the post's content.

If the author were affiliated with the Recording Industry Association of America (RIAA) a trade group representing the U.S recording industry, or the Electronic Frontier Foundation (EFF), a non-profit legal organisation focused on defending 'digital rights', heavily involved in fighting bad uses of Digital Rights Management technology, and opposing limitations on fair use, the statement is likely to be much less objective than content posted by a Harvard law professor. While an agent or search tool couldn't necessarily flag such resources as potentially biased without additional information about the affiliate organisation, it would still be very useful to present these additional facts to the user when returning search results.

The metadata community has a number of initiatives underway for describing people, both as agents of resource creation and for the utility of describing relationships between people, describing connections between people and organisations, and for capturing other contact information and other descriptive information about individuals and groups. Examples of such initiatives include the Dublin Core Agents Working Group's work on defining a metadata standard for agent description and identification. Ultimately, this work should result in the development of an Application Profile for agent description.

Also, work has been completed on 'Reference Models for Digital Libraries: Actors and Roles' within the DELOS/NSF Working Group. This work culminated in Final Report, issued in July 2003. Interestingly, this work goes well beyond the scope of authors and content creators; instead the DELOS/NSF model categorises Actors as Users, Professionals, and Agents. In this context, agents are the traditional content creators that help populate a digital library and professionals are the developers of the digital library itself and the providers of digital library services.

The scope of their work may be much deeper than is necessarily relevant to discussions of authority control on the Semantic Web, although the models used and conclusions drawn may prove to play an important role in future discussions about authority control for names. Another initiative, the Friend Of A Friend (FOAF) project described earlier, is of particular use to the Semantic Web community, because it was conceived with the Semantic Web in mind and is built upon the RDF data model.

FOAF expresses identity through any property value pair, allowing you to aggregate data about individuals using any unique property, such as an e-mail address or the URL for a home page. FOAF is primarily designed for community building, but when the possible privacy issues of sharing personal data are resolved there is much potential for FOAF to help aggregate public information about individuals. FOAF could be used to aggregate all sorts of resources, both by and about individuals–Again, resources such as, Wikipedia entries, journal articles, Who's Who biographical info, the individual's homepage, their blog, or their place of work.

This information could be glommed into a programme like Piggy Bank–a FireFox extension for viewing, collecting and merging RDF encoded data, developed by the Simile project –or any other Semantic Web enabled tool, and processed along with other local or remote data stores. For example, a local data store of vcards and/or FOAF data might include private data, such as phone number, calendaring system, and e-mail address. The very presence of that particular identifier in a local store of RDF data about people might change the context of any information interaction with a Wikipedia or Who's Who entry.

Using any 'unique' property to identify entities will certainly help to aggregate most of them, but it would miss entities that are not described using a particular piece of identifying information. Inferences about which descriptions represent the same entity will only go so far in establishing a positive match. The ability to completely aggregate such data becomes even more powerful when the identifying properties can be referenced against the VIAF to determine alternate forms of name and representations in alternate scripts. This allows a query of available RDF data to be much more comprehensive when deciding what pieces of data should be aggregated.

MARKUP AND ENCODING OF AUTHORITY DATA

One of the most valuable activities that libraries and librarians can engage in, both to help realise the Semantic Web and to generally increase the findability of electronic resources in general, is the process of creating versions of vocabularies in machine-readable format. Thesauri, authority files, classifications schemes, and subject heading lists–collectively referred to as Knowledge Organisation Systems–have enormous potential for enhancing the discoverability and organisation of resources in a networked environment.

The potential only increases when such systems are provided in formats designed for emerging Web technology, such as OWL and SKOS–two of the ontology schema of the Semantic Web.

- Knowledge organisation systems can enhance the digital library in a number of ways. They can be used to connect a digital library resource to a related resource. The related information may reside within the KOS itself or the KOS may be used as an intermediary file to retrieve the key needed to access it in another resource. A KOS can make digital library materials accessible to disparate communities. This may be done by providing alternate subject access, by adding access by different modes, by providing multilingual access, and by using the KOS to support free text searching.

The perceived benefits of knowledge organisation systems are of particular importance, and apply to networked resources beyond the scope of digital library materials. The availability of machine-readable representations of various thesauri and other controlled vocabulary enables more effective search and retrieval, better browse functionality and general organisation of materials online, and the automatic creation of context sensitive linkages between available resources and data sets. Additionally, and most importantly for Semantic Web development, providing controlled vocabularies outside of traditional library systems enables a variety of applications to more effectively merge and manipulate data and information from disparate sources. There are many steps that need to be taken to realise this set of goals. Firstly, the library and Semantic Web communities must agree on how best to encode these vocabularies.

Many of the subject schemes already exist in one or more machine-readable representations. Much of LCSH exists in MARC records in library catalogues and the databases of cataloging services such as OCLC's WorldCat and RLIN 21. All of the LC controlled vocabularies are available as complete files of MARC 21 or MARCXML formatted authority records through the Cataloguing Distribution Service of the Library of Congress.

The Getty provides licenced access to its vocabularies in three formats: XML, relational tables and MARC, and provides sample data from each vocabulary for free. At first glance, these formats do not appear to be of much use in the context of RDF, but the standardisation and global use of MARC makes it possible to convert these into RDF-friendly data. One approach is the creation of URIs to identify each terminal node on the source XML structure as a unique concept that can be used as a property in the RDF and DC Abstract Model sense. This prospect has the potential to retain as much of the detail available in the source format as possible, but may prove unnecessary and undesirable due to the complexity of the resultant sets of properties.

On the other hand, the information from MARC records may in fact be useful for automatic processes and machine activities. The richness of MARC authority data, and the time and effort invested in developing, encoding, and sharing this data, provides a unique and powerful set of vocabularies. However, it remains to be seen whether the complexity of the resulting XML records would be an impediment to intero-perability. An alternative approach involves simply cross-walking the XML data into an already defined RDF-friendly form.

Along the way, detail about relationships between terms will likely be lost, but the end product will probably be much simpler to work with. One possible target RDF vocabulary, the Simple Knowledge Organisation System (SKOS) Core has much potential in this context. SKOS Core provides a model for expressing the structure of what they refer to as a 'Concept Scheme'. "Thesauri, classification schemes, subject heading lists, taxonomies, terminologies, glossaries and other types of controlled vocabulary are all examples of concept schemes".

SKOS Core provides a means of expressing most of the semantic relationships included in most library subject vocabularies. For example, 'prefLabel' and 'altLabel' represent 'use' and 'use for' references, while 'broader' and 'narrower' are used to identify hierarchical relationships. SKOS allows for the creation of new labels and the encoding of more specific types of relationships as well. Additionally, SKOS provides mechanisms for various types of notes–scopeNote, definition, example and note.

The SKOS Core community has drafted documentation on 'Publishing a Thesaurus on the Semantic Web," which provides a guide for using SKOS to both describe and encode vocabularies in RDF. Converting large controlled vocabularies into RDF data is certainly a good way to get sample data sets to use to build prototype services. However, the long-term maintenance of such data stores may be problematic. As changes are made to the source vocabulary, those changes need to be propagated through to all the various formats that the vocabulary is made available in.

In the context of SKOS, this is a manageable task. SKOS extensions have been proposed to allow for versioning and the tracking of changes made to controlled vocabularies over time.

However, in cases where vocabularies are likely to be managed in a variety of different formats, the SKOS extensions are less helpful. Another approach is to harvest the source data in its native format and translate it into a variety of output formats either as nightly batch processes or on-the-fly as data is requested.

Progress is being made in this area, such as OCLC's work on exposing vocabularies in a variety of delivery formats, including MARCXML and SKOS. It doesn't matter whether the data store is MADS, MARC, RDF, or some arbitrary flavour of XML, it can be transformed into another format either on-the-fly or as a batch process. A centralised name authority database could be created from the national authority files available in various library communities and stored as normalised MARC 21.

If this data store is deemed useful to the Friend of a Friend (FOAF) community, the data can be turned into RDF. Similarly, Web services like Flickr could convert and makes use of Library of Congress Subject headings to augment both the searching and development of their folksonomies.

NATURAL-LANGUAGE PROCESSING AND AUTOMATIC INDEXING

Indexed books represent the most common example of a subject information retrieval system. Problems associ ated with both the quality and cost of human intellectual indexing have made automatic indexing an attractive goal. During the 1950s and early 1960s there was great optimism that this goal would be readily achieved. However, many of the ideas proposed for text analysis, indexing, and machine translation have proved to be simplistic; the complexity and richness of natural langu age defeated these workers. The indexing problem can be stated quite simply. It requires a content analysis of documents followed by characterisation of such content by descriptive labels.

This requires the following steps:

- Conceptual analysis of the significant content of a document.
- Expressing the analysis by a set of words or phrases to represent the subject.
- Translating the relevant subject descriptions into standard language.
- Arranging the standardised subject descriptions according to the syntax of the indexing language used in the information system.

The ease with which the problem can be expressed does not imply ease of solution. For example, a human indexer reads a section of text and can determine its subject content without conscious thought–reading the text normally involves understanding, which implies that content analysis has been accomplished. This can best be seen when the smooth flow of this process is interrupted, as may happen when the subject matter of text is both complex and unfamiliar. The indexer then has repeatedly to re read and examine text until understanding is acquired.

Then subject analysis is the relatively easy matter of selecting the most appropriate indexing phrase. For this solution to be a model for a computational approach to indexing, however, it must be expressed in algorithmic form: a major problem. To investigate how it has been tackled, a brief look at somc applications of statistical indexing techniques will be followed by a more extensivc survey of Natural Language Processing (NLP). No attempt will be made to survey the areas involved in expert systems and of knowledge representation; Walker's Knowledge Systems and Prolog provides a useful introduction to these areas.

DATABASE INDEXING

At present the literature dealing with indexing topics and concepts is mainly concerned with retrieving infor mation from texts stored in databases, whose function is usually to inform the user of some easily quantifiable fact and also to point the user to some relevant document. The pointing function may be either an abstract, or keywords removed from either the orig inal text or the abstract itself. In neither case is the text manipulated by the system similar to a book.Dealing with such texts is essentially easier than dealing with a book, for the following reasons: the texts normally involve only several sentences as opposed to tens or hundreds of thousands of words; they are usually in the form of abstracted data; and large num bers of significantly different texts are present in the database, and measures of dissimilarity and similarity between texts are thus normally easier to quantify than for a book. Comparisons between manual and automatic indexing systems show further data on the difficulties of indexing books.Cleverdon noted that:

- 'If two people or groups of people construct thesauri in a given subject area, only 60 per cent of the index terms may be common to both;

- If two experienced indcxers index a given docu ment using a given thesaurus, only 30 per cent of the index terms may be common to the two sets;
- If two intermediaries search the same question on the same database on the same host, only 40 per cent of the output may be common to both searches;
- If two scientists or engineers are asked to judge the relevance of a given set of documents to a given question, the area of agreement may not exceed 60 per cent.'

Although these are generalisations, and there are likely to be areas where the performance will exceed these figures, in others it will be considerably worse. Cleverdon suggested that many of these problems could be solved by eliminating the thesaurus and using instead the title or abstract of the article in free-text form; an approach which has had some success, and results from the work of Salton seem to show that performance exceeding that of manual indexing can regularly be achieved for many users, though Blair and Marron come to very different conclusions with the same data, claiming that fewer than 20 per cent of relevant documents are being retrieved.

ARTIFICIAL INTELLIGENCE (AT) APPROACHES TO INDEXING

Much of this work has been shown to be adequate for abstracts, particularly scientific or technical. Indeed, all current automated text-indexing systems are based largely on such statistical work, and hardly show even moderate sophistication in attempting any form of con tent analysis.

These techniques are less useful when applied to longer texts where keywords may form poor identifiers for the subject matter" and recourse still has to be made to the intellectual indexing process to identify correctly the 'aboutness' of a particular section of text, though even this may prove inadequate for research purposes.

For example, when it is necessary to determine whether a particular idea has been put forward by a given researcher it is often found that indexes, to books or to databases, form poor tools for solving this problem."

CONTENT ANALYSIS

Despite the incursions of a variety of non-textual forms requiring indexing, the bulk of the material that indexers are likely to deal with is the precursor of books–galleys and paste-ups. To mimic human intellectual analysis of these texts it is necessary to determine their content by attempting con tent analysis that implies comprehension by the pro gram.

It may seem curious that so little progress appears to have been made in content analysis of texts, when human indexers do such analysis with no apparent effort–syntax analysis; semantic analysis; and discourse analysis.

SYNTAX ANALYSIS

If the overall objective is to determine the intellectual content of tne text, then a sub-problem presents itself when we have to determine the meaning of a sentence. In most systems this means that sentence structure must be determined and possibly regularised in order to simplify the subsequent semantic analysis, which can now be designed to work with less rich forms of words–and therefore those that are more amenable to computational processing.

Syntax analysis performs two main functions in analysing natural language input:

- *Determining the Structure of the Input*: Syntax analysis should identify the subject and objects of each verb and determine what each modifying word or phrase modifies. This is most often done by assigning a tree structure to the input, in a process referred to as parsing;
- *Regularising the Syntactic Structure*:4 Subsequent processing can be simplified if we map the large number of possible input structures into a whatsoever, despite the amusing/apocryphal stories of the results of com puterised content analysis–for example, 'the editors of the new Macmillan Guide to Britain's Nature Reserves do realise the mammoth is extinct, even though it appears in the book's index. An over-zealous computer, working though the text, seised upon a sentence beginning: 'This guide is a mammoth work..."

This apparent lack of progress implies lack neither of effort nor of desire to attend to needs expressed by those involved in the literary field. Many of the problems are well known, if not well understood, for it is the challenge of natural-language processing that a text in its entirety may be less ambiguous than its individual parts. So a natural-language processor must resolve this ambiguity by applying context to select from the various possibili ties available, which are governed by the lexicon and grammar. This is hard because the text may contain the information required to resolve ambiguities, or it may be implicit in the shared background of the author and the reader.

To see more clearly the problems that arise when we look for meaning in text, three stages of text analysis will be examined. These are smaller number of structures. Some material in sentences can be, and usually is, omitted without changing the meaning: *e.g.,* 'She earns less than Mary1. By restoring the omitted text, the sentence structure can be regularised. Other transformations can relate sentences with normal word order to passive and cleft constructions: these will allow subsequent processing to concern itself with a much smaller number of structures. Thus, although there is no absolute need for regularisation, its absence will require usage of more complex semantic rules.

To determine whether regularisation, or even syn tactic analysis prior to semantic analysis, is required, computational linguists have looked at the work of psychologists interested in the way people deal with unusual or abnormal sentences, because such sentences may produce errors giving some understanding of how people deal with sentences in real life. It may be argued that people can use syntactically correct material which lacks any meaning; for example: 'Twas brillig, and the slithy toves'. Here syntax is the only factor giving an appearance of intelligibility. This shows that sentence parsing by humans can take place on the syntactic level with no need for semantics.

Sentences which are ungrammatical, but clear in their intended meaning, for instance 'She like go holiday.', show that semantics may drive an adequate interpretation of a sentence when syntax is poor. Thus we have two strategies used to give meaning to sentences: a syntactic-driven strategy which may be used when semantics are weak or non-existent; and a semantic-driven strategy when syntax is weak. Both methods may be used to extract meaning from a sentence if sections are not clear on the first reading.

In other attempts to explore ways of dealing with sentences in real life, psychologists have been interested in sentences where the reader is 'led up the garden path' in assuming that the sentence means one thing, then when the last word or two is read, sees that his assump tions were erroneous.

An example of this is: 'The horse raced past the barn fell.', where the reader thinks the horse was racing past the barn–until the last word is met, then backtracking occurs in an attempt to re analyse the meaning of the sentence, which is interpreted in the sense, 'The horse raced past the barn fell.' Marcus attempts computer-simulation of the human approach to this problem, and hopes to obtain insights into strategies used for sentence parsing. This should give not only an understanding of how people interpret the written word, but also possible strategies to be adopted by a computer/parsing programme.

PARSERS

Historically, parsing algorithms can be divided into three sections: context-free parsers; transformational parsers; and augmented context-free parsers such as the augmented transition network.

CONTEXT-FREE PARSERS

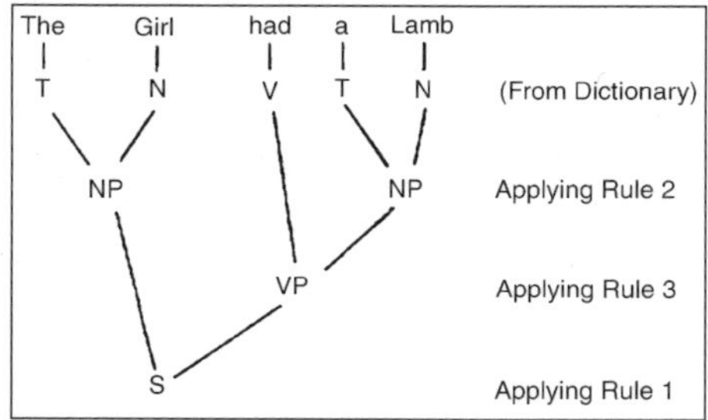

A context-free parser attempts to decompose a sentence by successively applying a series of derivations such as:

- Sentence (S) = noun phrase (NP) + verb phrase (VP).
- Noun phrase = article (T) + noun (N).
- Verb phrase = verb (V) + noun phrase.

With 'The girl had a lamb' the mapping would result in:

This type of parsing is known as bottom-up; the parse is started at the lowest level, that of individual words, and then built up towards a more complex construction. It could, however, start at the top of the tree and attempt to fit the structure to the sentence. Thus the task is to find a set of rules in the grammar of the language, which, correctly applied, produces the sentence being parsed. This is the top-down approach, always implemented with backtracking as a large number of possible parses at one level of the analysis turn out to be unsuccessful when the next level is attempted. The programme must be able to retrace its steps to a previous stage and re-commence an alternative parse. There are advantages and disadvantages in both approaches.

A top-down approach tends to be a poor choice for ambiguous sentences; a bottom-up approach reduces the possible number of interpretations the pro gram has to consider. Thus, if ambiguities arc not a feature of the document, a top-down approach would give a more efficient programme. Already many difficulties are manifest in this system; the grammar rules given are too simple for any real life situation, and extensions have to allow for more complex and variable sentence constructions. This may result in an unacceptable number of possible parses: for example, the sentence: 'Gravely concerned with spreading racial violence. President Kennedy used his press conference to issue counsel to both sides in the struggle' produced 136 possible analyses. An excessive number of pos sible solutions leads to the abandonment of this par sing strategy and the adoption of transformational grammars.

TRANSFORMATIONAL PARSERS

Harris proposed the theory of linguistic transformation, elaborated by his pupil Chomsky, which attempts to generate the deep structure of a sentence, representing its syntactic and semantic interpretation.

Thus a sentence such as 'The boy broke the window' can have a number of transformations:

- The window was broken by the boy (passive transformation);
- It was the boy who broke the window (cleft transformation);
- Was it the boy who broke the window? (question transformation).

All these sentences have constituents in common. If this underlying structure–the deep structure–can be uncovered, the difficulty of ascertaining the meaning may be reduced.

However, though the process of sentence generation from deep to surface structure can be accomplished using only a small number of transformations to produce an acceptable output, the converse does not hold. Hundreds of different reverse transformations apply to each given structure at the analysis step, making this a very ineffi cient process unless extra information is present to guide transformations into paths with a high likelihood of producing the correct deep structure.

Examples of systems which apply a series of reverse transformations may be seen in Petrick "and work by the MITRE group, all done in the 1960s. However, these types of parsers are no longer in common use, as not only were they found computationally inefficient, but a considerable amount of linguistic development has taken place since, the mid-1960s which is reflected in the greater sophistication in both concept and software. Many critiques of transformational grammar are available, but Wilks also postulates the alternative strategy of Preference Semantics," whose core is a system of preferential choice between deep semantic patterns with no conventional grammar analysis or generation.

Wilks argues that transformational grammar was devised independent of considerations of meaning, context and inference, and goes on to 'consider such an even apparently structural-grammatical matter as the ambiguity of prepositions; 'out of', for example, is highly ambiguous, which can be seen from any reflection on such sentences as: I live out of town. I hit her out of anger. I threw the ball out of the window. The statue is made out of marble.... Transformational grammar makes no suggestions whatever as to how the choice should be made.' Preference Semantics, oriented very much towards processing complex sentences, is suggested as a more plausible way of tackling this problem.

AUGMENTED TRANSITION NETWORK (ATM)

The last syntax analyser to be examined is the Aug mented transition network, which has the same power as a transformational grammar, but is considerably more straight forward. In a simple transition network (TN) the grammar is composed of states interconnected by branches specifying transitions between states. Thus a sentence could be represented by: that is, a sentence consists of a sequence of: noun phrase, verb, noun phrase. And a noun phrase consists of: article, adjective, noun.

This style of transition network is recursive; thus, repetitive patterns, for example a series of adjectives immediately preceding and modifying a noun, are catered for without recursion having to be implemented over the whole network. The TN can perform tests that govern the transition from one state to the next and can be programmed to query sentences where grammar might be suspect. So far, this is simply another variant on a regular grammar, but it has the advantage of recursion and of being represented in the form of a digraph, or directed graph, consisting of nodes joined by arcs.

The arcs are labelled by words or word categories; for example, noun (N) or noun phrase (NP), and it is the task of the parser to traverse the graph from node to node. In this example it can only move from node S, to S2 if the next item in the parse can be identified as a verb. Representing a gram mar as a digraph enables formal mathematical opera tions to be performed on the graph, as well as defining its properties. An augmented transition network (ATN) consists of this system with the addition of a system for generating deep structure and allowing grammatical constraints to be imposed, so that it has the important property of performing both surface and deep analysis simultaneously.

Generally, an ATN parser works in a similar way to the top-down context-free parser and uses the conventional backtracking routines to escape from possible parses which proved untenable. Examples of working grammars based on the ATN model include the Linguistic String Parser, - DIAGRAM, Proto-RELADES, and LAS. A com parison between an ATN and a two-stage parser–known as the sausage machine–may be found in the work of Wanner.

CONTEXT-SENSITIVITY

Despite considerable progress in parsing many major problems still remain, at least a proportion of them requiring context-sensitive grammars for their probable resolution in terms both of parsing and semantic pro cessing. An example of the type of difficulties which have proved hard to resolve can be gained by studying prob lems associated with parsing compound nouns.

The following closely follows Sparck Jones who states that three processes apply to compound nominals: they have to be:

- *Bracketed*: Wicker (bread basket) *vs* (wholemeal bread) basket;
- *Lexically disambiguated*: Bread = loaf vs bread = money;
- *Given a meaning characterisation*: Basket for bread *vs* basket with bread.

She states, 'various strategies, or rather non-strategies, have been adopted to deal with compound nouns. One, for example, is to put compound nouns in the lexicon. A second is to assume that restrictions on the possible interpretations of the constituents, for a specific universe of discourse, will force an appropriate interpretation on the whole. A third is not to attempt a full characteriza tion of the whole. And a fourth is to disregard elements which cannot be processed.

These are all unsatisfactory, for obvious reasons. We cannot put all the compounds, even for a limited domain, in the lexicon. We cannot rely on sense restrictions to give us an acceptable interpreta tion. We cannot assume that an explicit characterisation is unnecessary. And we cannot throw parts of the input away.'Furthermore, even with a considerable quantity of domain-specific knowledge, there must be differences in interpretation of:

- 'These border plants are expensive'–implying that the set of plants being considered are those normally found in a border; and

- These border plants have to be replaced'–that is, these plants in the border have to be replaced. The location of the plants is under consideration irrespective of the actual type of plant found there.

At present no system can cope with such nuances of meaning. We could take the matter still further. If we were to use the same core of words, but applied to a different domain: The IRA have done so much bombing that all the border plants have to be replaced' we have a situation where 'border plants' could apply to plants which grow, but is more likely to apply to factories (= plants) located at the Eire/N Ireland border. Disam biguation here would be a far from straightforward task.

The problem lies in parsing having been syntax-driven; most parsers are based on context-free grammar, whilst the underlying problems of ambiguous structures essen tially need semantic guidance not only from the context but also by using referents from domains of personal experience of the reader.

However, any conclusions formed from considering these facts can only be tentative, and influenced by the domain of discourse of any particular text. For example, much work has been done on the automatic indexing of chemical texts.

M The interest for many potential readers in this field is likely to be bound up with chemical structures, physical processes and chemical reactions. By their nature these are domain-restricted, and, due to the logical way chemical names are built up, eminently suitable for the application of stemming techniques– which in the process of stripping off prefixes and suffixes will be able to identify the structure, elements or con stituent groups of the compound under discussion–followed by statistical analysis. Few other subjects will be so amenable to this type of analysis.

INDEXING QUALITY

One also needs to ask 'How good an index do we need?' These ambiguities may simply be ignored, and reliance placed on other, clearer, sections of the text to fill in the doubtful areas, and/or human intervention for disambiguation. This crucial question could only be answered according to individual needs.

Factors to con sider include the costs of checking entries manually for possible errors; of running a programme that produces fewer errors than the one currently in use; and of errors–if the error rate is low enough users are likely to be satisfied with the performance.

At present, linguistic analysis of text by computer is not far enough advanced for such questions to be answered, but if we draw on results obtained from statistical, non-linguistic, indexing systems, we can surmise that 100 per cent accuracy is not needed for acceptable performance.' The caveat should be added that, as with most research on indexing, these results apply to large databases, and may well be inapplicable to texts such as books.

SEMANTIC AND DISCOURSE ANALYSIS

The object of parsing a sentence is only the first stage in a strategy to attempt to find some way in which the meaning of a sentence and the meanings inherent in a series of sentences could be represented in a computer with the aim of manipu-lating concepts and ideas inherent in the text with the same facility as the computer can manipulate characters.

It is only when text can be understood by a computer that we can hope to simulate the intellectual actions of a human indexer. As in the case of syntactic analysis, a realistic solution to the problem of semantic analysis must imply simplifi cation–in which case we need to specify a formal language on which to map natural language. Furthermore, in the case of indexing, we must decide also whether any other specialised needs must be met cither in the form of extra semantic information, or, conversely, whether all the information obtained from a full seman tic analysis would be required for our purposes.

It has been suggested that the task is to examine the semantic component of:

- Methods of identifying meaningful units in the input document;
- The derivation of document descriptions from these;
- The construction and use of classifications and other forms of index language organisation.

Unfortunately none of these aims is achievable without the addition of substantial quantities of outside knowledge. Part of this may come from the text itself, but many more assumptions of knowledge common to the author and the intended audience are made than may initially be obvious. Difficulties arising here may be illustrated by reference to a straightforward description: 'Just before dawn, the Valiant sighted the Zwiebel and fired two torpedoes. It sank swiftly, leaving few survivors."

Understanding this simple story is more than under standing the sum of its parts. We have to consider what the 'it' refers to. There are four possible antecedents: dawn; Valiant; Zwiebel; torpedoes. Straightforward syntactic analysis enables us to exclude torpedoes and semantic analysis excludes dawn, but only general world knowledge enables us to surmise that Valiant and Zwiebel must both be ships, and there is a causal relationship between firing torpedoes and sinking another ship. This type of implicit information, inherent in all texts, must be recovered to enable an automated indexing system to make an intelligent assessment of the suit ability of particular phrases or concepts as index entries. This search for meaning is at the root of both semantic analysis and discourse analysis and this aspect of computational linguistics has so far proved intractable.

Most attempts to solve the prob lem have been restricted in their domain as a conse quence of the method used to overcome the problem, which is attempting to assemble all the knowledge needed to answer any particular problem. This knowl edge could be used at the syntactic analysis stage by removing some syntactically plausible but semantically unlikely parses. The organisation of such quantities of knowledge is no trivial undertaking, though it has been attempted. One notable method was that of frames, ' based on the observation that new knowledge tends to be assimilated by identifying at least a portion of it with patterns inherent in pre-existing information.

These frames may be:

- Prototypes, describing classes of objects, actions, or situations: *e.g.,* chairs, running, attending the theatre. They form a general framework of expectations–so whether one goes to a theatre in Edinburgh or Vienna, the general outlines of what one does, how one behaves, and the point of the visit remain broadly the same. Consequently the 'going to the theatre' frame is likely to remain valid;
- Instance frames, describing particular instances of action, etc., *e.g.,* yesterday's visit to the theatre.

There are obvious similarities between frames and context-free grammar: prototype frames correspond to the rules of the grammar itself and instance frames to detailed grammatical knowledge. The concept of frames may also be considered as a context-free description of world knowledge. Some frame-based knowledge representation langu ages have been developed and this type of work has lead to the development of scripts that attempt to contain the meta-knowledge needed to understand a given simple narrative. Thus, if a computer programme has the appropriate script for a particular scene, it is possible to arrange for it to query anomalous situations, ask apparently intelligent questions and make responses to queries that involve concepts not directly mentioned in the text.

The classic example of a script is that of a restaurant where information is present about the characters, scene and typical actions. Anaphoric resolution thus becomes easier. For example: 'The customer told the waiter that he would like some wine.' We know that waiters serve food and drink, and customers order it, so it is clear that he must refer to the customer, not the waiter; whereas 'The customer told the waiter that he should bring the wine list' would result in he applying to the waiter, as it is the job of the waiter to bring this and similar items. This example shows that scripts cannot be used in novel situations: for these plans can be used, with attempts made to construct a causal chain.

This is no trivial problem: many of the required connections may be implicit, rather than directly stated, in the text. However, a system has been implemented by Wilensky as PAM (plan applier module) and as a simplified system called micro-PAM. These systems produce a complex series of inferences that raise the problem of which inference should be followed. The database of rules and scripts needed is very large even for what would normally be considered as fairly trivial situations, such as the restaurant scenario. A system requires considerable development effort to 'understand' even those episodes which consist of a relatively low number of sentences, even only one sen tence.

Avoiding generalisation, it can be seen that if a large number of sentences deal with essentially the same concept, then processing of the information becomes easier than if rapid changes of content in the sentences necessitated the implementation of a large number of plans in the system. A natural-language indexing system might use semantic analysis of text to produce suitable index entries, but only if the domain of discourse was very restricted. Unfortunately, this is also the area where statistical analysis and word stemming techniques can be quite successfully applied; the more diffuse areas prove intractable both for statistical analysis and discourse analysis.

The former is unsuited to this work, as keyword extraction may have little relevance to the production of useful index entries, and the very vastness of the domain in the latter poses difficult problems despite efforts to produce generalisations of text. One way of dealing with this problem is to develop a system, goal subsumption, which tries to plan for the satisfaction of several goals at the same time. In spite of all these strategies, however, the problem has in essence remained unsolved, particularly in attempts to transfer laboratory results to the domain of ordinary texts.

SEARCHING IN ONLINE LIBRARY CATALOGUES

Traditionally library catalogues have provided somewhat limited capabilities for searching by subject. The replacement of the card catalogue by online public access catalogues has brought about a great resurgence of interest throughout the library profession in all aspects of subject access. For one thing, it has been found that the proportion of catalogue searches that are subject searches has tended to increase considerably as OPACs fall into place. LIPETZ and PAULSON confirm this trend in a 'before and after' study at the New York State Library.

FROST studied catalogue users at the University of Houston and concluded that students search more often by subject than do faculty. However, on the basis of a study at the City University prior to the automating of their catalogue, HANCOCK suggests that subject searching of manual catalogues may have been more prevalent than previously thought. KASKE has found great variability in the proportion of OPAC searches that are subject searches–by hour of day, day of week, and week of semester. In discussions of online catalogue development in libraries two approaches are particularly evident.

One is to improve the interface between user and system, and the other is to enhance or augment the system itself. An analysis of online subject searches led one group of librarians and information specialists to conclude that an online catalogue must compensate for a user's inability to match his or her subject headings exactly with those of LCSH, must provide more than one searching option, and should permit users to refine large retrieval sets. HILDRETH also argues for a more interactive interface between the user and the system.

One essential feature is to provide the user with information concerning the status of the search as it progresses. The Subject Access Project performed at Syracuse University in the late 1970s determined that augmenting subject headings of traditional bibliographic records with terms from tables of contents and back-of-the-book indexes may be an efficient and relatively inexpensive way to improve subject access in the catalogue. BYRNE and MICCO describe a study in which an average of 21 multiword terms, drawn from indexes or tables of contents, were added to MARC records for 6,000 books.

Results of their studies indicate that searches of these augmented records achieved much improved recall compared with searches on titles or subject headings. DIODATO considers the same issue from a slightly different point of view when he studies readers' descriptions of books to determine if the descriptions match terms from the tables of contents and indexes. He concludes that tables of contents and indexes are two sources of terms that are likely to reflect terms that the user would use in searching for the books.

JAMIESON *et al.* have compared the searching of uncontrolled keywords occurring in bibliographic records with the searching of controlled terms in the records. In recognition of the millions of bibliographic records presently in MARC format in libraries and information centers, CHITTY argues that the issue is not how to improve the information on the record but how best to use the information already present. In actuality, the approaches to improving online catalogues are not a choice between whether the content is enhanced or the interface is improved. The content, the system/user interface, and the user are all integral parts of the system.

DWYER points out that many developments in the bibliographic organisation of libraries over the years have resulted in split files; he proposes that a total retrospective conversion be implemented as one means towards building better catalogues. Quality cataloging is a necessity because the accuracy of a system's content ultimately determines the success of retrieval. Because any transition to an online catalogue involves choices and trade-offs, Dwyer stresses the importance of understanding the true costs involved and of understanding the users' requirements in order to make intelligent choices in questions of design.

LAWRY raises the question, 'Can online catalogues be too easy'? The question indicates a concern that a system that appears to 'think' for the user, by assisting the user in query formulation, search strategy selection, and evaluation of retrieved titles, is unintentionally misleading the user.

Lawry stresses the importance of user education to make effective use of all the tools available in the library.BATES presents a model of subject access in online catalogues based on three design principles:

- Uncertainty;
- Variety; and
- Complexity.

Bates argues that because indexing is characterised by variety, searching should no longer be based on the exact matching of terms but, instead, should help the searcher by displaying and 'making it easier to explore' a variety of terms. Two tools proposed for improving search performance are an end-user thesaurus and a 'front-end system mind'; the former is basically a vast entry vocabulary, and the latter is a semantic network, incorporating the entry terms, that allows a searcher to select from a variety of methods for generating semantic associations.

The design approach proposed is intended to be implemented in existing catalogues based on LCSH without the need for any reindexing. Bates seems optimistic about the future of subject access in online catalogues. Not so BORGMAN, her colleague at UCLA. Based on studies of user behaviour in subject searching–whether in library catalogues or in broader bibliographic databases–she concludes that "we do not yet have sufficient knowledge of user behaviour to make improvements in system design".

Using the OKAPI (Online Keyword Access to Public Information) system, WALKER and WALKER and JONES investigated possible methods for improving subject searches. Automatic word stemming, synonym and cross-reference tables, and techniques for the approximate matching of words were all studied. They concluded that weak stemming is beneficial but that strong stemming is of doubtful utility, that semiautomatic spelling correction should be used in online catalogues, and that cross-reference lists to allow automatic cross-referencing should be compiled using input from cooperating libraries.

The cross-reference lists investigated were extremely simple, incorporating abbreviations, noun-adjective pairs, alternative terminology, alternative spellings, irregular plurals, related terms, numbers, and phrases. The phrases category is a little different from the others in that it consists of word combinations that should not be split up by searching algorithms because the meaning of the individual words is quite different from that of their combination.

A much more comprehensive study was the doctoral research project of LESTER. Her objective was to determine what features would be needed in online catalogues to increase the success of users in matching their search terms with LCSH. Random samples of user subject terms, selected from the transaction logs associated with the NOTIS/LUIS online catalogue at Northwestern University were compared with LCSH. For user terms that failed to match the headings, 22 different strategies for achieving a match were investigated.Strategies that did *not* improve matching significantly were: use of a spelling checker, singular/plural conflation, phonetic spelling, exact matching in either subject or personal name authority files, and any process involving geographic name authority files.

The strategies of right truncation, string searching with adjacency, and searching of keywords with Boolean operators significantly improved the matching whether or not the database were augmented by the inclusion of subject and name authority files and/or the ability to search all fields of a bibliographic record. It is interesting to compare Lester's finding on authority files–that they would have little effect on subject retrieval–with the finding of VAN PULIS and LUDY–that subject authority files are little used even when made available online.

MICCO *et al.* report on a project at Chatham College to develop an expert system capable of searching for and providing access to knowledge at the same level as a skilled reference librarian. The project proposes a system that will develop a user profile and diagnose information need, then connect the user to the information through a network interface that will include the use of CD-ROM technologies. The system is envisioned as using a Macintosh-style interface with windows and a mouse. It would have a three-tiered structure: the first level providing access tools, the second providing access to monographs, and the third providing access to periodicals.

As currently projected, the system will use the same types of heuristics employed by expert human searchers rather than the textual keyword searching approach frequently used in computer-based systems. Several projects that have dealt with the use of classification schemes in OPACs were reviewed in the earlier section on classification schemes.

Information Requests

The effectiveness of a delegated search, of course, very much depends on how well a request made by a user actually reflects the user's information need. Much work has been done on user-intermediary interaction in information retrieval. AUSTER and LAWTON look at various characteristics of the pre-search interview as factors affecting the success of a search. ALLEN claims that the way users understand and express their needs will be affected by the cognitive structures by which they have organised their knowledge of the topic and by the schemata introduced in the questions that intermediaries ask. Differences in personal schemata may mean that the same problem could result in completely different questions as filtered through the minds of different individuals.

One major problem in user-intermediary interaction is that the personal schemata of the user and that of the information specialist may be quite far apart. Moreover, various 'external schemata' may also exert strong influence on the interactions between user and intermediary. Somewhat related to Allen's work is that of DERR, who identifies five types of expressions used by individuals in making demands on information services; he discusses the implications of the differences for practices in information retrieval. PETRUS points out that the imperfect nature of requests makes information retrieval an operation based on probability. The retrieval situation can be described by the theory of statistical solutions.

NATURAL-LANGUAGE SEARCHING

The searching of text by computer can be traced back to the late 1950s, but interest has continued to increase as more and more text becomes accessible online. Based on studies performed with the full text of popular magazines, TENOPIR presents a useful but brief discussion of the relative effectiveness of various types of strategies for full-text searching. COVE and WALSH look at the feasibility of a browsing approach to searching text online. They describe a system that will display text extracts to prompt the user to select words. These can then lead to 'associated words'–*i.e.,* words occurring as the 'nearest neighbours' of the words originally selected–which can generate further displays of text, from which additional 'browse words' can be selected, and so on.

The type of text that is generally accessible online consists of relatively brief items such as journal articles, abstracts, or patents. Because of rapidly declining costs, it is now becoming increasingly feasible to store and exploit the text of much longer items, but how useful would it be to be able to search the complete text of, say, monographs? Based on studies of how library patrons use non-fiction books, PRABHA and RICE conclude that systems that permit the searching of the full text of non-fiction books would be of value to the users of at least the academic libraries. Over the years a number of studies have compared the results of searches in humanly indexed bibliographic databases with results of searches in full-text databases.

The common finding is that full-text databases give greater recall but reduced precision. SIEVERT *et al.* confirm this by comparing results achieved in searching MEDLINE with those achieved through searching two full-text databases in medicine; RO comes to the same conclusion in a different environment.

Unfortunately, this type of result is frequently mis-interpreted. The fact that a full-text database gives better recall than a database of humanly indexed bibliographic records has nothing to do with the properties of text *per se*; it is simply due to the fact that text records tend to be longer and thus provide more access points.

A database of records indexed with an average of, say, 50 descriptors may well give better recall than a database of brief abstracts, but one could change these results dramatically by greatly increasing the length of the abstracts or drastically reducing the number of descriptors assigned. It is the length of the record that is the major determinant of what is and is not retrieved, but this fact is sometimes overlooked.

AUSTIN examines some of the implications of natural-language searching, illustrating cases in which natural-language searches have failed. These failures are analysed for possible solutions, leading the author to conclude that computers exacerbate rather than alleviate the need for vocabulary control. HOOD reaches a similar conclusion. Full-text searching tends to uncover details, whereas controlled-vocabulary searching tends to uncover broad concepts. He concludes that a comprehensive search would require more than one method. Investigators at Syracuse University have undertaken several related studies on what is assumed to be one of the problems of text searching–the implicit reference to topics through anaphora. For example, AIDS can be variously represented by 'the disease,' 'it,' and so on, in a text. In one study the anaphors occurring in abstracts were replaced by their referents. It was then determined what effect this replacement would have on term weighting, based on word frequency counts, and subsequently on retrieval.

The results were inconclusive: in some searches the replacement improved the ranking of documents in search outputs, while in others it actually caused a deterioration of the ranking. It was hypothesised that this anomaly might be caused by the fact that anaphors sometimes refer to topics that are integral to a text, while at other times they refer to topics that are peripheral. This hypothesis was tested. Using abstracts from the PsycINFO database, words or phrases serving as anaphors were judged as being integral in 52 per cent of the cases studied; the comparable value for abstracts from the INSPEC database was 68 per cent.

The authors concluded that the resolution of anaphora may indeed be important if the effectiveness of text searching is to be improved. This is an example of a conclusion that is based on the processing of abstracts but that may not apply to the full-text situation. Presumably, the redundancy of full text will create a situation wherein the frequency with which a topic occurs *explicitly* will generally reflect its importance in the text regardless of how many implicit references may be missed. DOSZKOCS gives a useful general overview of natural-language processing in information retrieval.

The relative merits of natural-language *vs.* controlled-vocabulary approaches to information retrieval are still debated. DUBOIS compares the two approaches, and SVENONIUS looks at the history of the issue and suggests areas for research that "would clarify it in such a way as to contribute to a rational basis for the design of retrieval tools such as thesauri".BAER and JOHNSON, considering in particular the OP AC situation, conclude that vocabulary control is even more important in the online environment than it is in manual systems. As full-text databases become the norm, there looms a danger that the mere presence of the complete text may be viewed as a labour-saving substitute for subject indexing. YANCEY points out that the growth of information through full-text services will place even more importance on relevance and warns of the loss of retrieval capability through lack of subject indexing. A combination of full-text and subject-searching techniques to link past and present knowledge is presented as the preferable alternative. TEUFEL describes an approach to text retrieval that he refers to as '*n*-gram indexing.' The texts of abstracts are reduced to significant words through use of a stop list, then reduced further to word stems.

The stems are converted into trigrams; 'high noise' trigrams are replaced by tetragrams or even pentagrams. Natural-language queries are processed in the same way. Retrieval consists of looking for the best matches between *n*-gram representations of documents and of requests. Teufel presents some results of tests using abstracts from the INSPEC database. Problems in the portability of natural-language queries from one database to another are addressed by DAMERAU.

THE ALPHABETICAL INDEXING LANGUAGES OF UNIVERSITY LIBRARIES' ONLINE CATALOGUES

Indexing languages are support tools for indexing and information retrieval, which are a fundamental component of automated information systems for organising and disseminating information in specialised scientific areas that require a greater control of terminology. Fernández Molina and Moya Anegón consider online catalogues as automated retrieval systems of information that are more generally available and which are the first to be used by any user when there is a need for information.

In the First Meeting of Experts on an International Cataloguing Code, held in 2003, also known as 'Principles of Frankfurt', the functions of the catalogue were organised, corresponding to the environment of online catalogues, hence, the Paris principles were expanded to the field of bibliographic description by subject and to the conceptual models established by IFLA–International Federation of Library Associations. The evolution of representation and information retrieval, made possible by technological advances, can also be evidenced by the agility of the description activity, through cooperative cataloging that enables importing standard records in other retrieval information systems from various libraries, in accordance with international standards, aiming to interchange them, hence, contributing to the formation of online Bibliographic Database. This process offers advantages in terms of time, as the cataloging of a specific work will be much faster and easier, resulting in a lower cost.

Cooperative cataloging must be carried out carefully and specifically, regarding the thematic processing of the information and considering the guiding principles to conduct quality indexing. This is a result of developing the indexation during cataloguing, according to a defined indexing policy adopted by the system and with the proper use of alphabetical indexing languages as knowledge organisation systems. It can be concluded that the proper use of indexing language is necessary to ensure the implementation of quality indexing and information retrieval processes used by indexers and by users.

The shifts in paradigms within the scope of indexing as a representation process of information for constructing online catalogues, from the proposed use of *FRBRs,* are collaborative in these processes. The construction of online catalogues focused on users and on social context that involves the processing of information must be performed by multidisciplinary and integrated teams: Librarians, users, authors, catalogue designers, systems analysts, among others, valorised by the presence of librarians as promoters in the design of access points, exemplified also by the analytical access of subjects, authors and titles and other resources applicable to the representation and information retrieval. From this perspective, it is important to use relevant indexing language that portrays not only the profile of the catalogue, but also its user communities and, therefore, the evaluation studies of indexing languages to assist in choosing the more suitable knowledge organisation system to meet such purposes.

EVALUATION STUDIES OF INDEXING LANGUAGES IN INFORMATION RETRIEVAL SYSTEMS

When discussing the research work and evaluation methods of indexing languages in information retrieval systems, we verify a correlation between these themes and the epistemology of science information that includes independent outlooks to consolidate this scientific field. Several aspects influenced the development of this area, defining different epistemological paradigms, yet interrelated and comple-mentary. They are characterised by the existence of physical views, cognitive views and socio-cognitive views in the process of information retrieval.

The physical paradigm values the information retrieval system and the message transmitting process, and inserted in this context, we consider the online collective catalogue as 'physical' and the bibliographic record as the transmitter, which transmits the information to the user that receives the message. This information will be encoded to be transmitted as a message by the indexing language, which is then decoded by the user, sharing the same code of the bibliographic record. The communication design enables the feedback of the process, which may cause noise or silence in the recovery process of the information recorded on index supports. In contrast, the evaluation studies with a quantitative approach, from the 1970s, illustrate a shift from the physical view to the cognitive view, signaling the development of evaluation studies focussed on the user.

In the cognitive paradigm, the user is placed in an active position to elaborate ideas, concepts, etc. within an individual context. This scenario is viewed through the human dimension outlook, that is, the perspective focussed on the user, because the information retrieval systems should be modelled according to the user, in the framework of their information needs and their behaviour patterns in the search and use of information. However, since, the 1990s, the cognitive approaches have been analysed and criticised by many researchers which, in addition to divulging the cognitive processes of individuals to carry out indexing processes and designing building systems for information retrieval, aggregate 'context' as an important element, emphasising a social-cognitive view, hence, rendering this process effective.

Our view, supported by Capurro, leads us to presume that the construction of a retrieval information system holds users and their information needs as its focal point. The users, in turn, playing an active role in the socio-cultural context, enable the storage and perform the recovery and interpretation of the available bibliographic records. Consequently, the individual is seen as a part of a society and thus, the studies developed from the socio-cognitive approach regard the phenomena as embedded in a social context.

In the research development of information science, especially in the evaluation of indexing language thematic, we see that the theories about the quantitative and qualitative methods are part of this important scientific-theoretical scenario depicted by the physical and cognitive paradigms. This demonstrates the applicability of these approaches in the evaluation studies focussed on the system and on the user and not considering evaluation studies of indexing languages by the socio-cognitive approach based on epistemological ideas resulting from the social paradigm.

The quantitative methodology, representative of the physical paradigm, enables gathering information from a larger number of respondents, statistical analyses and, usually, the comparison and generalisation of results. From this perspective, we emphasise the classical indexing language evaluation studies; the Cranfield I and Cranfield II Projects, which were developed in 1957 and 1963, respectively,; the Lancaster study, which established the parameters and quantitative indices of precision and recall, which are applicable to assessing information retrieval systems exemplified by the MEDLARS system and the Aberystwyth Test.

These were developed in 1970 inscribing the issue of specificity as a substantially important matter in the development of alphabetical indexing languages, in addition to the research of Torres and of Oliveira, the object of whose empirical study was the Subject Headings List of the BIBLIODATA network, the particular interest of our study. The qualitative methodology works with a plethora of interpretations, meanings, beliefs, values and attitudes, establishing close relationships with the theoretical and conceptual foundations arising from the cognitive paradigm in the Information Science area, showing the change from physical view to the cognitive view, and characterising the elaboration of evaluation studies guided by the user. Qualitative evaluation studies on indexing languages developed by Owens and Cochrane and Toews are examples of this methodology scenario, depicting the importance of using international guidelines and standards in the construction of knowledge organisation systems that are compatible with the users search needs. Qualitative methodology provides direct involvement with individuals, places and interactive processes; starting a descriptive collection guided the accuracy that must exist during the analysis of data interpretation.

It should be noted that in the context of qualitative methodology, the cognitive approach is present in the area of information science when conducting searches on thematic processing and information retrieval, showing the actions undertaken by librarians and users during the development of these processes. Thus, studies using the qualitative-cognitive methodology show the subjectivity of the librarians and users mental activity during their professional activity. This is seen from actions that intend to reveal the implicit aspects in the knowledge structures of these professionals and users.

The studies of Dervin on the sense-making approach, initially applied to the communication sciences area, contributed to developing cognitive approaches. The data collection technique called Focus group was also used in qualitative-cognitive research work, initially in the marketing area and then in social sciences, ergonomics, health sciences, information science, and others. In the field of information science, the research work of Connaway applied the focus group technique to analyse the performance of the online catalogue of the University of Wisconsin-Madison, with emphasis on the evaluation of indexing language adopted by the system from the users perspective.

The introspective technique of the Verbal Protocol or 'Think Aloud' is applied to qualitative evaluation studies where the individuals express, aloud, what they think and what goes on in their minds while performing a task. These statements are recorded, and the individuals behaviour, such as facial expressions are also recorded. Thus, the language of thought performs many cognitive processes such as perception and reasoning. In Brazil, the pioneer research work using the technique, developed by Fujita and Fujita, in observing indexed reading, shows excellent results in the use of the verbal protocol, illustrating new aspects of indexed reading, among other contributions.

By using the verbal protocol technique, users can 'think aloud' by producing opinions and comments about the object being evaluated, hence, carrying out a cooperative and participatory evaluation: The users participate by identifying and understanding problems of information retrieval and by using the system in their own work environment. Thus, Boccato and Fujita developed a research work to evaluate, from the users perspective, indexing language DeCS-Descriptors in Health Sciences, used for information retrieval in the LILACS system produced by BIREME, in order to obtain indicators to outline language improvement strategies in the area of speech and language therapy. The study led to the consideration of the statements issued by the four participants and the results of the analysis revealed that the DeCS language in speech therapy demonstrated the search had unsatisfactory results on information retrieval.

In summary, regarding research development in the information science area, especially the thematic evaluation of indexing languages, we saw that the quantitative and qualitative methods are part of this important scientific-theoretical scenario portrayed by the physical and cognitive paradigms. This demonstrated the applicability of these approaches in evaluation studies focussed on the system and the user, not considering evaluation studies of indexing languages by the socio-cognitive approach based on the epistemological ideas resulting from the social paradigm that regards users inserted into their social environment.

THE SOCIO-COGNITIVE CONTEXT OF INDEXERS AND USERS IN UNIVERSITY LIBRARIES

The socio-cognitive context concerns representation and information retrieval from the perspective of individuals in their socio-cultural-historical context, on the assumption that the users information needs are constructed from outside to inside, that is, the users environment influence and contribute to constructing this need, which will be represented by their mental models associated with their conception of the world, reflected on their real information interest. Boccato and Fujita The context performs the mediation between the real situation in the library, guided by the analysis concepts used by the indexers, and the linguistic system, the indexed language adopted by the system, characterised by the representation of the indexed documents.

The socio-cognitive context of indexers refers to " a prior knowledge that such professionals have their working tools and the real needs of users". The activity of indexing leads to the indexer adopting a conception of the matter which should be intimately related to their established institutional objectives and to the information retrieval system itself, detailed in the indexing policy. These conceptions of subject analysis, which we believe affect the performance of the indexer, are classified according to Albrechtsen in simplist conception, content-oriented conception and requirements-oriented conception. The users previous knowledge is characterised by the university, by the research groups and by the online collective catalogue, elements that guide and influence the expression of their need for information, concomitant with the cognitive processes to meet this need.

Thus, the socio-cognitive context is a factor to be considered in the indexing process development, from indexing reading, aimed at the analysis and representation of information consistent with the users search needs. Associated with the socio-cognitive aspect, the physical aspects, to which the institution and/or the information system are linked through the mission, objectives, the strategic plans and philosophy, and the psychological aspects are fundamental to form the indexers context, as very significant variables in the construction of this process.The indexing language seen as the indexers expertise and prior knowledge, should enable highly accurate content matching of the documents and the users information needs expressed by their repertoire, resulting from prior knowledge constituted by the university, the research groups, the curriculum classification of scientific and academic disciplines and by the information retrieval system itself. In this case, the holistic and collective views of indexers and users are favoured, as they contribute to the definition of a thematic processing of information and to the modelling and construction of information retrieval systems.

Based on this concept, the information science area turns to a theoretical dimension brought into focus by interpretive approaches, focused on the semantic factors and the information social context of indexers and users. In this sense, our research work is contextualised between the shift of cognitive paradigm to the social paradigm, which puts the context of indexers and users in the center of the informational processes, characterised by the representation and information retrieval and knowledge.

Therefore, this research focuses on the socio-cognitive context of indexers and users, based on the theoretical perspectives of Hjørland, which approves a 'methodological collectivistic approach' for the proposal of conducting an assessment study on the use of indexing language in online catalogues of specialised scientific areas of university libraries, focusing on technologies of representation and information retrieval, using the verbal protocol as a data collection technique.

The verbal protocol technique, viewed by the socio-cognitive approach, focuses on the individual when performing a particular activity and its cognition related to its production context. With regards to the indexers, the interest is the thematic processing of information, specifically the indexing and the use it will make of indexing language when representing the information. From the users perspective, the focus is on information retrieval by subject, by using language to search for information and interacting with their environment.

MATERIALS AND METHODS

The data collections were performed on a sample of nine libraries of the UNESP in the three knowledge areas, exact sciences, humanities and biological sciences, of the civil engineering, education, and dentistry courses. The empirical study objective was the Subject Headings List of the Bibliodata Network used in the processes of indexing and information retrieval in the online collective catalogue ATHENA is demons-trated in table.The methodology consisted of a three-part diagnostic study:

- Operation and procedures in the processing of indexed information in the UNESP Libraries Network based on the perspective of the General Coordinator of Libraries;

- Operation and procedures in the processing of information in the UNESP Network of Libraries from the cataloguers outlook;
- The users evaluation on access and retrieval of online information.

Table. Selection of UNESP University Libraries and their Tespective Identifications.

City	Course	Area Identification	Libraries/Brazilian
Civil	Exact sciencesBauru		E1
	engineering	Guaratinguetá	E2
Ilha Solteira		E3	
Education	Humanities	Presidente Prudente	H1
	Rio Claro		H2
			São José do Rio Preto
	H3		
	Dentistry	Biological	Araçatuba
	B1		
		sciences	Araraquara
	B2		
			São José dos Campos
	B3		

To perform the first part, organisational diagnostic questionnaires were administered to the directors of university libraries. The preparation of the questionnaire was essential for the organisational diagnosis, consisting of a total of twenty-six open, closed and mixed questions.

In the second part, for the operation and procedures for the processing of information in the UNESP Network of Libraries from the cataloguers outlook, we used the cognitive approach with the verbal protocol introspection technique, as follows:

- *Group Verbal Protocol* (GVP) with the heads of libraries, cataloguers, reference librarians, faculty staff users, head researchers and research group staff, and student body users for accessing the participants knowledge on the processing of indexing content of university libraries as a source of qualified data collection in the diagnosis.
- Individual Verbal Protocol was conducted with by Cataloguers to identify the procedures of subject analysis and representation in cataloguing books, as well as to identify the difficulties and restrictions.

In the third part, regarding the evaluation of user access and retrieval of online information, Individual Verbal Protocols were performed with undergraduate freshmen and senior Users, of the aforementioned courses. In the introspective technique of verbal protocol " the individuals, talk aloud, and express what occurs in their minds during the execution of a task". These statements are recorded and transcribed verbatim to be analysed later through the establishment of categories. In the context of this study, the verbal protocol, seen from the socio-cognitive approach, focuses on the individual at the moment of undertaking a specific activity and his cognition in relation to his context of production.

In addition to this, it should be pointed out that the participation of the cataloguer is evidenced in the development of the indexing in the cataloguing via the use he makes of indexing language during this activity.

With respect to the user, the focus is centred on the search and retrieval by subject, by means of the use of language in the satisfaction of his research needs integrated with his environment consisting of the university, research group, syllabus and catalogue. Individual verbal protocol consists of the recording of the 'think aloud' of a single individual during the undertaking of a task, and group verbal protocol itemises the discussion of a copy-text on the subject that involves the task to be observed and, consequently, collected from the utterances of the individuals and from their cognitions of the theme being dealt with and evaluated. The different modalities of verbal protocols follow similar procedures in their application:

Procedures that Anticipated Application of Verbal Protocol

Definition of the universe of the research:

- *GVP and IVP*: University libraries of the UNESP Library Network Brazil.

Selection of copy-text:

- *GVP*: Passage between pages 205 and 208 of the following article: Dias, EW, Naves, MML, Moura, MA. The information-seeking behaviour of researchers and subject analysis.
- *IVP-C*: The bibliographical record itself to be catalogued for inclusion in the ATHENA catalogue of the UNESP Library Network.
- *IVP-U*: The bibliographical record itself retrieved from the ATHENA catalogue of the UNESP Library Network.

Definition of the task:

- *GVP*: Discussion of the copy-text previously referenced.
- *IVP-C*: Undertaking of the by cataloguers of the indexing for the cataloguing of books on dentistry, civil engineering and education, highlighting the use of the LCARB in the process of the representation of information.
- *IVP-U*: Undertaking by the users of information retrieval on topics determined by them in dentistry, civil engineering and education, in the collective Athena catalogue, by subject field, using the LCARB indexing language.

Selection of the individuals:

- *GVP*: Three librarians, one teacher and one student.
- *IVP-C*: Population of by cataloguers from the three knowledge areas,

biological, exact and human sciences, respectively, dentistry, civil engineering and education, amounting to nine individuals from UNESP libraries.

- *IVP-U*: Population of undergraduate users from the first and last year of the dentistry, civil engineering and education courses in nine libraries of UNESP, totaling eighteen participants.

Informal Conversation with the Individuals

In this conversation, the researchers contacted the individuals through the General Coordination of Libraries explaining the objectives of the research, the methodology used and agreeing a date for the collection of data. The anonymity of all the participants was protected.

Procedures Adopted During the Application of Verbal Protocol

- *GVP*: After the reading of the copy-text, a discussion was initiated, in which the researcher made the necessary interventions so as to prompt the participants. The entire discussion was recorded and transcribed verbatim.
- *IVP-C*: Every expression of thought uttered by the cataloguer during the execution of indexing in the cataloguing task and recorded with the aid of an MP3 device.
- *IVP-U*: Every expression of thought uttered by the user during the development of indexing in the bibliographic search and recorded with the aid of an MP3 device.

Procedures Following the Application of the Verbal Protocol

Transcription of the recordings:

- *GVP*: After the recording of the discussion of the text by the individuals, a literal transcription was made with the identification of the sources of the individual statements. This identification was made in the following way: Head of Library, reference librarian, cataloguer, Faculty Staff Users/teachers, Student Body Users.
- *IVP-C*: After the recording of the 'think aloud' during the indexing in the cataloguing, a literal transcription was made of the recordings of the individuals statements.
- *IVP-U*: After the recording of the 'think aloud' during the information retrieval, a literal transcri-ption was made of the recordings of the individuals statements.

Analysis of the Transcriptions

- With the transcriptions ready, a detailed reading of the data was undertaken in search of significant and recurring phenomena for the construction of the categories. Following the construction of the categories, we returned again to the data to extract passages from the transcription that exemplified each category. Thus, the procedures adopted for the organisation diagnosis applications in university libraries, and the individual and group verbal protocols were conducted in order to characterise the organisational/academic context in the UNESP Library Network and to observe the views of cataloguers and users to analyse the actions and opinions of the participating individuals regarding indexing during cataloguing and information retrieval. Thirty-six data collections were held for nine groups of verbal protocols, nine individual verbal protocols with cataloguers and eighteen individual verbal protocols with student body users. The total number of individuals participating in this research was seventy-two persons, with forty five in the group of verbal protocol; nine cataloguers and eighteen students. The collections began in May 2006 and concluded in September 2007; they were conducted in the individuals work or study environments, namely the premises of the nine UNESP Library Networks that were previously scheduled to participate in our study. In addition, we should highlight the difficulty of bringing all the participants together in the same place on the same day and at the same time, since, the execution of the data collection was possible only when all of them were in the same field of observation. The transcripts of the data collection generated a substantial amount of data. Considering the socio-cognitive approach to the interaction of the organisational environment and the different perspectives arising from the different participants involved in the data collection indicated the complexity in analysing these transcripts, thus, the reading in full of the verbal protocols were performed, since, the language used by the individuals is not always the same used in the literature. For the collected data analysis procedures and to meet our study proposals, twelve categories were elaborated based on the theoretical frameworks, the research objectives and the statements made by the participants who contributed to exemplifying each phenomenon; each category was systematised into three themes:

- Indexing language by content: indexing procedures:
  a. Procedures for indexing representation;
  b. Language selection;
  c. Choosing terms;
  d. Performance of language in the indexing representation process;
  e. Indexing language by usage: knowledge/importance of language;

f. Search strategy;
g. Performance of language in the information retrieval process;
h. System precision and recall ability;
i. Evaluation of the information retrieval system;
j. Indexing language by form: procedures for construction, upgrading and maintenance of language;
k. The role of the librarian in the construction, upgrading and maintenance of language.

RESULTS AND DISCUSSION

The results presented aim to demonstrate the vision of the context in which the by cataloguers and the users are inserted and, consequently, of the use that is made of indexing language in the indexing in the cataloguing and in the information retrieval. To this effect, we analysed the organisational diagnostics questionnaires completed by the heads of libraries and the individual and group verbal protocols.

The analysis of the organisational diagnostics question-naires revealed a picture of administratively consolidated university libraries, promoting a participative management, many involving the users in the process of the planning of products and services. With regard to the activity of indexing in cataloguing, it was confirmed that the libraries are aware that the LCARB is an instrument of terminological control adopted for the representation and information retrieval in the ATHENA catalogue. In addition, when asked whether the referred indexing language meets the needs of representation, the replies varied between 'does not meet' or 'partially meets'.

In the information retrieval process, almost all the libraries concurred in responding that the language does not meet the needs of users searches by subject, although all of them provide formal and informal training of users which includes the use of the ATHENA catalogue in the information retrieval process by subject field.

The qualitative analyses of the data collected with the application of the verbal protocol technique, in the individual and group modalities, were undertaken on the basis of the selection of the statements uttered by the individuals in this study in the choice of twelve categories, systematised in three thematic axes regarding the use of the Subject Headings List of the BIBLIODATA Network.

The indexing language has been widely discussed by cataloguers and users, teachers and students, in group and individual verbal protocols in the three knowledge areas and has given rise to many questions and concerns about the performance and importance of this mediation and communication instrument between indexing and information retrieval in online collective catalogues of the specialised scientific areas of university libraries.

The socio-cognitive context of UNESP Library Network cataloguers, comprised by the university, library, UNESP quality standard for bibliographic records, Subject Headings List of the BIBLIODATA Network, parallel indexing languages, ATHENA catalogue and the teachers and undergraduate students of specialised scientific areas influenced the indexing, which provided us important results on the use of LCARB for the information representation in the online collective catalogue ATHENA.

Such results arrived from the declarations uttered by the participating individuals in the Group (PVG) and Individual (PVI) Verbal Protocols may also be verified, in their entirety, identified in the following way: Heads of Libraries (HL), by Cataloguer participant in the group verbal protocol (C), by Cataloguer participant in the Individual verbal protocol (C-I), Reference Librarians (RL), Faculty Staff Users/teachers (FS-U) and Student Body Users (SB-U) and accompanied also by the identification of the respective libraries.

In a synthetic analysis, the use of LCARB proved to be a 'required' instrument in the UNESP Network, which was used for confirmation and validation of subject headings to be described in field 650. This important finding is associated with some aspects, also explicit by the obtained results.

As a first aspect, due to the fact that LCARB does not have a specialised and updated vocabulary and as it does not provide a consistent syntactic and semantic structure, it was observed that the use of parallel knowledge organisation systems was a frequent practice in the search for specificity that is required by the thematic processing of information in scientific areas, through the description in field 690, reflecting the plethora of knowledge in which the university library is inserted.

8

Librarian's Computer Awareness and Use of it Application in College Libraries

Dramatic changes in information technology and society are having a considerable impact on educational institutions and their libraries. Information is a vital and indispensable product of the modern society. Availability of right information accurately, precisely and timely is of critical importance. IT is the synthesis of computers and communication. Rapid advances in computer and communication technology enable storing, processing and transmission of huge amount of information easily, quickly and inexpensively. Develop-ments in science and technology ha4ve brought about reduction in size and cost of IT and tremendous increase in its capabilities. The use of IT enables provision of specialised, user oriented library and information products and services effectively and efficiently.

INFORMATION TECHNOLOGY

Information Technology (IT) can be defined as those processes and technologies which are used in acquisition and dissemination of information based on some electronic technology. Somerville has stated 'Information technology has resulted from a convergence of computing technology and communications technology'. This means it is essentially the result of advances in the three important areas of computing, telecommunication and microelectronics. Information Technology is the application of a wide variety of electronic technologies to the information-handling activities. In the domain of library information service, information technologies such as computer, telecommunications, word processing, micro-graphics, reprographics, video recordings and other electronic devices for the storage, retrieval, reproduction and dissemination of information are used.

NEED AND PURPOSE OF INFORMATION TECHNOLOGY IN LIBRARIES

The application of information technology in libraries results in increased operational efficiency. The IT increases productivity of library staff. It relieves professional staff from mundane jobs that involves a lot of duplication so that they can be fruitfully used for user-oriented library services.

It improves quality of services rendered by the library. Use of information technology ensures ease of functioning, accuracy and economy in human labour with greater speed. The exponential growth of information has made manual system redundant giving way to computerised information storage and retrieval tools.

Effective and efficient handling of huge quantum of information is only possible by using computers, which have the added advantage of being highly accurate and efficient that adds value to information. Moreover, the technology also helps in rendering services that were hitherto not possible using traditional means. The new information technology facilitates improved management of physical and financial resources. The advances in technology and its availability at lower cost, has also raised expectations of users from librarians and libraries.

The new information technology, on one hand, facilitate wider access to information for the library users, on other hand, it facilitates wider dissemination of information products and services generated by the library. The availability of networks facilitates resource sharing and high-speed communication with other libraries.

DEVELOPMENTS IN COMPUTER AND MICROPROCESSOR TECHNOLOGY

Dramatic reductions in the size and cost of computer components and equally impressive gains in the speed, storage capacity and reliability of hardware components have expanded their use rapidly in all activities and functions of a library and information centre. Notable reductions in the size of microprocessors combined with dramatically enhanced capacity have added new dimensions to the computer new hardware technology.

Initially, small silicon chips contained only few components and circuits, but the average number of components has doubled each year Since, 1965. Early small-scale integration efforts first gave way to large-scale integration (LSI) chips that contained thousands of components, very large-scale integration (VLSI) chips that contained hundreds of thousands of components and circuits, and now ultra large-scale integration (ULSI) chips come with millions of components and circuits.

A microprocessor, also known as Central Processing Unit (CPU) of a computer, is a complete computation engine that is fabricated on a single chip. Microprocessors are manufactured by different companies like Intel, Advanced Micro Divices (AMD), Motorola, ,etc. However, most widely-used microprocessors are manufactured by Intel. The first microprocessor used in a PC was Intel 8080. Introduced in 1974, it was a complete 8-bit microprocessor on a single chip. Intel 8088 used in the IBM PC in 1979, was the first microprocessor that made its presence felt in the market. The PC market moved from the 8088, 80286, 80386, 80486, Pentium, Pentium-II, III, IV and now to Intel Dual Core and Quad Core. The new Intel Dual Core can execute any piece of code that ran on the original 8088, but the Dual Core runs about 3,000 times faster. The capacity of a microprocessor is measured in terms of the number of bits it can send or receive and the number of bits it can process internally.

The 8088 was an 8/16 bit processor, indicating that it can send or receive 8 bits of data and internally process 16 bits of data at a time. The 80286 was a 16/16 bit processor and 80386 chip had a 32-bit processor with a 32-bit data path and, as a result, was much faster than either the 8088 or the 80286 chip. The 80486 chip, introduced by Intel in late 1989, had a 32- bit processor.

It has architectural enhancements, Hence, it performed better than the 80386 chip. The Pentium is a 32-bit processor with a 32-bit data path. It is three times faster than the 80486. The Pentium II and III had a 32-bit processor with a 64-bit data path. It was three times faster than the Pentium. The Pentium IV is a 32-bit processor with a 64-bit data path, and was introduced in 2000.

It is four times faster than the Pentium. Currently, PCs and laptops are equipped with Dual Core which is a 64-bit processor with 64-bit data path and processing speed of 3.0 Ghz. Like microprocessor technology, digital storage devices have also witnessed notable reductions in its size and cost with dramatically enhancement in capacity of storage.

There are two types of data storage devices, *i.e.,* removable data storage devices and Non-removable data storage devices. The data storage devices come in many sizes and shapes. The storage devices can also be categorised based on media used for storage, for example magnetic storage media, optical storage media, metal-oxide semiconductors or flash memory devices (popularly known as Pen drives or USB drives). Magnetic storage media are commonly used for large volumes of data (*e.g.,* video, image, or remote sensing data). Large amounts of data are stored through tape drives because the capacity on the drives is huge - three billion (or three gigabits) of data per square inch can fit on a single magnetic disk.

Hard discs, floppies, tapes, cartridges, ,etc., are example of magnetic media. CD-ROMs and DVD ROMs are example of optical storage media which can again be of two types, , *i.e.,* i) write-once, read-many: data once written cannot be erased; and ii) Rewritable: the data that is once written can be erased completely and the same storage device can be used again for storing different data. A typical disc used in a computer-based CD drive stores 650 MB.

Digital Versatile Disk or DVD, initially stood for Digital Video Disc. Like a CD, DVD is an optical storage system for read-only, recordable and rewritable applications. The DVD format provides several configurations of data layers, moving from 2D storage to 3D storage. Each configuration is designed to provide additional storage capacity. The similarity between the DVD and the CD gets smaller with each upgraded configuration, however, DVDs in contrast to CDs has storage capacity of 4.7 GB.

Metal-oxide semiconductors-based storage devices, popularly known as pen drives or USB drives or flash memory devices, is Non-volatile computer memory that can be electrically erased and reprogrammed. It is a technology that is primarily used in memory cards and USB flash drives for general storage and transfer of data between computers and other digital products. Flash memory stores information in an array of memory cells made from floating-gate transistors.

In traditional single-level cell (SLC) devices, each cell stores only one bit of information. Some newer flash memory, known as multi-level cell (MLC) devices, can store more than one bit per cell by choosing between multiple levels of electrical charge to apply to the floating gates of its cells. Flash drives are now available with 8 GB storage capacity. Digital collections that are too large to store entirely on a disk use hierarchical storage mechanisms (HSM). In an HSM, the most frequently used data is kept on fast disks while less frequently used data is kept in nearline such as an automated (robotic) tape library.

An HSM can automatically migrate data from tape to disk and vice-versa as required. Intelligent storage networks and snap-servers are now available in which the physical storage devices are intelligently controlled and made available to a number of servers.

A number of RAID (Redundant Array of Inexpensive Disks) models are also available for greater security and performance. The RAID technology distributes the data across a number of disks in a way that even if one or more disks fail, the system would still function while the failed component is replaced.

DEVELOPMENTS IN COMMUNICATION AND NETWORK TECHNOLOGY

Communication technology, with its ability to transmit data and information from one location to another, serve as a tool to exploit potentials and ability of computer to store and process vast amount of information. A computer communica-tion network is an interconnection of a collection of several computers from which the user can select the service required and communicate with any computer as a local user.

A computer communication networks can be viewed as a collection of nodes with computing resources and nodal-switching computers that facilitate communication through a set of transmission links. Developments in communication technology have made it possible to interconnect geographically dispersed computing resources of different kinds and makes.

Users can access the network through PCs and terminals attached to a node and messages traverse these networks through the switching nodes. Since, computer communicates using digitised signals instead of electric signals, it requires different transmission facilities than those used for transmitting analogue electrical signals. It is, however, a common practice to use conventional telecommunication links for data transmission by converting digital signals into analogue signals using a process called 'Modulation' and the device that performs the conversion is called the MODEM (MOdulator - DEModulator).

Currently, terrestrial, satellite-based data networks, Integrated Service Digital Network (ISDN) and wireless networks are available that can handle all kinds of communication requirements (, *i.e.,* voice, data, telemetry, facsimile and video) without discrimination.

The computer networks can be grouped into four categories based on geographical locations of its computer terminals, , i.e.,

- *Local Area Network (LAN)*: interconnection of many computers within a given local area, more often premises of a single organisation building. A very high speed of data transmission can be attained within a limited geographic area. LANs are typically configured in a star, bus or ring. Low speed LANs use telephone wires or copper cables, optical fibre cables are used to achieve high-speed transmission of data.
- *Wide Area Network (WAN)*: WAN is used to interconnect a number of widely dispersed computers in various cities of a country or different countries. WANs use communication media maintained by telegraph or telephone companies. These networks usually have land telephone lines, underground coaxial cables, microwave communication and satellite communications.
- *Metropolitan Area Network (MAN)*: MAN refers to inter- connection within geographical limits of a city or town.
- *Gateways*: Gateways consist of software and hardware that are required to interconnect networks amongst themselves. Gateways contend with any differences in packet sizes, protocols and addressing methods between the two networks it connect. Gateways are also used to connect LANs to WANs and WANs, in turn, can be linked through gateways to create national and international data communication networks.

The communications networks can be grouped into the following three categories based on the technology and communication media used by them:

- *Public Switched Telephone Network*: PSTN are managed by common carriers usually telephone companies/departments the world over. The PSTN generally provide two basic services, the normal dial-up connections to the subscribers and permanent leased connection between two subscriber's points. The permanent leased connections provide single traceable line between two subscriber points. The leased lines are generally less prone to noise than dial-up lines.

- *Public Data Network*: Analogous to the public telephone network, many domestic common carriers provide data communications services via a specialised network called a Public Data Network (PDN). Most Internet Service Providers (ISPs) use combination of PDN and PSTN for providing Internet connectivity.
- *Integrated Services Digital Networks* (ISDN): An ISDN is a network that provides end-to-end digital connectivity to support a wide range of services, including voice and Non-voice services.

Computer networks use physical channels through which information is transmitted between computers in a network. Media may be classified as bounded , *i.e.,* wires (twisted pair telephone wires or UTP CAT 5), cables (co-axial) and optical fibres; or unbounded , *i.e.,* radio waves or microwaves. Data communication is an integral part of the modern information storage and retrieval systems in terms of their online access. Today, network technology works on client server architecture with middleware used for connecting software components or applications on clients and servers.

Technique of packet switching, evolved in 1960s, is used for transferring data between computer systems with an objective to facilitate networked computers to communicate seamlessly across multiple, geographically dispersed locations. The Transmission Control Protocol (TCP) and Internet Protocol (IP), called TCP/ IP suite, is the backbone of Internet and other TCP/ IP based networks.

With developments in communication technology, institutions have options to set-up fibre optic-based gigabit LAN or wireless LAN. Depending on the geographical location, institutions have options to buy terrestrial or satellite-based Internet bandwidth its combinations from a number of Internet Service Providers (ISPs).

APPLICATION OF IT IN COLLEGE LIBRARIES

The main functions of a library are acquisition, technical processing, storage, retrieval and dissemination. The traditional methods of doing these result in slow, laborious and repetitive manual routines. With the advent of modern technologies and their applications, manual routines have transformed into machine oriented ones.

The application of modern technology has allowed access to and storage of information quickly. The availability of computers has gradually changed the library scene. The convegence of computers with new developments in telecommunication techniques and equipment is considered as new information technology. The new information technology has a wide range of services which libraries can avail themselves of and offer to supplement the existing ones to users. Some of the areas to which the modern technology could be applied in day to day activities of the libraries are acquisition, cataloguing, circulation, indexing and abstracting of articles ,etc.

NEED FOR IT

Twentieth century has been the century of explosions. It has witnessed the population explosion, socio-cultural explosion, and nuclear explosion. The information explosion is due to the fact that information generation is a continuous process.

The interdisciplinary research and multidisciplinary research has led to the creation of new ideas, new knowledge and unprecedented growth in information particularly in science and technology. In this era of information explosion, in which large amount of information needs to be processed, application and use of new technology , *i.e.,* information technology is essential.

COMPUTER AWARENESS

Nowhere has the impact of the computer been felt greater than in the field of library and information services. Already most of the libraries are flooded with documents and records that they simply can not handle efficiently without computers. Computers are changing the way in which libraries collect, store, retrieve and disseminate information. The libraries that can not adjust to these trends will not survive. So computers will come and stay forever in all the library and information centres that wish to function efficiently here after.

ROLE OF COLLEGE LIBRARIAN IN IT ERA

The problem we face today is not of dearth of information, but of excessive information. The developing countries are making an earnest effort to concentrate more on developing and using new electronic gadgets to provide better access to information. With the use of new information technology, the libraries can provide nascent information quickly in great volume.

Today, the librarian plays a significant role in information handling and information transfer. He is rightly known as the information officer and is supposed to provide an active service for maximum use of information with minimum cost and time.

Information technology demands trained personnel to handle information storage and retrieval in libraries. A modern librarian has to play a very important role in the process of communication in the contemporary time, for which he must be well educated, highly qualified and professionally competent.

Bibliography

A Rajagopal Kamath and B Manmadhan: *Management Information Systems : Critical Success Factors*, Dominant Publication, Delhi, 2008.

A. Neelameghan and K.N. Prasad: *Computer-Based Library Information Systems: Designing Techniques*, Ess Ess Publication, Delhi, 2006.

Aaron, E.: *Abstracts Produced Using Computer Assistance,* Washington: National Academy Press, 2000.

Aghatise, E.: *Automation and Academic Library Structure*, Maharashtra: Pune Publication, 2004.

Anderson, B.: *Library Management Styles and Structures: A Need to Rethink*, Toronto: Thomson Nelson, 2008.

Arora Kanu *: University Library System : Centralization and Decentralization*, Regal, Delhi, 2008.

Bidyut Mal: *Library Sciences and Documentation*, Shree Publication, Delhi, 2004.

Chattopadhyay, A.: *Principles of Information Systems for Management*, Hyderabad: Economic and Political Weekly Press, 2005.

Cockburn, A.: *Management Information Systems can Help Senior Library Managers,* New Delhi: Long Life Publication, 2006.

Cohen, M.: *Maintaining the Privacy of Library Records*, London: Waverly Book Company, 2003.

Doezema, J.: *Measuring Academic Library Performance: A Practical Approach*, Maharashtra: Pune Publication, 2000.

George, R.: *String Indexing*, Expanded, Baltimore, MD: Johns Hopkins University Press, 2003.

Giorgi, A.: *Computerized Monitoring and Online Privacy*, Pittsburgh: Duquesne University Press, 2005.

Glaser, B.: *Confidentiality in the Use of Library Materials*, Mill Valley: Sociology Press, 2001.

Jyotindra Zaveri and Nitin C. Kamat: *Management Information Systems*, Himalaya Publishing House, Delhi, 2011.

K S Dhawan: *Readings in Library Science (4 Vols-Set)*, Commonwealth Publication, New Delhi, 2001.

K.G. Rastogi: *Reference Services in Library Science*, Alfa Publications, Delhi, 2006.

K.G. Rastogi: *The Functions of Cataloguing in Library Science*, Alfa Publications, Delhi, 2006.

R.S. Khochar: *Library Science Today*, Discovery Publishing House, Delhi, 1999.

Raghunath Pandey and M.N. Velayudhan Pillai: *Library Science Research*, Jnanada Prakashan, Delhi, 2011.

Raghunath Pandey and M.N. Velayudhan Pillai: *World Famous Public Libraries*, Jnanada Prakashan, Delhi, 2011.

Sreenidhi Iyengar: *Researches in Library Science*, Anmol Publication, Delhi, 1996.

Strauss, A.: *Assistive Technology in Special Libraries*, San Francisco: Harper Bowling Green State University, 2000.

Sudha Azhikodan: *Public Libraries in Malabar*, Serials Publication, Delhi, 2010.

T C Mohanti: *Research Methodology in Library Science*, Alfa Publication, Delhi, 2008.

Van Maanen, J.: *Library Assistive Technology: Predictions and Trends*, Chicago: The Hotel Monthly Press, 2006.

Vygotsky, L.: *Adaptive Technology Equipment for the Library*, New York: Columbia Press, 2001.

Index

I

L

M

O

P

Q

R

S

T

V